CROCHET SNAILS AND MUSHROOM SPRITES

MEGAN LAPP,
Creator of
Crafty Intentions

STACKPOLE BOOKS
Essex, Connecticut
Blue Ridge Summit, Pennsylvania

STACKPOLE BOOKS

An imprint of The Globe Pequot Publishing Group, Inc.
64 South Main Street
Essex, CT 06426
globepequot.com
Distributed by NATIONAL BOOK NETWORK
800-462-6420

Copyright © 2025 by Megan Lapp
Additional photography by Lauren Lewis
Bookplate created and used with permission by Kelly Bastow. © Kelly Bastow, 2025.

All rights reserved. No part of this book may be reproduced in any form or by any electronic or mechanical means, including information storage and retrieval systems, without written permission from the publisher, except by a reviewer who may quote passages in a review.

The contents of this book are for personal use only. Patterns herein may be reproduced in limited quantities for such use. Any large-scale commercial reproduction is prohibited without the written consent of the publisher.

We have made every effort to ensure the accuracy and completeness of these instructions. We cannot, however, be responsible for human error, typographical mistakes, or variations in individual work.

An errata will be provided for this and all Crafty Intentions books (https://craftyintentions.com/errata).

British Library Cataloguing in Publication Information available

Library of Congress Cataloging-in-Publication Data available

ISBN 978-0-8117-7164-1 (paper : alk. paper)
ISBN 978-0-8117-7165-8 (electronic)

♾️™ The paper used in this publication meets the minimum requirements of American National Standard for Information Sciences—Permanence of Paper for Printed Library Materials, ANSI/NISO Z39.48-1992.

First Edition

CONTENTS

INTRODUCTION . . . 1

Where to Begin 1
   Materials 1

Tips and Tricks 2

Mushroom Sprite Planning Sheet . . . 4

Snail Planning Sheet 5

Glossary of Terms and Stitches 6

MUSHROOM SPRITES . . 11

Mushroom Sprite Arms 15
   Options. 15
   Arms Style 1: Nubbin 16
   Arms Style 2: Short and Thin. 16
   Arms Style 3: Medium and Thin 17
   Arms Style 4: Medium and Thick 19
   Arms Style 5: Medium and Pointed 20
   Arms Style 6: Long and Thin 21
   Arms Style 7: Long and Thick. 23
   Arms Style 8: Long with Elbow Joint. 24
   Arms Style 9: Extra Long and Thick 25
   Arms Style 10: Extra Long and Thick with
      Elbow Joint 28

iii

Mushroom Sprite Feet and Legs . . . 29

Options. .29
Feet/Legs Style 1: Nubbin Feet. 31
Feet/Legs Style 2: Oval-Soled Sitting Feet . . .31
Feet/Legs Style 3: Large Oval-Soled
    Sitting Feet 32
Feet/Legs Style 4: Round-Soled Sitting Feet. .34
Feet/Legs Style 5: Large Round-Soled
    Sitting Feet 35
Feet/Legs Style 6: Short Pointed Feet/Legs. . .36
Feet/Legs Style 7: Medium Pointed
    Feet/Legs 37
Feet/Legs Style 8: Thick Medium Pointed
    Feet/Legs 38
Feet/Legs Style 9: Oval-Soled Sitting Legs
    with Knees 39
Feet/Legs Style 10: Round-Soled Sitting Feet
    with Knees 40
Feet/Legs Style 11: Oval-Soled Dangly Legs . .42
Feet/Legs Style 12: Round-Soled
    Dangly Legs. 44

Mushroom Sprite Bodies 49

Options. .49
Body Style 1: Tall Large with Built-In
    Standing Legs 51
Body Style 2: Tall Double-Headed with
    Built-In Standing Legs. 58
Body Style 3: Medium-Tall 65
Body Style 4: Medium 70
Body Style 5: Short Small 76
Body Style 6: Short and Wide 80
Body Style 7: Chanterelle Body and Cap. . . .85
Body Style 8: Morel Body and Cap 90

Mushroom Sprite Caps 98

Options. .98
Cap Style 1: Large Round 101
Cap Style 2: Large Pointed 102
Cap Style 3: Large Uneven 103
Cap Style 4: Small Cone 105
Cap Style 5: Cone. 107

Cap Style 6: Small Ruffle. 109
Cap Style 7: Round 111
Cap Style 8: Tall and Pointy. 113
Cap Style 9: Gumdrop Shape 115
Cap Style 10: Small Round 116
Cap Style 11: Straight Pointed 117
Cap Style 12: Curved Pointed 119
Cap Style 13: Wavy. 121
Cap Style 14: Ruffly 122
Cap Style 15: Fairy Cap Spiral Curling 123
Cap Style 16: Fairy Cap, Wavy and
    Pointing Up. 126
Cap Style 17: Inky Cap
    (*Coprinopsis atramentaria*). 128
Cap Style 18: Fly Agaric (*Amanita muscaria*),
    Solid Color 131
Cap Style 19: Fly Agaric (*Amanita muscaria*),
    Two Colors 132
Cap Style 20: Picot Edge Bell 135
Cap Style 21: Ruffle Edge 137
Cap Style 22: Wide Cap. 138
Cap Style 23: Wavy Edge 140
Optional Spots/Dots for Caps 141

SMALL SNAILS . . 146

Options. 147

Small Snail Bodies 148

Small Snail Body Style 1:
    Horizontal Bottom 148
Small Snail Body Style 1: Horizontal Top . . . 149
Small Snail Body Style 2: Upright Bottom . . 152
Small Snail Body Style 2: Upright Top. 154

Small Snail Antennae 158

Small Snail Antennae Style 1 158
Small Snail Antennae Style 2 158

Small Snail Shells 160

Small Snail Shell Style 1: Pointed 160
Small Snail Shell Style 2: Round. 168

Small Snail Assembly. 170

MEDIUM SNAILS . . 177
Options. 178

Medium Snail Body 178
Medium Snail Body Bottom. 178
Medium Snail Body Top. 181

Medium Snail Antennae 187

Medium Snail Shells 188
Medium Snail Shell Style 1: Pointed 188
Medium Snail Shell Style 2: Round. 205
Medium Round Snail Shell
   Optional Closure 208

Medium Snail Assembly 209

GIANT SNAILS . . 217
Options. 218

Giant Snail Body. 219
Giant Snail Body Bottom. 219
Giant Snail Body Top. 223

Giant Snail Antennae 232
Giant Snail Short Antennae 232
Giant Snail Long Antennae 232

Giant Snail Shells 233
Giant Snail Shell Style 1: Pointed 233
Giant Snail Shell Style 2: Round 254
Giant Round Snail Shell Optional Closure . . 260

Giant Snail Assembly. 261

SADDLES AND OTHER ACCESSORIES . . . 266
Options. 267

Leashes 268
Removable Leash 268
Sew-to-Attach Leash 269

Saddle and Accessories for Giant Snail 274
Saddle Blanket for Giant Round Snail Shell . . 274
Saddle Blanket for Giant Pointed Snail Shell. .275
Saddle Seat 275
Saddle Flap 277
Seat Back 277
Seat Handle 280
Saddle Horn 281
Saddle Support 282
Saddle Bags 284
Saddle Straps 284
Saddle Assembly 285

Reins 289

Acknowledgments 290

About the Author. 291

Mushroom Sprite with Arms Style 7, Feet/Legs Style 10, Body Style 8

INTRODUCTION

Where to Begin

Mushroom Sprites and Snails go together like ice cream and a hot summer day. You can have either one separately, but together they're magic. Mushroom Sprites come in many varieties, from different sizes to options with or without limbs, to an array of caps, and more! Snails come small, medium, or large, with different shell and antennae options. Then, to encourage their partnership, starting on page 266 you can find leashes, reins, and saddles that the Mushroom Sprites can use to take their Snails for a walk, run, or slow gallop through the meadow. This book contains simpler mushroom shapes for those with less experience, as well as spiraling shells and colorwork for more advanced crocheters.

There are many things that will impact the size of your finished creatures, including your choice of yarn, your personal tension, how much fiberfill you use to stuff your creature, and the options you ultimately select. Approximate yardage is given for all pieces. Mushroom Sprites range from 4 to 8 inches tall for most selections (without dangly legs) created with the suggested materials. Small Snails are approximately 4 inches tall and 6 inches long. Medium Snails are approximately 6 inches tall and 8 inches long. Giant Snails are approximately 9 inches tall and 12 inches long. It is important to use the same weight yarn for all parts of your creature. Using a different weight yarn for one piece may result in that piece being a different scale than the others.

To help you plan, each section includes a photo gallery with all the available options for that attribute. Look through the book, note the options that you'd like to use for your Mushroom Sprite or Snail, use the Planning Sheets on pages 4 and 5 to design your garden sprite and steed, and track your progress as you complete each piece.

Take a moment to familiarize yourself with the Glossary of Terms and Stitches on page 6 to note any stitches or techniques that may be new to you, and refer to it as needed while you work.

MATERIALS

NOTE: All yarn amounts and sizing measurements are approximate.

* Worsted weight #4 medium yarn
* Sport weight #2 light yarn for the Morel Mushroom Cap (Body Style 8's cap)
* Crochet hook, size G-6 (4 mm)

- * Safety eyes: Sizing ranges from 8 mm to 12 mm black safety eyes or 15 mm to 16 mm colored iris safety eyes. I purchase safety eyes from two sources: Darkside Crochet and Suncatcher Craft Eyes. Darkside Crochet is UK based and Suncatcher is US based, but both ship worldwide. Both are also women-owned businesses.
  - You can find Darkside here: https://darksidecrochet.bigcartel.com
  - You can find Suncatcher here: https://suncatchercrafteyes.com
  - For a visual guide of different sizes of eyes used on Body Style 1, see page 54.
- * Scissors
- * Stitch markers
- * Pins
- * Tapestry/darning needles
- * Fiberfill
- * Something to add weight to the bottom of legs and bodies like flat glass marble gems, clean stones, pellets in nylon stockings, and so on

Optional:
- * Hemostats/forceps (for stuffing small places with fiberfill)
- * Screw-back metal rivets, studs, or spikes to use on leashes/collars or for general decoration
- * Plastic canvas
- * Bottle caps and/or felt furniture pads (or similar) to reinforce bottoms of feet or the flat under-cap of Mushroom Sprites
- * Craft glue
- * Starch

NOTE: Adding metal rivets, safety eyes, or weights will make the creature unsafe for small children. If the creature is meant for a child, avoid adding weights or metal rivets. If the creature is meant for children under the age of three, you should also avoid safety eyes and opt for crocheted, felt, or embroidered eyes instead.

Tips and Tricks

1. Make sure as you work that you are crocheting right side out versus inside out. This technique is explained in the Glossary beginning on page 6.
2. Make sure as you work that you are working the "Sl St to beginning stitch, Ch 1" join correctly. This technique is explained in the Glossary beginning on page 6, which includes a YouTube tutorial link.
3. Worsted weight yarn with a 4 mm crochet hook is recommended for these patterns. You can, however, use any yarn weight you prefer as long as you adjust your hook size so the fabric you create has a tight enough weave to not show the fiberfill through the crochet work. If you change the yarn weight you are using, you will also need to adjust the safety eye size to be proportional to your work.
4. It is important to use the same weight yarn for all parts of each cohesive creature. This issue can especially affect your work if your Mushroom Cap turns out too big or too small for your Mushroom Body or if your Snail Body top or bottom turns out too big or too small for its corresponding bottom or top. Make sure you are using the same weight yarn for each piece unless specifically told otherwise (for example, the Morel Mushroom Cap is meant to be a lighter weight yarn than the body).
5. Flat glass marble gems are optional and can be added in some of the Mushroom arms and legs, or in the bottoms of Mushroom bodies, but it should be done in limbs before they narrow. You do not need to use flat glass marble gems specifically. You could use an alternative material like a clean bottle cap, plastic canvas cut to size, felt furniture pads cut to size, or something similar. You can also use a combination of these materials, like inserting a clean bottle cap first and then putting a weighted material on top of it inside the limb. Including weight in the Mushroom Sprite arms (or legs) is entirely optional. The weight can help the arms hang more naturally/limply at the Mushroom Sprite's sides, but it is not a necessary step to completing a Mushroom Sprite. The weight at the bottom of the body of the Mushroom Sprite can help with fundamental balance and stability and is more strongly recommended.
6. Hemostats are an excellent tool for stuffing hard-to-reach places inside your amigurumi. Consider using a pair as needed!

7. If you have any issues following a YouTube video link, you can go to the Crafty Intentions YouTube Channel here: https://youtube.com/CraftyIntentions.

8. Stitch count is shown at the end of each row in brackets like this: [6]

   The "Sl St to beginning stitch, Ch 1" join is not counted in the stitch count.

   Chain stitches are not counted in the stitch count unless specified.

9. Optional: You may add metal spikes that screw in place as spikes on the leashes. Place the screw through the stitch in the desired location and twist the spike onto the end of the screw. Tighten as much as possible. Once it is fully placed, you can further cement the screw in place by putting some craft glue on the head of the screw and the crochet work surrounding it to fasten it more permanently. If the screw won't stay in place because the stitches are too open, you can use a washer, or you can fashion a washer from a small piece of plastic canvas or felt to prevent the screw from slipping through the stitches. Please note that adding metal spikes makes the piece unsafe for children.

10. Optional: Particularly for the Inky Mushroom Cap, a starch or a clear-drying nontoxic craft glue may be helpful in securing its position to hang down in "drips."

11. How to attach the yarn to a new spot: Slip Stitch to attach into the indicated stitch, Ch 1, and start your first stitch into the same stitch you attached the yarn to.

12. "Sl St, Ch 1" join seams on arms should be on the inside of the arm positioned against the Mushroom Sprite's body. "Sl St, Ch 1" join seams on legs will be positioned on the back of the legs and body.

13. It might be helpful to make the Medium Snail before making the Giant Snail as practice before tackling such a large-scale project.

14. Consider using stitch markers for rows with large stitch counts, placing a stitch marker every 10 stitches to help keep track of your stitch count.

15. If you are making a Mushroom Sprite rider for your Giant Snail with a saddle, it is recommended to use with Bodies 3, 4, 5, or 6 and Feet/Legs Styles 9, 10, 11, or 12.

16. For community support, troubleshooting, and other resources, you can go here: https://linktr.ee/CraftyIntentions.

INTRODUCTION • 3

Mushroom Sprite Planning Sheet

Here's an easy-to-use planning guide to copy, photograph, or scan and use as a template for noting the styles and options you want for each Mushroom Sprite you make. There is also a printable version of this planning sheet available on the Crafty Intentions website.

Arms _____

Legs and Feet _____

Body _____

Cap _____

Other Notes _____

If you are making Mushroom Sprite Body Style 1 or 2, skip the feet/legs instructions, as these Mushroom Sprites have built-in legs in their patterns.

Chart Illustrating Body Styles and Cap Styles That Work Together

	Body Style 1	Body Style 2	Body Style 3	Body Style 4	Body Style 5	Body Style 6
Cap Style 1	○	■	■	■	■	■
Cap Style 2	○	■	■	■	■	■
Cap Style 3	○	■	■	■	■	■
Cap Style 4	■	○	■	■	■	■
Cap Style 5	■	■	■	○	■	■
Cap Style 6	■	■	■	○	■	■
Cap Style 7	■	■	■	○	■	■
Cap Style 8	■	■	■	○	■	■
Cap Style 9	■	○	■	■	■	■
Cap Style 10	■	○	■	■	○	■
Cap Style 11	■	○	■	■	○	■
Cap Style 12	■	○	■	■	○	■
Cap Style 13	■	○	■	■	○	■
Cap Style 14	■	○	■	■	○	■
Cap Style 15	■	■	○	■	■	○
Cap Style 16	■	■	○	■	■	○
Cap Style 17	■	■	○	■	■	○
Cap Style 18	■	■	○	■	■	○
Cap Style 19	■	■	○	■	■	○
Cap Style 20	■	■	○	■	■	○
Cap Style 21	■	■	○	■	■	○
Cap Style 22	■	■	○	■	■	○
Cap Style 23	■	■	○	■	■	○

All open spaces indicate a body and cap style that will work well together. All darkened spaces indicate that those options will not work together.

Snail Planning Sheet

Here's an easy-to-use planning guide to copy, photograph, or scan and use as a template for noting the styles and options you want for each Snail you make. There is also a printable version of this planning sheet available on the Crafty Intentions website.

Snail Size _____

Body Top Color _____

Body Bottom Color _____

Shell Style _____

Shell Main Color _____

Shell Accent Color _____

Antennae Style _____

Leash _____

Saddle Parts and Colors _____

_____

Reins _____

Giant Snails are the perfect size for a Mushroom Sprite to ride. Medium Snails are the perfect companion size for Mushroom Sprites, and Small Snails make great lap-sized cuddle buddies.

Glossary of Terms and Stitches

[Brackets]	Brackets that come after BLO or FLO indicate that these stitches are back loop only or front loop only. Ex.: "BLO [SC 6]" Brackets at the end of the row indicate the stitch count for the row. Ex.: [6]; this means there are 6 stitches in the row.
&	Located between two stitches, the "&" indicates that both stitches are made into the same stitch, as an increase, but with two different types of stitches. Go here for video demonstration: https://youtube.com/watch?v=jGA2nAzL2cU&t=16s
< or >	Indicates the stitch will start (<) or finish (>) in the same stitch as the last stitch or the next stitch.
<Dec>	Beginning in the same stitch as your last stitch, make a decrease stitch into that and the next stitch, and then, into the same stitch that the decrease stitch ends in, begin your next stitch. This technique creates an increase using a decrease stitch and can apply to a regular Dec, a Half Double Crochet Dec, or any other kind of decrease. Go here for video demonstration: https://youtube.com/watch?v=Ni2ZM1cXJI4
<HDC Dec>	Beginning in the same stitch as your last stitch, make a HDC Dec (see page 8) stitch into that and the next available stitch, and then, into the same stitch that the decrease stitch ends in, begin your next stitch. See the <Dec> entry for a link to a video demonstration of the technique.
<DC Dec>	Beginning in the same stitch as your last stitch, make a DC Dec (see page 7) stitch into that and the next available stitch, and then, into the same stitch that the decrease stitch ends in, begin your next stitch. See the <Dec> entry for a link to a video demonstration of the technique.
2 Dec in 3 SC	Make one decrease as normal, and then make the second decrease starting in the same stitch as the first decrease and in the next stitch. Go here for video demonstration: https://youtube.com/watch?v=vWRuWd689KQ
AC [ ]	Accent Color [ ] This note indicates that you will work the stitches inside the brackets in the Accent Color yarn.
Bobble	Different Bobble stitches are used throughout the book. Each time a Bobble stitch is used, the exact definition of that specific Bobble stitch will be explained below the row.
BLO [ ]	Back Loop Only **NOTE:** The rows with FLO or BLO stitches will be structured with brackets [ ]. The brackets will enclose any and all stitches that the FLO or BLO instruction should apply to. Ex.: "FLO [SC 3], SC 3" means 3 SC stitches in the FLO and then 3 normal SC.
Ch	Chain

6 • INTRODUCTION

Colorwork	For a seamless color change, switch to the new color during the final stitch before the color change. To switch colors at the end of a row, switch to the new color when you make the slip stitch join. When you make the final yarn over to complete the last stitch before the new color (or the slip stitch join at the end of the row), use the new color for that final yarn over, and pull up. Doing so will produce a seamless transition to that new color. As you work the next stitches, hold the unused color on top of the previous row of stitches and crochet around it as you work. Go here for a video demonstration: https://youtube.com/watch?v=1XReLVEjZCo
DC	Double Crochet YO, insert into next stitch, YO, pull up, YO, pull through 2 loops, YO, pull through 2 loops
DC Dec	YO, insert into next stitch, YO, pull up, YO, pull through 2 loops, YO, insert into next stitch, YO, pull up, YO, pull through 2 loops, YO, pull through all 3 loops
DC/HDC Dec	YO, insert into next stitch, YO, pull up, YO, pull through 2 loops, YO, insert into next stitch, YO, pull up, YO, pull through all 4 loops
DC Triple Inc	Double Crochet Triple Increase Three double crochet stitches worked into one stitch
Dec	Decrease: 1 stitch combining 2 spaces. All decreases are single crochet decreases unless otherwise specified. Insert your hook into the next stitch, YO, pull up, insert your hook into the next stitch, YO, pull up, YO, pull through all 3 loops **NOTE:** Do not use an invisible decrease unless explicitly told to do so.
FLO [ ]	Front Loop Only **NOTE:** The rows with FLO or BLO stitches will be structured with brackets [ ]. The brackets will enclose any and all stitches that the FLO or BLO instruction should apply to. Ex: "FLO [SC 3], SC 3" means 3 SC in the FLO and then 3 normal SC.
FP DC	Front Post Double Crochet YO, insert hook from front to back to front around post of corresponding stitch below, YO, pull up, YO, pull through 2 loops, YO, pull through all remaining loops
FP HDC	Front Post Half Double Crochet YO, insert hook from front to back to front around post of corresponding stitch below, YO, pull up, YO, pull through all remaining loops
Half Trip	Half Triple Crochet YO twice, insert into next stitch, YO, pull up, YO, pull through 2 loops, YO, pull through all remaining loops

HDC	Half Double Crochet YO, insert hook into next stitch, YO, pull up, YO, pull through all 3 loops
HDC Dec	Half Double Crochet Decrease Both versions are interchangeably usable. Easier version (fewer loops held on hook, looser stitch): YO, insert into next stitch, YO, pull up, YO, pull through 2 loops, YO, insert into next stitch, YO, pull up, YO, pull through all 4 loops More difficult version (more loops held on hook, tighter stitch): YO, insert into next stitch, YO, pull up, YO, insert into next stitch, YO, pull up, YO, pull through all 5 loops
HDC Inc	Half Double Crochet Increase Two HDC stitches worked into one stitch
HDC/SC Dec	Half Double Crochet and Single Crochet Decrease Both versions are interchangeably usable. Easier version (fewer loops held on hook, looser stitch): YO, insert into next stitch, YO, pull up, YO, pull through 2 loops, insert into next stitch, YO, pull up, YO, pull through all 3 loops More difficult version (more loops held on hook, tighter stitch): YO, insert into next stitch, YO, pull up, insert into next stitch, YO, pull up, YO, pull through all 4 loops
Inc	Increase: Create 2 stitches in 1 space Assume all increases are single crochet increases unless otherwise specified.
MC [ ]	Main Color [ ] This note indicates that you will work the stitches inside the brackets in the Main Color yarn.
OC	Original Chain This note refers to the very first set of chain stitches you made to start the piece you're working on.
Picot	Chain 3, slip stitch in the third Ch from hook
Right side/ Outside vs. Wrong side/ Inside	To crochet right side out, insert your hook from the outside/right side of the work to the inside/ wrong side of the work; if you are right-handed, you will be working in a clockwise direction. Here is a video on this technique: https://youtube.com/watch?v=beReNFWQPAs

SC	Single Crochet
	Insert into next stitch, YO, pull up, YO, pull through 2 loops
SC/HDC Dec	Single Crochet/Half Double Crochet Decrease
	Insert into next stitch, YO, pull up, YO, insert into next stitch, YO, pull up, YO, pull through all remaining stitches
	Here is a video on this stitch: https://youtube.com/watch?v=h4wkxMOMqXg&t=12s
Sl St	Slip Stitch
Sl St to beginning stitch, Ch 1	Most of the patterns are written with a "Slip Stitch, Chain 1" joining method for each row. This does affect the shape of each piece, as the piece was written with the seam shift in mind. If you prefer to crochet in spiral/in the round, you are welcome to try it, but I do not guarantee that all asymmetrical sections will come out as shown. The "Sl St, Ch 1" join is not counted in the stitch count.
	To end the row, after you have worked the entire row, you will Sl St into the first stitch you worked in the row and then chain 1. Begin the next row by crocheting into the same stitch you slip stitched into.
	For video demonstration, go here: https://youtube.com/watch?v=Qqu5N7TCt3U
St	Stitch
Triple Crochet	YO twice, insert into next stitch, YO, pull up, YO, pull through 2 loops, YO, pull through 2 loops, YO, pull through all remaining loops
Triple SC Inc	Triple Single Crochet Increase: 3 SC worked into 1 stitch
YO	Yarn Over

INTRODUCTION • 9

Three Mushroom Sprites, left to right: ❶ Mushroom Sprite with Arms Style 7, Feet/Legs Style 10, Body Style 8; ❷ Mushroom Sprite with Arms Style 6, Body Style 2, Cap Style 11; ❸ Mushroom Sprite with Arms Style 2, Feet/Legs Style 1, Body Style 4, Cap Style 6

MUSHROOM SPRITES

❶ Mushroom Sprite with Arms Style 3, Feet/Legs Style 4, Body Style 6, Cap Style 23; and ❷ Mushroom Sprite with Body Style 1, Cap Style 2

Mushroom Sprite with Arms Style 7, Feet/Legs Style 10, Body Style 4, Cap Style 6

Mushroom Sprite with Arms Style 6, Feet/Legs Style 11, Body Style 3, Cap Style 19

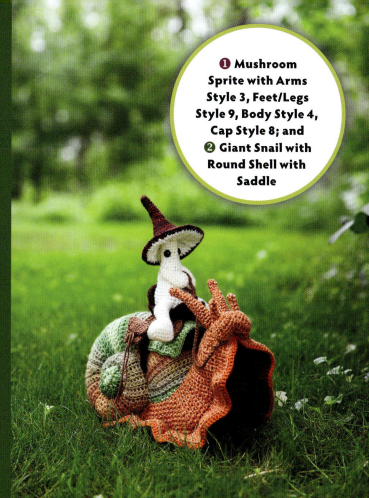

❶ **Mushroom Sprite with Arms Style 3, Feet/Legs Style 9, Body Style 4, Cap Style 8;** and ❷ **Giant Snail with Round Shell with Saddle**

❶ **Mushroom Sprite with Arms Style 7, Feet/Legs Style 10, Body Style 4, Cap Style 6;** and ❷ **Giant Snail with Pointed Shell with Saddle**

Mushroom Sprite with Arms Style 9, Body Style 1, Cap Style 1, optional dots

Mushroom Sprite Arms

Decide whether you want your Mushroom Sprite to have arms. If you do, make two arms, and then follow one of the styles of Body instruction patterns, including the Body instructions for incorporating the optional arms. If you do not want the arms, skip the arm instructions.

OPTIONS

Arms Style 1: Nubbin . . . 16

Arms Style 2: Short and Thin . . . 16

Arms Style 3: Medium and Thin . . . 17

Arms Style 4: Medium and Thick . . . 19

Arms Style 5: Medium and Pointed . . . 20

Arms Style 6: Long and Thin . . . 21

Arms Style 7: Long and Thick . . . 23

Arms Style 8: Long with Elbow Joint . . . 24

Arms Style 9: Extra Long and Thick . . . 25

Arms Style 10: Extra Long and Thick with Elbow Joint . . . 28

MUSHROOM SPRITE ARMS • 15

ARMS STYLE 1: NUBBIN (MAKE 2)

Mushroom Body Color Yarn: Approximately 4 yd/3.75 m worsted/medium weight yarn for two arms

> All arms are optional. All Mushroom bodies can be made either with or without arms.

1. SC 6 in Magic Circle, Sl St to beginning stitch, Ch 1 [6]
2. SC 6, Sl St to beginning stitch, Ch 1 [6]
3. SC 3, Dec, SC, Sl St to beginning stitch [5]

Fasten off with a short yarn tail.

Do not stuff.

Mushroom Sprite with Arms Style 1, Feet/Legs Style 1, Body Style 5, Cap Style 9

ARMS STYLE 2: SHORT AND THIN (MAKE 2)

Mushroom Body Color Yarn: Approximately 6 yd/5.5 m worsted/medium weight yarn for two arms

> All arms are optional. All Mushroom bodies can be made either with or without arms.

1. SC 6 in Magic Circle, Sl St to beginning stitch, Ch 1 [6]
2-3. (2 rows of) SC 6, Sl St to beginning stitch, Ch 1 [6]
4. SC 2, Dec, SC 2, Sl St to beginning stitch, Ch 1 [5]
5. SC 5, Sl St to beginning stitch, Ch 1 [5]
6. SC 5, Sl St to beginning stitch [5]

Fasten off with a short yarn tail.

Optional: Stuff the arms lightly with fiberfill (the arms in the photos have not been stuffed).

Mushroom Sprite with Arms Style 2, Feet/Legs Style 1, Body Style 6, Cap Style 23

Mushroom Sprite with Arms Style 2, Feet/Legs Style 1, Body Style 4, Cap Style 6

Mushroom Sprite with Arms Style 4, Feet/Legs Style 12, Body Style 4, Cap Style 6

Mushroom Sprite with Arms Style 3, Feet/Legs Style 10, Body Style 4, Cap Style 7

ARMS STYLE 3: MEDIUM AND THIN (MAKE 2)

***Mushroom Body Color Yarn:** Approximately 22 yd/20 m worsted/medium weight yarn for two arms*

All arms are optional. All Mushroom bodies can be made either with or without arms.

1. SC 6 in Magic Circle, Sl St to beginning stitch, Ch 1 [6]

2. (SC, Inc) x 3, Sl St to beginning stitch, Ch 1 [9]

3–4. (2 rows of) SC 9, Sl St to beginning stitch, Ch 1 [9]

5. SC 3, Dec, SC 4, Sl St to beginning stitch, Ch 1 [8]

Optional: Insert one glass gem (or alternative weight) in the bottom of the arm.

6. SC 3, Dec, SC 3, Sl St to beginning stitch, Ch 1 [7]

7. SC 2, Dec, SC 3, Sl St to beginning stitch, Ch 1 [6]

8. SC 2, Dec, SC 2, Sl St to beginning stitch, Ch 1 [5]

9. SC 5, Sl St to beginning stitch [5]

Fasten off with a short yarn tail.

Optional: Stuff the arms lightly with fiberfill (the arms in the photos have not been stuffed).

MUSHROOM SPRITE ARMS • 17

ARMS STYLE 4: MEDIUM AND THICK (MAKE 2)

Mushroom Body Color Yarn: Approximately 15 yd/13.75 m worsted/medium weight yarn for two arms

> All arms are optional. All Mushroom bodies can be made either with or without arms.

1. SC 6 in Magic Circle, Sl St to beginning stitch, Ch 1 [6]
2. Inc x 6, Sl St to beginning stitch, Ch 1 [12]
3–4. (2 rows of) SC 12, Sl St to beginning stitch, Ch 1 [12]
5. (SC 2, Dec, SC 2) x 2, Sl St to beginning stitch, Ch 1 [10]
6. SC 10, Sl St to beginning stitch, Ch 1 [10]
7. (SC 3, Dec) x 2, Sl St to beginning stitch, Ch 1 [8]

Optional: Insert one glass gem (or alternative weight) in the bottom of the arm.

8. SC 8, Sl St to beginning stitch, Ch 1 [8]
9. (SC, Dec, SC) x 2, Sl St to beginning stitch, Ch 1 [6]
10. SC 6, Sl St to beginning stitch, Ch 1 [6]
11. SC 2, Dec, SC 2, Sl St to beginning stitch, Ch 1 [5]
12. SC 5, Sl St to beginning stitch [5]

Fasten off with a short yarn tail.

Optional: Stuff the arms lightly with fiberfill (the arms in the photos have not been stuffed).

Mushroom Sprite with Arms Style 4, Feet/Legs Style 12, Body Style 4, Cap Style 6

① Mushroom Sprite with Arms Style 3, Feet/Legs Style 9, Body Style 4, Cap Style 8, ② riding on a Giant Snail with a Round Shell and saddle, ③ followed by a Medium Snail with a Pointed Shell and a ④ Small Snail with a Pointed Shell and Style 1 Antennae

Giving your Mushroom Sprite arms can mean they'll be able to safely hold their saddle and reins more easily when riding their snail!

ARMS STYLE 5: MEDIUM AND POINTED (MAKE 2)

Mushroom Body Color Yarn: Approximately 15 yd/13.75 m worsted/medium weight yarn for two arms

> All arms are optional. All Mushroom bodies can be made either with or without arms.

1. SC 5 in Magic Circle, Sl St to beginning stitch, Ch 1 [5]
2. SC 2, Inc, SC 2, Sl St to beginning stitch, Ch 1 [6]
3. SC 6, Sl St to beginning stitch, Ch 1 [6]
4. SC 5, Inc, Sl St to beginning stitch, Ch 1 [7]
5. SC 7, Sl St to beginning stitch, Ch 1 [7]
6. SC 3, Inc, SC 3, Sl St to beginning stitch, Ch 1 [8]

Optional: Insert one glass gem (or alternative weight) in the bottom of the arm.

7. SC 8, Sl St to beginning stitch, Ch 1 [8]
8. SC 7, Inc, Sl St to beginning stitch, Ch 1 [9]
9. SC 9, Sl St to beginning stitch, Ch 1 [9]
10. SC 4, Inc, SC 4, Sl St to beginning stitch, Ch 1 [10]
11. SC 10, Sl St to beginning stitch, Ch 1 [10]
12. Dec x 5, Sl St to beginning stitch [5]

Fasten off with a short yarn tail.

Optional: Stuff the arms lightly with fiberfill (the arms in the photos have not been stuffed).

Mushroom Sprite with Arms Style 5, Feet/Legs Style 8, Body Style 3, Cap Style 16

Mushroom Sprite with Arms Style 6, Feet/Legs Style 10, Body Style 5, Cap Style 10

ARMS STYLE 6: LONG AND THIN (MAKE 2)

Mushroom Body Color Yarn: Approximately 30 yd/27.5 m worsted/medium weight yarn for two arms

> All arms are optional. All Mushroom bodies can be made either with or without arms.

1. SC 6 in Magic Circle, Sl St to beginning stitch, Ch 1 [6]
2. (SC, Inc) x 3, Sl St to beginning stitch, Ch 1 [9]
3–5. (3 rows of) SC 9, Sl St to beginning stitch, Ch 1 [9]
6. SC 7, Dec, Sl St to beginning stitch, Ch 1 [8]

Optional: Insert one glass gem (or alternative weight) in the bottom of the arm.

7. SC 8, Sl St to beginning stitch, Ch 1 [8]
8. SC 3, Dec, SC 3, Sl St to beginning stitch, Ch 1 [7]
9. SC 7, Sl St to beginning stitch, Ch 1 [7]
10. SC 5, Dec, Sl St to beginning stitch, Ch 1 [6]
11. SC 6, Sl St to beginning stitch, Ch 1 [6]
12. SC 2, Dec, SC 2, Sl St to beginning stitch, Ch 1 [5]
13–14. (2 rows of) SC 5, Sl St to beginning stitch, Ch 1 [5]
15. SC 5, Sl St to beginning stitch [5]

Fasten off with a short yarn tail.

Optional: Stuff the arms lightly with fiberfill (the arms in the photos have not been stuffed).

MUSHROOM SPRITE ARMS • **21**

Mushroom Sprite with Arms Style 6, Feet/Legs Style 11, Body Style 3, Cap Style 19

ARMS STYLE 7: LONG AND THICK (MAKE 2)

Mushroom Body Color Yarn: Approximately 25 yd/ 22.75 m worsted/medium weight yarn for two arms

> All arms are optional. All Mushroom bodies can be made either with or without arms.

1. SC 6 in Magic Circle, Sl St to beginning stitch, Ch 1 [6]
2. Inc x 6, Sl St to beginning stitch, Ch 1 [12]
3. (SC 3, Inc) x 3, Sl St to beginning stitch, Ch 1 [15]
4–7. (4 rows of) SC 15, Sl St to beginning stitch, Ch 1 [15]
8. (SC 3, Dec) x 3, Sl St to beginning stitch, Ch 1 [12]
9. SC 12, Sl St to beginning stitch, Ch 1 [12]
10. (SC, Dec, SC) x 3, Sl St to beginning stitch, Ch 1 [9]
11–12. (2 rows of) SC 9, Sl St to beginning stitch, Ch 1 [9]

Optional: Insert one or two glass gems (or alternative weight) in the bottom of the arm.

13. (SC, Dec) x 3, Sl St to beginning stitch, Ch 1 [6]
14–16. (3 rows of) SC 6, Sl St to beginning stitch, Ch 1 [6]
17. SC 2, Dec, SC 2, Sl St to beginning stitch, Ch 1 [5]
18. SC 5, Sl St to beginning stitch [5]

Fasten off with a short yarn tail.

Optional: Stuff the arms lightly with fiberfill (the arms in the photos have not been stuffed).

This Mushroom Sprite can reach anything on the highest mushroom shelves: Arms Style 7, Body Style 2, Cap Style 4

Arms Style 7, Body Style 2, Cap Style 13, optional dots

MUSHROOM SPRITE ARMS • 23

ARMS STYLE 8: LONG WITH ELBOW JOINT (MAKE 2)

Mushroom Body Color Yarn: Approximately 30 yd/27.5 m worsted/medium weight yarn for two arms

> All arms are optional. All Mushroom bodies can be made either with or without arms.

1. SC 6 in Magic Circle, Sl St to beginning stitch, Ch 1 [6]
2. Inc x 6, Sl St to beginning stitch, Ch 1 [12]
3. (SC 3, Inc) x 3, Sl St to beginning stitch, Ch 1 [15]
4–7. (4 rows of) SC 15, Sl St to beginning stitch, Ch 1 [15]
8. (SC 3, Dec) x 3, Sl St to beginning stitch, Ch 1 [12]
9. SC 12, Sl St to beginning stitch, Ch 1 [12]
10. (SC, Dec, SC) x 3, Sl St to beginning stitch, Ch 1 [9]

Optional: Insert one or two glass gems (or alternative weight) in the bottom of the arm.

11. SC 9, Sl St to beginning stitch, Ch 1 [9]
12. (SC, Dec) x 3, Sl St to beginning stitch, Ch 1 [6]
13. SC 6, Sl St to beginning stitch, Ch 1 [6]
14. FLO [(SC, Inc) x 3], Sl St to beginning stitch, Ch 1 [9]
15. SC 4, Inc, SC 4, Sl St to beginning stitch, Ch 1 [10]
16–18. (3 rows of) SC 10, Sl St to beginning stitch, Ch 1 [10]
19. Dec x 5, Sl St to beginning stitch, Ch 1 [5]
20. SC 5, Sl St to beginning stitch [5]

Fasten off with a short yarn tail.

Optional: Stuff the arms lightly with fiberfill (the arms in the photos have not been stuffed).

This Mushroom Sprite never skips arm day.

Arms Style 8, Feet/Legs Style 9, Body Style 7

❶ Mushroom Sprite with Arms Style 8, Body Style 1, Cap Style 2; ❷ Giant Snail with Pointed Shell and Saddle with Reins

ARMS STYLE 9: EXTRA LONG AND THICK (MAKE 2)

Mushroom Body Color Yarn: Approximately 35 yd/32 m worsted/medium weight yarn for two arms

> All arms are optional. All Mushroom bodies can be made either with or without arms.

1. SC 6 in Magic Circle, Sl St to beginning stitch, Ch 1 [6]
2. Inc x 6, Sl St to beginning stitch, Ch 1 [12]
3. SC 12, Sl St to beginning stitch, Ch 1 [12]
4. (SC, Inc, SC) x 4, Sl St to beginning stitch, Ch 1 [16]
5-9. (5 rows of) SC 16, Sl St to beginning stitch, Ch 1 [16]
10. (SC 3, Dec, SC 3) x 2, Sl St to beginning stitch, Ch 1 [14]
11. SC 14, Sl St to beginning stitch, Ch 1 [14]
12. (SC 5, Dec) x 2, Sl St to beginning stitch, Ch 1 [12]
13. SC 12, Sl St to beginning stitch, Ch 1 [12]
14. (SC 2, Dec, SC 2) x 2, Sl St to beginning stitch, Ch 1 [10]

Optional: Insert one or two glass gems (or alternative weight) in the bottom of the arm.

15-16. (2 rows of) SC 10, Sl St to beginning stitch, Ch 1 [10]
17. (SC 3, Dec) x 2, Sl St to beginning stitch, Ch 1 [8]
18-19. (2 rows of) SC 8, Sl St to beginning stitch, Ch 1 [8]
20. (SC, Dec, SC) x 2, Sl St to beginning stitch, Ch 1 [6]
21-22. (2 rows of) SC 6, Sl St to beginning stitch, Ch 1 [6]
23. SC 2, Dec, SC 2, Sl St to beginning stitch, Ch 1 [5]
24. SC 5, Sl St to beginning stitch [5]

Fasten off with a short yarn tail.

Optional: Stuff the arms lightly with fiberfill (the arms in the photos have not been stuffed).

Mushroom Sprite with Arms Style 9, Body Style 2, Cap Style 10

MUSHROOM SPRITE ARMS • 25

Mushroom Sprite with Arms Style 10, Body Style 1, Cap Style 1

ARMS STYLE 10: EXTRA LONG AND THICK WITH ELBOW JOINT (MAKE 2)

Mushroom Body Color Yarn: Approximately 40 yd/36.5 m worsted/medium weight yarn for two arms

> All arms are optional. All Mushroom bodies can be made either with or without arms.

1. SC 6 in Magic Circle, Sl St to beginning stitch, Ch 1 [6]
2. Inc x 6, Sl St to beginning stitch, Ch 1 [12]
3. SC 12, Sl St to beginning stitch, Ch 1 [12]
4. (SC, Inc, SC) x 4, Sl St to beginning stitch, Ch 1 [16]
5–9. (5 rows of) SC 16, Sl St to beginning stitch, Ch 1 [16]
10. (SC 3, Dec, SC 3) x 2, Sl St to beginning stitch, Ch 1 [14]
11. SC 14, Sl St to beginning stitch, Ch 1 [14]
12. (SC 5, Dec) x 2, Sl St to beginning stitch, Ch 1 [12]
13. SC 12, Sl St to beginning stitch, Ch 1 [12]

Optional: Insert one or two glass gems (or alternative weight) in the bottom of the arm.

14. (SC 2, Dec, SC 2) x 2, Sl St to beginning stitch, Ch 1 [10]
15. SC 10, Sl St to beginning stitch, Ch 1 [10]
16. (SC 3, Dec) x 2, Sl St to beginning stitch, Ch 1 [8]
17. SC 8, Sl St to beginning stitch, Ch 1 [8]
18. (SC, Dec, SC) x 2, Sl St to beginning stitch, Ch 1 [6]
19. SC 6, Sl St to beginning stitch, Ch 1 [6]
20. FLO [(SC, Inc) x 3], Sl St to beginning stitch, Ch 1 [9]
21. SC 4, Inc, SC 4, Sl St to beginning stitch, Ch 1 [10]
22–24. (3 rows of) SC 10, Sl St to beginning stitch, Ch 1 [10]
25. Dec x 5, Sl St to beginning stitch, Ch 1 [5]
26. SC 5, Sl St to beginning stitch [5]

Fasten off with a short yarn tail.

Optional: Stuff the arms lightly with fiberfill (the arms in the photos have not been stuffed).

Mushroom Sprite with Arms Style 10, Feet/Legs Style 9, Body Style 8

Mushroom Sprite Feet and Legs

If you are making Mushroom Sprite Body Style 1 or 2, skip the feet/legs instructions, as these Mushroom Sprites have built-in legs in their patterns. If you are making Mushroom Sprite Body Styles 3–8, decide which feet/legs you want your Mushroom Sprite to have. Follow the crochet instructions for one of the styles of feet/legs, and then proceed to your chosen style of body instructions pattern. If you are not sure where to start, Feet/Legs Style 1 is recommended. Feet/Legs Styles 9, 10, 11, and 12 are recommended for Snail riders.

OPTIONS

Feet/Legs Style 1: Nubbin Feet . . . 31

Feet/Legs Style 2: Oval-Soled Sitting Feet . . . 31

Feet/Legs Style 3: Large Oval-Soled Sitting Feet . . 32

Feet/Legs Style 4: Round-Soled Sitting Feet . . . 34

Feet/Legs Style 5: Large Round-Soled Sitting Feet . . 35

Feet/Legs Style 6: Short Pointed Feet/Legs . . . 36

Feet/Legs Style 7: Medium Pointed Feet/Legs . . . 37

Feet/Legs Style 8: Thick Medium Pointed Feet/Legs . . 38

Feet/Legs Style 9: Oval-Soled Sitting Legs with Knees . . . 39

Feet/Legs Style 10: Round-Soled Sitting Feet with Knees . . . 40

Feet/Legs Style 11: Oval-Soled Dangly Legs . . . 42

Feet/Legs Style 12: Round-Soled Dangly Legs . . . 44

Counterclockwise from top:
❶ Mushroom Sprite with Feet/Legs Style 12, Body Style 7; ❷ Mushroom Sprite with Feet/Legs Style 6, Body Style 6, Cap Style 22; ❸ Mushroom Sprite with Feet/Legs Style 1, Body Style 5, Cap Style 11

The right legs will carry your Mushroom Sprite to hang out with buddies. They may even form a fairy circle. If they do, don't step inside.

Mushroom Sprite with Arms Style 2, Feet/Legs Style 1, Body Style 4, Cap Style 6

FEET/LEGS STYLE 1: NUBBIN FEET (MAKE 2)

Mushroom Body Color Yarn: Approximately 10 yd/9 m worsted/medium weight yarn for two feet/legs

1. SC 8 in Magic Circle, Sl St to beginning stitch, Ch 1 [8]
2. SC 5, Inc x 2, SC, Sl St to beginning stitch, Ch 1 [10]
3. SC 10, Sl St to beginning stitch, Ch 1 [10]
4. SC 4, Dec, SC 2, Dec, Sl St to beginning stitch [8]

Fasten off with a short yarn tail. Mark the 4th stitch of the final row of both feet.

When you attach the feet/legs to the body, you can insert a flat glass marble gem (or alternate weight) in each foot/leg to fill it out and add a bit of extra weight. Optional: Stuff the foot/leg lightly with fiberfill (the feet in the photos have not been stuffed).

Mushroom Sprite with Arms Style 1, Feet/Legs Style 1, Body Style 5, Cap Style 9

FEET/LEGS STYLE 2: OVAL-SOLED SITTING FEET (MAKE 2)

Mushroom Body Color Yarn: Approximately 20 yd/18.25 m worsted/medium weight yarn for two feet/legs

1. Ch 5, starting in the 2nd Ch from hook, Inc, SC 2, work SC 4 in the final available Ch stitch, continue to crochet around to the other side of the OC, SC 2, Inc in the same Ch stitch as your first Inc, Sl St to beginning stitch, Ch 1 [12]
2. SC, Inc, SC 2, HDC Inc x 4, SC 2, Inc, SC, Sl St to beginning stitch, Ch 1 [18]
3. BLO [SC 18], Sl St to beginning stitch, Ch 1 [18]
4. SC 18, Sl St to beginning stitch, Ch 1 [18]
5. SC 5, Dec x 4, SC 5, Sl St to beginning stitch, Ch 1 [14]
6. SC 5, Dec x 2, SC 5, Sl St to beginning stitch, Ch 1 [12]
7. SC 4, Dec x 2, SC 4, Sl St to beginning stitch, Ch 1 [10]
8. SC 3, Dec x 2, SC 3, Sl St to beginning stitch, Ch 1 [8]
9. SC 8, Sl St to beginning stitch, Ch 1 [8]
10. SC 8, Sl St to beginning stitch [8]

Fasten off with a short yarn tail. Mark the 3rd stitch of the final row of both feet/legs.

Before stuffing the foot/leg, you can insert a flat glass marble gem (or alternative weight) in the bottom of each foot/leg to add a bit of extra weight and keep the bottom of the foot/leg flat.

Stuff the foot/leg lightly with fiberfill to fill out the shape.

Mushroom Sprite with Arms Style 6, Feet/Legs Style 2, Body Style 4, Cap Style 7

Mushroom Sprite with Feet/Legs Style 2, Body Style 6, Cap Style 21

FEET/LEGS STYLE 3: LARGE OVAL-SOLED SITTING FEET (MAKE 2)

Mushroom Body Color Yarn: Approximately 30 yd/27.5 m worsted/medium weight yarn for two feet/legs

1. Ch 5, Starting in the 2nd Ch from hook, Inc, SC 2, work SC 4 in the final available Ch stitch, continue to crochet around to the other side of the OC, SC 2, Inc in the same Ch stitch as your first Inc, Sl St to beginning stitch, Ch 1 [12]

2. SC, Inc, SC 2, HDC Inc x 4, SC 2, Inc, SC, Sl St to beginning stitch, Ch 1 [18]

3. Inc, SC, Inc, SC 3, (Inc, SC, Inc) x 2, SC 3, Inc, SC, Inc, Sl St to beginning stitch, Ch 1 [26]

Mushroom Sprite with Arms Style 7, Feet/Legs Style 3, Body Style 3, Cap Style 18

32 • MUSHROOM SPRITE FEET AND LEGS

4. BLO [SC 26], Sl St to beginning stitch, Ch 1 [26]
5. SC 26, Sl St to beginning stitch, Ch 1 [26]
6. SC 8, Dec x 5, SC 8, Sl St to beginning stitch, Ch 1 [21]
7. SC 5, Dec x 2, 2 Dec in 3 SC, Dec x 2, SC 5, Sl St to beginning stitch, Ch 1 [16]

> The "2 Dec in 3 SC" is a special stitch and is defined in the Glossary beginning on page 6.

8. SC 5, Dec x 3, SC 5, Sl St to beginning stitch, Ch 1 [13]
9. SC 4, Dec, SC, Dec, SC 4, Sl St to beginning stitch, Ch 1 [11]
10. SC 3, Dec, SC, Dec, SC 3, Sl St to beginning stitch, Ch 1 [9]
11. SC 3, 2 Dec in 3 SC, SC 3, Sl St to beginning stitch, Ch 1 [8]
12–13. (2 rows of) SC 8, Sl St to beginning stitch, Ch 1 [8]
14. SC 8, Sl St to beginning stitch [8]

Fasten off with a short yarn tail. Mark the 3rd stitch of the final row of both feet.

Before stuffing the foot/leg, you can insert a flat glass marble gem (or alternative weight) in the bottom of each foot/leg to add a bit of extra weight and keep the bottom flat.

Stuff the foot/leg lightly with fiberfill to fill out the shape.

Mushroom Sprite with Arms Style 2, Feet/Legs Style 3, Body Style 5, Cap Style 10

❶ Mushroom Sprite with Arms Style 3, Feet/Legs Style 4, Body Style 6, Cap Style 15;
❷ Mushroom Sprite with Arms Style 7, Feet/Legs Style 5, Body Style 3, Cap Style 18;
❸ Mushroom Sprite with Arms Style 4, Feet/Legs Style 2, Body Style 5, Cap Style 13

FEET/LEGS STYLE 4: ROUND-SOLED SITTING FEET (MAKE 2)

Mushroom Body Color Yarn: Approximately 22 yd/20 m worsted/medium weight yarn for two feet/legs

1. SC 6 in a Magic Circle, Sl St to beginning stitch, Ch 1 [6]
2. Inc x 6, Sl St to beginning stitch, Ch 1 [12]
3. (SC, Inc) x 6, Sl St to beginning stitch, Ch 1 [18]
4. BLO [SC 18], Sl St to beginning stitch, Ch 1 [18]
5. SC 18, Sl St to beginning stitch, Ch 1 [18]
6. (SC 7, Dec) x 2, Sl St to beginning stitch, Ch 1 [16]
7. (SC 3, Dec, SC 3) x 2, Sl St to beginning stitch, Ch 1 [14]
8. (SC 5, Dec) x 2, Sl St to beginning stitch, Ch 1 [12]
9. (SC 2, Dec, SC 2) x 2, Sl St to beginning stitch, Ch 1 [10]
10. (SC 3, Dec) x 2, Sl St to beginning stitch, Ch 1 [8]
11. SC 8, Sl St to beginning stitch, Ch 1 [8]
12. SC 8, Sl St to beginning Stitch [8]

Fasten off with a short yarn tail. Mark the 3rd stitch of the final row of both feet.

Before stuffing the foot/leg, you can insert a flat glass marble gem (or alternative weight) in the bottom of each foot/leg to add a bit of extra weight and keep the bottom of the foot/leg flat.

Stuff the foot/leg lightly with fiberfill to fill out the shape.

Mushroom Sprite with Feet/Legs Style 4, Body Style 3, Cap Style 5

Mushroom Sprite with Arms Style 4, Feet/Legs Style 5, Body Style 4, Cap Style 5

FEET/LEGS STYLE 5: LARGE ROUND-SOLED SITTING FEET (MAKE 2)

Mushroom Body Color Yarn: Approximately 28 yd/25.5 m worsted/medium weight yarn for two feet/legs

1. SC 6 in a Magic Circle, Sl St to beginning stitch, Ch 1 [6]
2. Inc x 6, Sl St to beginning stitch, Ch 1 [12]
3. (SC, Inc) x 6, Sl St to beginning stitch, Ch 1 [18]
4. (SC, Inc, SC) x 6, Sl St to beginning stitch, Ch 1 [24]
5. BLO [SC 24], Sl St to beginning stitch, Ch 1 [24]
6. SC 24, Sl St to beginning stitch, Ch 1 [24]
7. (SC 5, Dec, SC 5) x 2, Sl St to beginning stitch, Ch 1 [22]
8. (SC 9, Dec) x 2, Sl St to beginning stitch, Ch 1 [20]
9. (SC 4, Dec, SC 4) x 2, Sl St to beginning stitch, Ch 1 [18]
10. (SC 7, Dec) x 2, Sl St to beginning stitch, Ch 1 [16]
11. (SC 3, Dec, SC 3) x 2, Sl St to beginning stitch, Ch 1 [14]
12. (SC 5, Dec) x 2, Sl St to beginning stitch, Ch 1 [12]
13. (SC 2, Dec, SC 2) x 2, Sl St to beginning stitch, Ch 1 [10]
14. (SC 3, Dec) x 2, Sl St to beginning stitch [8]

Fasten off with a short yarn tail. Mark the 3rd stitch of the final row of both feet.

Before stuffing the foot/leg, you can insert a flat glass marble gem (or alternative weight) in the bottom of each foot/leg to add a bit of extra weight and keep the bottom flat.

Stuff the foot/leg lightly with fiberfill to fill out the shape.

MUSHROOM SPRITE FEET AND LEGS • 35

Mushroom Sprite with Arms Style 7, Feet/Legs Style 5, Body Style 3, Cap Style 18

Mushroom Sprite with Feet/Legs Style 6, Body Style 6, Cap Style 22

FEET/LEGS STYLE 6: SHORT POINTED FEET/LEGS (MAKE 2)

Mushroom Body Color Yarn: Approximately 16 yd/ 14.5 m worsted/medium weight yarn for two feet/legs

1. SC 6 in a Magic Circle, Sl St to beginning stitch, Ch 1 [6]

2. (SC, Inc, SC) x 2, Sl St to beginning stitch, Ch 1 [8]

3. (SC 3, Inc) x 2, Sl St to beginning stitch, Ch 1 [10]

4. (SC 2, Inc, SC 2) x 2, Sl St to beginning stitch, Ch 1 [12]

5. (SC 5, Inc) x 2, Sl St to beginning stitch, Ch 1 [14]

6. (SC 3, Inc, SC 3) x 2, Sl St to beginning stitch, Ch 1 [16]

7. SC 16, Sl St to beginning stitch, Ch 1 [16]

8. SC 2, Dec x 6, SC 2, Sl St to beginning stitch, Ch 1 [10]

9. SC 2, (2 Dec in 3 SC) x 2, SC 2, Sl St to beginning stitch [8]

> The "2 Dec in 3 SC" is a special stitch and is defined in the Glossary beginning on page 6.

Fasten off with a short yarn tail. Mark the 2nd stitch of the final row of both feet/legs.

Before stuffing the foot/leg, you can insert a flat glass marble gem (or alternative weight) in the bottom of each foot/leg to add a bit of extra weight.

Stuff the foot/leg lightly with fiberfill to fill out the shape.

Mushroom Sprite with Arms Style 2, Feet/Legs Style 6, Body Style 6, Cap Style 15

36 • MUSHROOM SPRITE FEET AND LEGS

FEET/LEGS STYLE 7: MEDIUM POINTED FEET/LEGS (MAKE 2)

Mushroom Body Color Yarn: Approximately 20 yd/18.25 m worsted/medium weight yarn for two feet/legs

1. SC 6 in a Magic Circle, Sl St to beginning stitch, Ch 1 [6]
2. (SC, Inc, SC) x 2, Sl St to beginning stitch, Ch 1 [8]
3. SC 8, Sl St to beginning stitch, Ch 1 [8]
4. (SC 3, Inc) x 2, Sl St to beginning stitch, Ch 1 [10]
5. SC 10, Sl St to beginning stitch, Ch 1 [10]
6. (SC 2, Inc, SC 2) x 2, Sl St to beginning stitch, Ch 1 [12]
7. SC 12, Sl St to beginning stitch, Ch 1 [12]
8. (SC 5, Inc) x 2, Sl St to beginning stitch, Ch 1 [14]
9. SC 14, Sl St to beginning stitch, Ch 1 [14]
10. (SC 3, Inc, SC 3) x 2, Sl St to beginning stitch, Ch 1 [16]
11. SC 16, Sl St to beginning stitch, Ch 1 [16]
12. SC 2, Dec x 6, SC 2, Sl St to beginning stitch, Ch 1 [10]
13. SC 2, (2 Dec in 3 SC) x 2, SC 2, Sl St to beginning stitch [8]

The "2 Dec in 3 SC" is a special stitch and is defined in the Glossary beginning on page 6.

Fasten off with a short yarn tail. Mark the 2nd stitch of the final row of both feet/legs.

Before stuffing the foot/leg, you can insert a flat glass marble gem (or alternative weight) in the bottom of each foot/leg to add a bit of extra weight.

Stuff the foot/leg lightly with fiberfill to fill out the shape.

Mushroom Sprite with Arms Style 2, Feet/Legs Style 7, Body Style 5, Cap Style 13

Did you know that some Mushroom Sprites can glow in the dark? Not these. But some can.

❶ Mushroom Sprite with Arms Style 4, Feet/Legs Style 5, Body Style 4, Cap Style 5; ❷ Mushroom Sprite with Arms Style 2, Feet/Legs Style 6, Body Style 5, Cap Style 9

FEET/LEGS STYLE 8: THICK MEDIUM POINTED FEET/LEGS (MAKE 2)

***Mushroom Body Color Yarn:** Approximately 23 yd/ 21 m worsted/medium weight yarn for two feet/legs*

1. SC 6 in a Magic Circle, Sl St to beginning stitch, Ch 1 [6]
2. (SC, Inc, SC) x 2, Sl St to beginning stitch, Ch 1 [8]
3. (SC 3, Inc) x 2, Sl St to beginning stitch, Ch 1 [10]
4. (SC 2, Inc, SC 2) x 2, Sl St to beginning stitch, Ch 1 [12]
5. (SC 5, Inc) x 2, Sl St to beginning stitch, Ch 1 [14]
6. (SC 3, Inc, SC 3) x 2, Sl St to beginning stitch, Ch 1 [16]
7. (SC 7, Inc) x 2, Sl St to beginning stitch, Ch 1 [18]
8. (SC 4, Inc, SC 4) x 2, Sl St to beginning stitch, Ch 1 [20]
9. SC 20, Sl St to beginning stitch, Ch 1 [20]
10. SC 2, (SC, Dec, SC) x 4, SC 2, Sl St to beginning stitch, Ch 1 [16]
11. SC 2, Dec x 6, SC 2, Sl St to beginning stitch, Ch 1 [10]
12. SC 2, (2 Dec in 3 SC) x 2, SC 2, Sl St to beginning stitch [8]

> The "2 Dec in 3 SC" is a special stitch and is defined in the Glossary beginning on page 6.

Fasten off with a short yarn tail. Mark the 2nd stitch of the final row of both feet/legs.

Before stuffing the Foot/Leg, you can insert a flat glass marble gem (or alternative weight) in the bottom of each foot/leg to add a bit of extra weight.

Stuff the foot/leg lightly with fiberfill to fill out the shape.

If you would prefer for the legs to be positioned pressed together (in this or any style leg), as in the photos on this page, you can position the legs and pin them in place, and then sew to tack them together with a yarn tail or separate piece of yarn to make that positioning permanent.

Mushroom Sprite with Arms Style 3, Feet/Legs Style 8, Body Style 7

Mushroom Sprite with Arms Style 5, Feet/Legs Style 8, Body Style 3, Cap Style 16

38 • MUSHROOM SPRITE FEET AND LEGS

FEET/LEGS STYLE 9: OVAL-SOLED SITTING LEGS WITH KNEES (MAKE 2)

Mushroom Body Color Yarn: Approximately 30 yd/27.5 m worsted/medium weight yarn for two feet/legs

Part 1: Knee (Make 1 per Leg)

1. SC 6 in Magic Circle, Sl St to beginning stitch [6]

Fasten off with a short yarn tail.

Part 2: Foot/Leg

1. Ch 5, starting in the 2nd Ch from hook, Inc, SC 2, work SC 4 in the final available Ch stitch, continue to crochet around to the other side of the OC, SC 2, Inc in the same Ch stitch as your first Inc, Sl St to beginning stitch, Ch 1 [12]
2. SC, Inc, SC 2, HDC Inc x 4, SC 2, Inc, SC, Sl St to beginning stitch, Ch 1 [18]
3. BLO [SC 18], Sl St to beginning stitch, Ch 1 [18]
4. SC 18, Sl St to beginning stitch, Ch 1 [18]
5. SC 5, Dec x 4, SC 5, Sl St to beginning stitch, Ch 1 [14]
6. SC 5, Dec x 2, SC 5, Sl St to beginning stitch, Ch 1 [12]
7. SC 4, Dec x 2, SC 4, Sl St to beginning stitch, Ch 1 [10]

> Before stuffing the foot/leg, you can insert a flat glass marble gem in the bottom of each foot/leg (or use an alternative like plastic canvas cut to size) to add a bit of extra weight and keep the bottom of the foot/leg flat. Stuff the foot/leg lightly with fiberfill. This instruction is here because the leg will begin to narrow at this point, and it will become too difficult to insert a flat glass marble gem or stuff the foot/leg after Row 7.

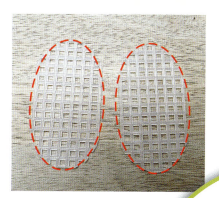

8. SC 3, Dec x 2, SC 3, Sl St to beginning stitch, Ch 1 [8]
9-11. (3 rows of) SC 8, Sl St to beginning stitch, Ch 1 [8]
12. SC 3, starting by working into any stitch on the knee and the next available stitch on the foot/leg, SC 3 (through both pieces), continuing in the next available stitch on the foot/leg only, SC 2, Sl St to beginning stitch, Ch 1 [8]

> When you work into the knee piece, insert your hook into the wrong side/inside of the knee piece first, and then insert your hook into the right side/outside of the foot/leg's next available stitch and complete a SC through both at the same time. Do not work into the slip stitch join from the knee piece. See this video for more information on this technique:
> https://youtu.be/paLzIAi--vk

If you know you want your Mushroom Sprite to be a good Snail rider, then legs with knees or dangly legs work best for staying in the saddle!

❶ **Mushroom Sprite with Arms Style 3, Feet/Legs Style 9, Body Style 4, Cap Style 8,** ❷ **riding a Giant Snail with a Round Shell and saddle, herding (from left to right) an** ❸ **Upright Small Snail with Style 1 Antennae and a Round Shell, an** ❹ **Upright Small Snail with Style 1 Antennae and a Pointed Shell, and a** ❺ **Medium Snail with a Pointed Shell**

13. Inc, SC, start a decrease in the next available stitch on the foot/leg, complete the decrease in the first available stitch on the knee, Inc in the knee, start a decrease in the last available stitch on the knee, complete the decrease in the first available stitch on the foot/leg, SC, Sl St to beginning stitch, Ch 1 [8]
14–17. (4 rows of) SC 8, Sl St to beginning stitch, Ch 1 [8]
18. SC 8, Sl St to beginning stitch [8]

Fasten off with a short yarn tail.

For "sitting" position: If you want the legs to sit knees up, feet/legs down, mark the 4th stitch of the final row of both legs.

> A sitting position is sitting with the knees bent, feet hanging downward. This is an ideal position for sitting at the edge of a shelf or table or as a Snail rider.

For "ring sitting" position, mark the 6th stitch on the first leg (this will be the first to be connected to the body) and the 3rd stitch on the second leg (this will be the second to be connected to the body).

> A ring sitting position is sitting with the knees bent slightly so that the legs form a ring and the feet are sole to sole. Crochet tension may affect the sitting position; adjust the marked stitches if necessary.

Stuff the foot/leg lightly with fiberfill to fill out the shape.

Mushroom Sprite with Arms Style 6, Feet/Legs Style 9, Body Style 5, Cap Style 10

FEET/LEGS STYLE 10: ROUND-SOLED SITTING FEET WITH KNEES (MAKE 2)

Mushroom Body Color Yarn: Approximately 32 yd/29.25 m worsted/medium weight yarn for two feet/legs

Part 1: Knee (Make 1 per Leg)

1. SC 6 in Magic Circle, Sl St to beginning stitch [6]

Fasten off with a short yarn tail.

Part 2: Foot and Leg

1. SC 6 in a Magic Circle, Sl St to beginning stitch, Ch 1 [6]
2. Inc x 6, Sl St to beginning stitch, Ch 1 [12]
3. (SC, Inc) x 6, Sl St to beginning stitch, Ch 1 [18]
4. BLO [SC 18], Sl St to beginning stitch, Ch 1 [18]
5. SC 18, Sl St to beginning stitch, Ch 1 [18]
6. (SC 7, Dec) x 2, Sl St to beginning stitch, Ch 1 [16]
7. (SC 3, Dec, SC 3) x 2, Sl St to beginning stitch, Ch 1 [14]
8. (SC 5, Dec) x 2, Sl St to beginning stitch, Ch 1 [12]
9. (SC 2, Dec, SC 2) x 2, Sl St to beginning stitch, Ch 1 [10]

> Before stuffing the foot/leg, you can insert a flat glass marble gem (or alternative weight) in the bottom of each foot/leg to add a bit of extra weight and keep the bottom flat. Stuff the foot/leg lightly with fiberfill. This instruction is here because the leg will begin to narrow at this point and it will become too difficult to insert a flat glass marble gem or stuff the foot/leg after Row 9.

10. (SC 3, Dec) x 2, Sl St to beginning stitch, Ch 1 [8]

11–13. (3 rows of) SC 8, Sl St to beginning stitch, Ch 1 [8]

14. SC 3, starting by working into any stitch on the knee and the next available stitch on the foot/leg, SC 3 (through both pieces), continuing in the next available stitch on the foot/leg only, SC 2, Sl St to beginning stitch, Ch 1 [8]

> When you work into the knee piece, insert your hook into the wrong side/inside of the knee piece first, and then insert your hook into the right side/outside of the foot/leg's next available stitch and complete a SC through both at the same time. Do not work into the slip stitch join from the knee piece. See this video for more information on this technique:
> https://youtu.be/paLzIAi--vk

15. Inc, SC, start a Dec in the next available stitch on the foot/leg, complete the decrease in the first available stitch on the knee, Inc in the knee, start a Dec in the last available stitch on the knee, complete the decrease in the first available stitch on the foot/leg, SC, Sl St to beginning stitch, Ch 1 [8]

> In Row 15, when you work into the knee, only crochet around the outside available stitches on the knee; ignore the stitches that you made to connect the knee with the foot/leg in Row 14.

16–19. (4 rows of) SC 8, Sl St to beginning stitch, Ch 1 [8]

20. SC 8, Sl St to beginning stitch [8]

For "sitting" position: If you want the legs to sit knees up, feet down, mark the 4th stitch of the final row of both feet/legs.

> A sitting position is sitting with the knees bent, feet hanging downward. This is an ideal position for sitting at the edge of a shelf or table or as a Snail rider.

For "ring sitting" position, mark the 6th stitch on the first foot/leg (this will be the first to be connected to the body) and the 3rd stitch on the second foot/leg (this will be the second to be connected to the body).

> A ring sitting position is sitting with the knees bent slightly so that the legs form a ring and the feet are sole to sole. Crochet tension may affect the sitting position; adjust the marked stitches if necessary.

Stuff the foot/leg lightly with fiberfill to fill out the shape.

Mushroom Sprite with Arms Style 7, Feet/Legs Style 10, Body Style 8

MUSHROOM SPRITE FEET AND LEGS • 41

❶ Mushroom Sprite with Arms Style 3, Feet/Legs Style 10, Body Style 4, Cap Style 1; ❷ Giant Snail with Round Shell plus optional saddle

FEET/LEGS STYLE 11: OVAL-SOLED DANGLY LEGS (MAKE 2)

Mushroom Body Color Yarn: Approximately 48 yd/44 m worsted/medium weight yarn for two feet/legs

1. Ch 5, starting in the 2nd Ch from hook, Inc, SC 2, work SC 4 in the final available Ch stitch, continue to crochet around to the other side of the OC, SC 2, Inc in the same Ch stitch as your first Inc, Sl St to beginning stitch, Ch 1 [12]

2. SC, Inc, SC 2, HDC Inc x 4, SC 2, Inc, SC, Sl St to beginning stitch, Ch 1 [18]

3. Inc, SC, Inc, SC 3, (Inc, SC, Inc) x 2, SC 3, Inc, SC, Inc, Sl St to beginning stitch, Ch 1 [26]

4. BLO [SC 26], Sl St to beginning stitch, Ch 1 [26]

5. SC 26, Sl St to beginning stitch, Ch 1 [26]

6. SC 8, Dec x 5, SC 8, Sl St to beginning stitch, Ch 1 [21]

7. SC 7, Dec, 2 Dec in 3 SC, Dec, SC 7, Sl St to beginning stitch, Ch 1 [18]

The "2 Dec in 3 SC" is a special stitch and is defined in the Glossary beginning on page 6.

8. SC 6, Dec x 3, SC 6, Sl St to beginning stitch, Ch 1 [15]

9. SC 4, Dec, 2 Dec in 3 SC, Dec, SC 4, Sl St to beginning stitch, Ch 1 [12]

10. SC 12, Sl St to beginning stitch, Ch 1 [12]

11. SC 5, Dec, SC 5, Sl St to beginning stitch, Ch 1 [11]

12. SC 11, Sl St to beginning stitch, Ch 1 [11]

13. SC 5, 2 Dec in 3 SC, SC 3, Sl St to beginning stitch, Ch 1 [10]

14–18. (5 rows of) SC 10, Sl St to beginning stitch, Ch 1 [10]

Before stuffing with fiberfill, you can insert a flat glass marble gem (or alternative weight) into the bottom of each foot/leg to add a bit of extra weight and to help keep the bottom of the foot/leg flat. Stuff the piece medium-light with fiberfill. You will want to fill out the shape with the stuffing, but do not make it overly dense; it should be very light and squishy. This instruction is here because the leg will become too narrow to insert a flat glass marble gem or easily stuff the foot/leg after Row 18.

The "Sl St, Ch 1" join seam on the back of the leg will present diagonally from the center of the back of the heel up to the right side of the back of the knee when you crochet the knee joint in Row 19 for right-handed crocheters (the opposite is true for left-handed crocheters).

19. To create the knee joint, fold the opening of the leg in half, aligning the edges. Now, working through both sides of the fold: First start a SC by inserting your hook (from the right side/outside of the work to the inside/wrong side of the work) into the first available stitch, and then insert your hook into the last SC you made in the previous row (from the inside/wrong side of the work to the outside/right side of the work) and complete the SC. Repeat this process in the next available stitch, working your way across the folded edge for a total of 5 SC stitches, Ch 1, Turn [5]

Be careful to ignore and do not crochet into the "Sl St, Ch 1" join from the previous row when you complete Row 19.

Mushroom Sprite with Arms Style 6, Feet/Legs Style 11, Body Style 3, Cap Style 19

20. FLO [SC 5], pivot work, SC 5 in the unworked (back) loops, Sl St to beginning stitch, Ch 1 [10]

> In Row 20, you are working into the front loops and then the back loops of the 5 SC from Row 19. First you will work into the front loops of the SC and then continue around the other side of the piece to work into the remaining back loops.

21. Working into all the stitches from Row 20, SC 6, 2 Dec in 3 SC, SC, Sl St to beginning stitch, Ch 1 [9]
22. SC 9, Sl St to beginning stitch, Ch 1 [9]
23. SC 6, 2 Dec in 3 SC, Sl St to beginning stitch, Ch 1 [8]
24. SC 8, Sl St to beginning stitch, Ch 1 [8]
25. SC 8, Sl St to beginning stitch [8]

Fasten off with a short yarn tail.

For "ring sitting" position, mark the 3rd stitch of the final row of the first foot/leg (this will be the first to be connected to the body) and the 7th stitch of the final row of the second foot/leg (this will be the second to be connected to the body).

> A ring sitting position is sitting with the knees bent slightly so that the legs form a ring and the feet are sole to sole. Crochet tension may affect the sitting position; adjust the marked stitches if necessary.

For "sitting" position: Mark the 2nd stitch on the final row of both legs.

> A sitting position is sitting with the knees bent, feet hanging downward. This is an ideal position for sitting at the edge of a shelf or table or as a Snail rider.

FEET/LEGS STYLE 12: ROUND-SOLED DANGLY LEGS (MAKE 2)

Mushroom Body Color Yarn: Approximately 36 yd/33 m worsted/medium weight yarn for two feet/legs

1. SC 6 in Magic Circle, Sl St to beginning stitch, Ch 1 [6]
2. Inc x 6, Sl St to beginning stitch, Ch 1 [12]
3. (SC, Inc) x 6, Sl St to beginning stitch, Ch 1 [18]
4. BLO [SC 18], Sl St to beginning stitch, Ch 1 [18]
5. SC 6, (2 Dec in 3 SC) x 2, SC 6, Sl St to beginning stitch, Ch 1 [16]

> The "2 Dec in 3 SC" is a special stitch and is defined in the Glossary beginning on page 6.

6. SC 7, Dec, SC 7, Sl St to beginning stitch, Ch 1 [15]
7. SC 15, Sl St to beginning stitch, Ch 1 [15]
8. SC 6, 2 Dec in 3 SC, SC 6, Sl St to beginning stitch, Ch 1 [14]
9. SC 14, Sl St to beginning stitch, Ch 1 [14]
10. SC 6, Dec, SC 6, Sl St to beginning stitch, Ch 1 [13]
11. SC 5, 2 Dec in 3 SC, SC 5, Sl St to beginning stitch, Ch 1 [12]
12. SC 5, Dec, SC 5, Sl St to beginning stitch, Ch 1 [11]
13. SC 4, 2 Dec in 3 SC, SC 4, Sl St to beginning stitch, Ch 1 [10]

44 • MUSHROOM SPRITE FEET AND LEGS

14–16. (3 rows of) SC 10, Sl St to beginning stitch, Ch 1 [10]

> Before stuffing with fiberfill, you can insert a flat glass marble gem (or alternative weight) into the bottom of each foot/leg to add a bit of extra weight and to help keep the bottom flat. Stuff the piece medium-light with fiberfill. You will want to fill out the shape with the stuffing, but do not make it overly dense; it should be very light and squishy. This instruction is here because the leg will become too narrow to insert a flat glass marble gem or easily stuff the foot/leg after Row 16.

Front

Side

17. SC 4. To create the knee joint, fold the opening of the leg in half, aligning the edges. Now, working through both sides of the fold: First start a SC by inserting your hook into the next available stitch from Row 16 (from the right side/outside of the work to the inside/wrong side of the work), and then insert your hook into the last SC you made in this row (from the inside/wrong side of the work to the outside/right side of the work) and complete the SC. Repeat this process in the next available stitch, working your way across the folded edge for a total of 5 SC stitches, Ch 1, Turn [5]

> The stitch count reflects the number of stitches available to work into in the next row. Be careful to ignore the "Sl St, Ch 1" join from the previous row when you complete Row 17.

Mushroom Sprite with Feet/Legs Style 12, Body Style 7

18. FLO [SC 5], pivot work, SC 5 in the unworked (back) loops from Row 17, Sl St to beginning stitch, Ch 1 [10]

> In Row 18, you are working into the front loops and then the back loops of the 5 SC from Row 17; first you will work into the front loops of the SC and then continue around the other side of the piece to work into the remaining back loops.

19. Working into all the stitches from Row 18, SC 6, 2 Dec in 3 SC, SC, Sl St to beginning stitch, Ch 1 [9]

20. SC 9, Sl St to beginning stitch, Ch 1 [9]

21. SC 6, 2 Dec in 3 SC, Sl St to beginning stitch, Ch 1 [8]

22. SC 8, Sl St to beginning stitch, Ch 1 [8]

23. SC 8, Sl St to beginning stitch [8]

Fasten off with a short yarn tail. Mark the 5th stitch of the final row of both legs.

Mushroom Sprite with Arms Style 10, Body Style 1, Cap Style 1

Mushroom Sprite with Arms Style 6, Feet/Legs Style 12, Body Style 4, Cap Style 8, optional dots

Mushroom Sprite Bodies

If you are making Mushroom Sprite Body Style 1 or 2, skip the feet/legs instructions, as these Mushroom Sprites have built-in legs in their patterns. If you are making Mushroom Sprite Body Styles 3–8, decide which feet/legs you want your Mushroom Sprite to have.

While arms and feet/legs are interchangeable between all bodies, caps are not. Each body can be used only with specific caps, so decide in advance what type of cap you want your Mushroom Sprite to have and follow the body instructions that are compatible with that cap.

OPTIONS

Body Style 1: Tall Large with Built-In Standing Legs . . . 51

Without Arms   With Arms

Body Style 2: Tall Double-Headed with Built-In Standing Legs . . . 58

Without Arms   With Arms

Body Style 3: Medium-Tall . . . 65

Without Arms   With Arms

Body Style 4: Medium . . . 70

Without Arms   With Arms

Body Style 5: Short Small . . . 76

Without Arms   With Arms

Body Style 6: Short and Wide . . . 80

Without Arms   With Arms

Body Style 7: Chanterelle Body and Cap . . . 85

Without Arms   With Arms

Body Style 8: Morel Body and Cap . . . 90

Without Arms   With Arms

MUSHROOM SPRITE BODIES • 49

Mushroom Sprite With Arms Style 8, Body Style 1, Cap Style 2

BODY STYLE 1: TALL LARGE WITH BUILT-IN STANDING LEGS (MAKE 1)

For use with Cap Style 1, 2, or 3

Mushroom Body Color Yarn: Approximately 125 yd/114.25 m worsted/medium weight yarn

> Body Style 1 does not use separate legs. It can use separate arms or no arms. The bottom of the feet in the legs of this Mushroom Sprite can be reinforced with either circles of plastic canvas cut to fit or clean plastic bottle caps. This approach can help fill out the shape and keep the bottom of the feet flat. Any weight used can be dropped inside the leg on top of this reinforcement. The weight helps make the Mushroom Sprite stable enough to stand by itself. You can use flat glass marble gems (or alternative weight) to balance the Mushroom Sprite. You will be filling the rest of the body medium-firm with fiberfill. You can do this as you go, or you can leave it until you have finished with the body.

Legs

1. SC 6 in Magic Circle, Sl St to beginning stitch, Ch 1 [6]
2. Inc x 6, Sl St to beginning stitch, Ch 1 [12]
3. (SC, Inc) x 6, Sl St to beginning stitch, Ch 1 [18]
4. (SC, Inc, SC) x 6, Sl St to beginning stitch, Ch 1 [24]
5. BLO [SC 24], Sl St to beginning stitch, Ch 1 [24]

6–8. (3 rows of) SC 24, Sl St to beginning stitch, Ch 1 [24]
9. (SC 5, Dec, SC 5) x 2, Sl St to beginning stitch, Ch 1 [22]
10. SC 22, Sl St to beginning stitch, Ch 1 [22]

> At this point you can add something to flatten and reinforce the bottom of the inside of the foot/leg.

11. (SC 9, Dec) x 2, Sl St to beginning stitch, Ch 1 [20]
12. SC 20, Sl St to beginning stitch, Ch 1 [20]
13. (SC 4, Dec, SC 4) x 2, Sl St to beginning stitch, Ch 1 [18]
14. SC 18, Sl St to beginning stitch, Ch 1 [18]
15. (SC 7, Dec) x 2, Sl St to beginning stitch, Ch 1 [16]
16. SC 16, Sl St to beginning stitch, Ch 1 [16]
17. SC 16, Sl St to beginning stitch [16]

Fasten off the first leg with a short yarn tail. Mark the 6th stitch on the first leg.

Work Rows 1–17 again to make a second leg and do not fasten off; continue with the instructions below.

> As a reminder, the stitches made in the following row are all made by inserting the hook from the right side (outside) of the work to the wrong side (inside) of the work. Do not work into the "Sl St, Ch 1" join.

18A. Ch 1, SC 15, Inc in the current piece (leg 2), Ch 2

18B. Starting in the marked stitch on the first leg, Inc, SC 14, Inc, around the first leg

18C. SC in each of the 2 Ch stitches from 18A, SC in the same stitch as where you worked the first SC in 18A, continue in spiral, do not Sl St or Ch 1 [38]

> The final SC of Row 18C shares a stitch with the first SC of Row 18A—this basically creates an increase.

> Row 19 will be worked around all available stitches from Row 18. You will first work along the 17 stitches on leg 2, then into the chain side of the 2 Ch stitches; next you will work into the 18 stitches on leg 1, then into the 2 SC worked into Ch stitches, and then into the 1 stitch on leg 2. This makes 40 available stitches to work into in Row 19.

19. (SC 4, Dec, SC 4) x 4 [36]
20. SC 36 [36]
21. (SC 7, Dec) x 4 [32]
22. SC 32 [32]
23. (SC 3, Dec, SC 3) x 4 [28]
24. SC 28 [28]
25. (SC 5, Dec) x 4 [24]
26–27. (2 rows of) SC 24 [24]

> At this point you can fill the legs with glass gems (or alternative weight) to balance the Mushroom Sprite and help it stand by itself. Begin to fill the legs and body medium-firm with fiberfill.

28. (SC 2, Dec, SC 2) x 4 [20]
29–30. (2 rows of) SC 20 [20]

52 • MUSHROOM SPRITE BODIES

> In Rows 31–35, follow the instructions for either the "Without Arms" body or the "With Arms" body, based on whether you are incorporating arms. Ignore the set of instructions you do not need/are not using.

31. Without Arms: SC 20 [20]
With Arms: SC 6 in the body only, SC in the first arm and body simultaneously, SC 9 in the body only, SC in the second arm and body simultaneously, SC 3 in the body only [20]

> When you crochet into the arm and the body simultaneously, position the arm piece so you are inserting your hook first from the inside of the arm to the outside of the arm and then into the right side of the body (as normal), and make that stitch into both pieces at the same time. You can use any stitch on the arm to begin attaching the arm to the body. Make sure you do not crochet into the "Sl St, Ch 1" join space on the arm, and aim to orient the arm's join seam to the back side of the Mushroom Sprite.

32. Without Arms: (SC 3, Dec) x 4 [16]
With Arms: SC 6 in the body, SC 4 in the first arm, starting in the next available body stitch, SC, Dec, SC 6, SC 4 in the second arm, starting in the next available body stitch, SC, Dec [24]

> When you crochet Row 32, work along the unused stitches of the arm and ignore the stitch used to connect the arm with the body from Row 31.

33. Without Arms: SC 16 [16]
With Arms: (SC 2, Dec, SC 2) x 4 [20]

34. Without Arms: SC 16 [16]
With Arms: (SC 4, Dec, SC 4) x 2 [18]

35. Without Arms: SC 16 [16]
With Arms: (SC 7, Dec) x 2 [16]

36–44. (9 rows of) SC 16 [16]

MUSHROOM SPRITE BODIES • 53

For a Mushroom Sprite *without arms*, add 8 mm–12 mm safety eyes between Rows 37 and 38 with 2 stitch spaces between the posts, centered on the front of the body, *or* 16 mm safety eyes between Rows 37 and 38 with 3 or 4 stitch spaces between the posts (if they are sinker eyes, keep in mind that they will sink into the crochet work as you attach them).

8 mm eyes

12 mm eyes

9 mm eyes

16 mm eyes

For a Mushroom Sprite *with arms*, add 8 mm–12 mm safety eyes between Rows 38 and 39 with 2 stitch spaces between the posts, centered on the front of the body, *or* 16 mm safety eyes between Rows 38 and 39 with 3 or 4 stitch spaces between the posts (if they are sinker eyes, keep in mind that they will sink into the crochet work as you attach them).

8 mm eyes

12 mm eyes

9 mm eyes

16 mm eyes

The legs have seams created by the "Sl St, Ch 1" join method. Those seams mark the "back" of the body.

45. FLO [(SC, Inc) x 8], Sl St to beginning stitch, Ch 2 [24]

You will not crochet into the Ch 2 at the end of Row 45 (and in future rows), and the Ch 2 is not counted in the stitch count. The under-cap/gills will continue to use the "Slip St, Ch 2" join seam.

46. (DC, FP DC, DC & FP DC) x 8, Sl St to beginning stitch, Ch 2 [32]

Check the Glossary beginning on page 6 for the definition of the "FP DC" and the "&" symbol. Each of the repeats from Row 46 will be worked into each of the sets of "(SC, Inc)" from Row 45. Work the first DC as normal into the first SC. Work the first FP DC around the post of the first SC in the Inc. Work the next DC as normal into the 2nd SC in the Inc. Work the "& FP DC" around the post of the same 2nd SC in the Inc. Repeat these instructions around the row. For a video on the "FP DC" stitch and the "FP DC & DC," go here: https://youtube.com/watch?v=DvBWZ9dCnYk&t=3s

54 • MUSHROOM SPRITE BODIES

47. (DC & FP DC, DC & FP DC, DC, FP DC) x 8, Sl St to beginning stitch, Ch 2 [48]

Each of the repeats from Row 47 will be worked into each of the sets of "(DC, FP DC, DC & FP DC)" from Row 46. Work the first DC as normal into the first DC. Work the first "& FP DC" around the post of the same DC you worked into with the first DC. Work the next DC as normal into the first FP DC from Row 46. Work the second "& FP DC" around the post of the same FP DC you just worked into from Row 46. Work the next DC as normal into the next DC stitch from Row 46. Work the last FP DC around the post of the last FP DC in the stitch set from Row 46. You will repeat these instructions around the row.

48. (DC Inc, FP DC) x 24, Sl St to beginning stitch, Ch 2 [72]

The DC Inc stitches in Row 48 are worked into the regular DC stitches in Row 47. The FP DC stitches are worked around the posts of the FP DC stitches from Row 47.

49. (DC 2, FP DC) x 24, Sl St to beginning stitch, Ch 2 [72]

The DC stitches in Row 49 are worked into the DC Inc stitches from Row 48. The FP DC stitches are worked around the posts of the FP DC stitches from Row 48.

50. (DC, <DC Dec>, DC, FP DC) x 24, Sl St to beginning stitch, Ch 2 [96]

The "(DC, <DC Dec>, DC)" instructions in Row 50 will be worked across the "DC 2" stitches from Row 49. Check the Glossary beginning on page 6 for the definition of a "DC Dec," as well as what it means to make a "<Dec>" stitch. The FP DC stitches are worked around the posts of the FP DC stitches from Row 49. You will repeat these instructions around the row.

MUSHROOM SPRITE BODIES • 55

51. (DC 3, FP DC) x 24, Sl St to beginning stitch, Ch 2 [96]

> The "DC 3" will be worked across the "(DC, <DC Dec>, DC)" instructions from Row 50. The FP DC stitches are worked around the posts of the FP DC stitches from Row 50.

52. (DC 3, FP DC) x 24, Sl St to beginning stitch [96]

> It is optional to work Row 52 as "(DC, FP DC, DC, FP DC) x 24" instead. Doing so will result in even more ridges on the under-cap.

Fasten off with a short yarn tail, and tuck the yarn tail inside the body.

If you have not already done so, fill the legs with flat glass marble gems (or alternative weight) to balance the Mushroom Sprite and help it stand by itself. Fill the rest of the body firmly with fiberfill.

Body Closure (Make 1)

1. SC 8 in Magic Circle, Sl St to beginning stitch, Ch 1 [8]

2. Inc x 8, Sl St to beginning stitch, Ch 1 [16]

3. Hold this piece against the top opening of the Mushroom Sprite body, on top of the under-cap/gills. Working through the next available stitch on the current piece and the leftover back loops from Row 44 at the same time, (SC, Inc) x 8 around, Sl St to beginning stitch [24]

> In Row 3, you will insert your hook first through the next available stitch on the Body Closure piece, Row 2, and then you will insert your hook through a leftover BLO stitch from Row 44 on the Mushroom Sprite Body and complete a SC.

Fasten off with a short yarn tail and proceed to a suitable cap option for this body style (see chart on page 4).

Mushroom Sprite with Arms Style 6, Body Style 2, Cap Style 11

BODY STYLE 2: TALL DOUBLE-HEADED WITH BUILT-IN STANDING LEGS (MAKE 1)

For use with Cap Style 4, 9, 10, 11, 12, 13, or 14

Mushroom Body Color Yarn: Approximately 95 yd/87 m worsted/medium weight yarn

> The Body Style 2 Mushroom Sprite does not use separate legs. It can use separate arms or no arms. The bottom of the feet in the legs of this Mushroom Sprite can be reinforced with either circles of plastic canvas cut to fit or clean plastic bottle caps. This approach can help keep the bottom of the feet flat. Any weight can be dropped inside the leg on top of this reinforcement. The weight helps make the Mushroom Sprite stable enough to stand by itself. You can use flat glass marble gems (or alternative weight) to balance the Mushroom Sprite. Stuff the rest of the body medium-firm with fiberfill. You can do this as you go, or you can leave it until you have finished with the body.

Part 1: Legs (and Body)

1. SC 6 in Magic Circle, Sl St to beginning stitch, Ch 1 [6]
2. Inc x 6, Sl St to beginning stitch, Ch 1 [12]
3. (SC, Inc) x 6, Sl St to beginning stitch, Ch 1 [18]
4. (SC, Inc, SC) x 6, Sl St to beginning stitch, Ch 1 [24]
5. BLO [SC 24], Sl St to beginning stitch, Ch 1 [24]
6. SC 6, HDC Dec x 6, SC 6, Sl St to beginning stitch [18]
7–14. (8 rows of) SC 18, Sl St to beginning stitch, Ch 1 [18]
15. SC 18, Sl St to beginning stitch [18]

Fasten off the first leg with a short yarn tail. Mark the 16th stitch on the first leg.

Repeat Rows 1–15 to make a second leg and do not fasten off; continue with the instructions below.

> As a reminder, the stitches made in the following row are all made by inserting the hook from the right side (outside) of the work to the wrong side (inside) of the work.

16A. Ch 1, SC 7 in the leg you are working on (2nd leg), Ch 2

16B. Starting in the marked stitch, SC 18 around the first leg you made

16C. SC in each of the 2 Ch stitches from 16A, continuing in 2nd leg, SC 11, continue in spiral, do not Sl St or Ch 1 [38]

Row 17 will be worked around all available stitches from Row 16. You will first work along the 7 stitches on leg 2, then into the chain side of the 2 Ch stitches; next you will work into the 18 stitches on leg 1, then into the 2 SC worked into Ch stitches, and then into the 11 stitches on leg 2. This makes 40 available stitches to work into in Row 17.

17. SC 40 [40]
18. (SC 4, Dec, SC 4) x 4 [36]
19–20. (2 rows of) SC 36 [36]
21. (SC 7, Dec) x 4 [32]
22–24. (3 rows of) SC 32 [32]

At this point you can fill the legs with glass gems (or alternative weight) to balance the Mushroom Sprite and help it stand by itself. Begin to fill the legs and body medium-firm with fiberfill.

25. (SC 3, Dec, SC 3) x 4 [28]
26–29. (4 rows of) SC 28 [28]

Mark the 3rd skipped stitch in Row 30 (which is the 12th stitch of Row 29). Row 30 starts the first of two stems of the Mushroom Sprite's two heads. First you will complete this stem, and then you will return to the marked stitch to start the second stem.

In Rows 30 and 31, follow the instructions for either the "Without Arms" body or the "With Arms" body, based on whether you are incorporating arms. Ignore the set of instructions you do not need/are not using.

30. Without Arms: SC 9, Ch 4, Sk 14 stitches, starting in the next available stitch, SC 5 [14]

With Arms: SC in the arm and body simultaneously, SC 8, Ch 4, Sk 14 stitches, starting in the next available stitch, SC 5 [14]

When you crochet into the arm and body simultaneously, position the arm piece so you are inserting your hook first into the inside of the arm to the outside of the arm and then into the right side of the body (as normal), and make that stitch into both pieces at the same time. You can use any stitch on the arm to begin attaching the arm to the body, but aim to orient the arm's join seam to the back side of the Mushroom Sprite.

MUSHROOM SPRITE BODIES • 59

31. Without Arms: SC 9, SC 4 into the Ch stitches from Row 30, SC 5 [18]

With Arms: Working into the arm stitches, SC 4, continuing into the next available stitch on the body, SC, Dec, SC 5, working into the first 2 Ch stitches, work a Dec, continuing into the next 2 available Ch stitches, SC 2, continuing into the next available stitch on the body, SC 3, Dec [18]

When you crochet Row 31, work into the outside of the arm stitches and ignore the stitch used to connect the arm with the body from Row 30.

32. (SC 7, Dec) x 2 [16]

33. SC 16 [16]

34. (SC 3, Dec, SC 3) x 2 [14]

35–36. (2 rows of) SC 14 [14]

37. (SC 5, Dec) x 2 [12]

38–40. (3 rows of) SC 12 [12]

41. (SC 2, Dec, SC 2) x 2 [10]

42–44. (3 rows of) SC 10 [10]

45. SC 10, Sl St to beginning stitch, Ch 1 [10]

Add 8 mm–12 mm safety eyes between Rows 39 and 40 with 2 stitch spaces between the posts, centered on the front of the body, **or** 15 mm–16 mm safety eyes between Rows 39 and 40 with 3 or 4 stitch spaces between the posts (if they are sinker eyes, keep in mind that they will sink into the crochet work as you attach them). It is optional to trim the posts of the safety eyes—do this only if the item is not a toy intended for play, as trimming the post can marginally impact the structural integrity of the eye post. It is helpful to trim the posts of eyes that are applied to thinner Mushroom Sprite stems, which can help with stuffing and so forth. This is optional. Finish adding fiberfill to the body before you add the body closure.

Left to right: 9 mm eyes, 8 mm eyes

Left to right: 16 mm eyes, 12 mm eyes

The legs have seams created by the "Sl St, Ch 1" join method. Those seams mark the "back" of the body.

46. FLO [(SC, Inc) x 5], Sl St to beginning stitch, Ch 2 [15]

In Rows 46 and 47, you are creating the under-cap/gills of the Mushroom. End Row 46 with the "Sl St to beginning stitch, Ch 2" instruction. The Ch 2 is not included in the stitch count; do not crochet into it.

60 • MUSHROOM SPRITE BODIES

47. (DC & FP DC) x 15, Sl St to beginning stitch [30]

> In Row 47, work each DC as normal into the next available stitch, and then work the "& FP DC" around the post of the same SC that you worked the DC stitch into, repeat these instructions around the row. For a video on the "FP DC" stitch and the "FP DC & DC," go here: https://youtube.com/watch?v=DvBW-Z9dCnYk&t=3s

If you are using the Cap Style 4 for Body Style 2, fasten off here with a short yarn tail, and tuck the yarn tail inside when you crochet to attach the Mushroom Cap. If using Cap Style 9, 10, 11, 12, 13, or 14, continue to Row 48.

48. Ch 2, (DC, FP DC) x 15, Sl St to beginning stitch [30]

> In Row 48, work each DC as normal into the next available DC from the previous row, and then work the FP DC around the post of the next available FP DC from the previous row. Repeat these instructions around the row.

Fasten off with a short yarn tail, and tuck the yarn tail inside when you crochet to attach the Mushroom Cap.

Twice the heads can mean twice the need for pet snails—so prepare to give your double-headed mushrooms not just one snail but two.

❶ Mushroom Sprite with Arms Style 6, Body Style 2, Cap Style 11, petting a ❷ Medium Snail with Pointed Shell in a corral

MUSHROOM SPRITE BODIES • 61

Part 2: Second Stem

> In Rows 1 and 2, follow the instructions for either the "Without Arms" body or the "With Arms" body, based on whether you want to incorporate arms. Ignore the set of instructions you do not need/are not using.

1. *Without Arms:* Attach the yarn to the marked stitch on Row 29 in Part 1, SC 12, continuing in the unworked side of the Ch 4 from Row 30, SC in each chain for a total of 4 SC, continuing in the next available stitch, SC 2 [18]

With Arms: Attach the yarn to the marked stitch on Row 29 in Part 1, SC 4, SC in the arm and body simultaneously, SC 7, continue in the unworked side of the Ch 4 from Row 30, SC in each Ch for a total of 4 SC, continuing in the next available stitch, SC 2 [18]

> When you crochet into the arm and body simultaneously, position the arm piece so that you are inserting your hook first into the inside of the arm to the outside of the arm and then into the right side of the body (as normal), and make that stitch into both pieces at the same time. You can work into any arm stitch you want; aim to orient the arm's join seam to the back side of the Mushroom Sprite.

2. *Without Arms:* SC 18 [18]

62 • **MUSHROOM SPRITE BODIES**

With Arms: SC 4 in the body, continuing into the next available stitch on the arm, SC, Dec, SC, continuing into the next available stitch on the body, SC 4, Dec, SC 5, Dec [18]

> In Row 2 with arms, you will work around all the available stitches of Row 29, Part 1, plus the 4 available stitches from the arm.

> When you crochet Row 2 with arms, work into the outside of the arm stitches and ignore the stitch used to connect the arm with the body from Row 1.

3. SC 18 [18]
4. (SC 7, Dec) x 2 [16]
5–6. (2 rows of) SC 16 [16]
7. (SC 3, Dec, SC 3) x 2 [14]
8–10. (3 rows of) SC 14 [14]
11. (SC 5, Dec) x 2 [12]
12–15. (4 rows of) SC 12 [12]
16. (SC 2, Dec, SC 2) x 2 [10]

17–21. (5 rows of) SC 10 [10]
22. SC 10, Sl St to beginning stitch, Ch 1 [10]

> After Row 20, add 8 mm–12 mm safety eyes between Rows 16 and 17 with 2 stitch spaces between the posts, centered on the front of the body, *or* 16 mm safety eyes between Rows 16 and 17 with 3 or 4 stitch spaces between the posts (if they are sinker eyes, keep in mind that they will sink into the crochet work as you attach them). It is optional to trim the posts of the safety eyes—do this only if the item is not a toy intended for play, as trimming the post can marginally impact the structural integrity of the eye post. It is helpful to trim the posts of eyes that are applied to thinner Mushroom Sprite stems, which can help with stuffing and so forth. This is optional. Finish adding fiberfill to the body before you attach the body closure.

Left to right: 9 mm eyes, 8 mm eyes

Left to right: 16 mm eyes, 12 mm eyes

> The legs have seams created by the "Sl St, Ch 1" join method. Those seams mark the "back" of the body.

23. FLO [(SC, Inc) x 5], Sl St to beginning stitch, Ch 2 [15]

> In Rows 23 and 24, you are creating the under-cap/gills of the Mushroom. End Row 23 with the "Sl St to beginning stitch, Ch 2" instruction. The Ch 2 is not included in the stitch count, and you will not crochet into it.

24. (DC & FP DC) x 15, Sl St to beginning stitch [30]

> In Row 24, you will work each DC as normal into the next available stitch, and then you will work the "& FP DC" around the post of the same SC that you worked the DC stitch into. Repeat these instructions around the row.

If you are using the Cap Style 4 for Body Style 2, fasten off here with a short yarn tail, and tuck the yarn tail inside when you crochet to attach the Mushroom Cap. If using Cap Style 9, 10, 11, 12, 13, or 14, continue to Row 25.

MUSHROOM SPRITE BODIES • 63

25. Ch 2, (DC, FP DC) x 15, Sl St to beginning stitch [30]

> In Row 25, work each DC as normal into the next available DC from Row 24 and then work the FP DC around the post of the next available FP DC from Row 24. Repeat these instructions around the row.

Fasten off with a short yarn tail, and tuck the yarn tail inside when you crochet to attach the Mushroom Cap.

Body Closure (Make 2)

1. SC 5 in Magic Circle, Sl St to beginning stitch, Ch 1 [5]

2. Inc x 5, Sl St to beginning stitch, Ch 1 [10]

3. Hold this piece against one of the top hole openings of the Mushroom Sprite body, on top of the under-cap/gills. Working through the next available stitch on the current piece and the leftover back loops from Row 45 on Part 1 or Row 22 on Part 2, (SC, Inc) x 5 around, connecting this piece with the Mushroom Sprite's body, Sl St to beginning stitch [15]

> In Row 3, you will insert your hook first through the next available stitch on the Body Closure piece, Row 2, and then you will insert your hook through a leftover BLO stitch from Row 45 on Part 1 or Row 22 on Part 2 on the Mushroom Sprite Body, and complete a SC.

Fasten off with a short yarn tail. Proceed to a suitable cap option for this body style (see chart on page 4).

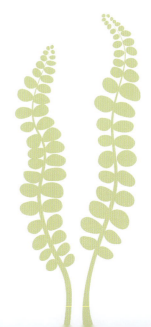

64 • MUSHROOM SPRITE BODIES

BODY STYLE 3: MEDIUM-TALL (MAKE 1)

For use with Cap Style 15, 16, 17, 18, 19, 20, 21, 22, or 23

Mushroom Body Color Yarn: Approximately 45 yd/41.25 m worsted/medium weight yarn

> This body can be made with or without arms and/or feet/legs. If you are using feet/legs, select one of the twelve styles of feet/legs and make those before beginning this body.

> You will be filling the base of the body with flat glass marble gems (or alternative weight) to balance the Mushroom Sprite and help it sit by itself. You will be filling the rest of the body firmly with fiberfill. You can do this as you go, or you can leave it until you have finished with the body.

1. SC 6 in Magic Circle, Sl St to beginning stitch, Ch 1 [6]
2. Inc x 6, Sl St to beginning stitch, Ch 1 [12]
3. (SC, Inc) x 6, Sl St to beginning stitch, Ch 1 [18]
4. (SC, Inc, SC) x 6, Sl St to beginning stitch, Ch 1 [24]
5. (SC 3, Inc) x 6, Sl St to beginning stitch, Ch 1 [30]

> Rows 6 and 7 include instructions on how to crochet to attach feet/legs to the body. Feet/legs help balance and stabilize your Mushroom Sprite and are recommended. Without feet/legs, you'll need to carefully weight the base of your mushroom for balance. If you do not want to include feet/legs, work the rows as follows:
> Row 6: BLO [SC 30], Sl St to beginning stitch, Ch 1
> Row 7: SC 30, Sl St to beginning stitch, Ch 1, and then continue with Row 8

> In Row 6, you will work into the back loops of the body to create a flat base. When attaching the foot/leg to the body, work through both loops of the foot/leg and the back loop of the body.

6. BLO [SC 6, starting in the marked stitch on the foot/leg, SC 4 in the foot/leg and body at the same time, SC 6 in the body only, starting in the marked stitch on the foot/leg, SC 4 in foot/leg and body at the same time, SC 10 in the body only], Sl St to beginning stitch, Ch 1 [30]

> When you crochet into the foot/leg and body simultaneously, position the foot/leg piece so you are inserting your hook first into the wrong side (inside) of stitch on the foot/leg and then into the BLO of the right side of the body (as normal), and make that stitch into both pieces at the same time. Make sure you **do not** crochet into the "Sl St, Ch 1" join space on the foot/leg.

7. SC 5, Dec starting the Dec in the next available stitch on the body and ending in the next available stitch on the foot/leg, Inc x 2, Dec starting the Dec in the next available stitch on the foot/leg and ending in the next available stitch on the body, SC 4, Dec starting the Dec in the next available stitch on the body and ending in the next available stitch on the foot/leg, Inc x 2, Dec starting the Dec in the next available stitch on the foot/leg and ending in the next available stitch on the body, SC 9, Sl St to beginning stitch, Ch 1 [30]

> All stitches in Row 7 are made into the right side of the work, working all the way around the outside edge of the body and the feet/legs. Do not crochet into the 4 SC stitches from each foot/leg that were used to connect the feet/legs with the body from Row 6.

MUSHROOM SPRITE BODIES • 65

8–9. (2 rows of) SC 30, Sl St to beginning stitch, Ch 1 [30]

10. (SC 4, Dec, SC 4) x 3, Sl St to beginning stitch, Ch 1 [27]

11. SC 27, Sl St to beginning stitch, Ch 1 [27]

12. SC 7, (Dec, SC 2) x 2, Dec, SC 10, Sl St to beginning stitch, Ch 1 [24]

13. SC 24, Sl St to beginning stitch, Ch 1 [24]

14. SC 6, (Dec, SC 2) x 2, Dec, SC 8, Sl St to beginning stitch, Ch 1 [21]

15–16. (2 rows of) SC 21, Sl St to beginning stitch, Ch 1 [21]

In Rows 17–19, follow the instructions for either the "Without Arms" body or the "With Arms" body, based on whether you are incorporating arms. Ignore the set of instructions you do not need/are not using.

17. Without Arms: (SC 5, Dec) x 3, Sl St to beginning stitch, Ch 1 [18]

With Arms: SC 4, SC in arm and body simultaneously, Dec, SC 5, Dec, SC, SC in arm and body simultaneously, SC 3, Dec, Sl St to beginning stitch, Ch 1 [18]

When you crochet into the arm and body simultaneously, position the arm piece so you are inserting your hook first into the inside of the arm to the outside of the arm and then into the right side of the body (as normal), and make that stitch into both pieces at the same time. You can use any stitch on the arm to begin attaching the arm to the body. Make sure you **do not** crochet into the "Sl St, Ch 1" join space on the arm, and aim to orient the arm's join seam to the back side of the Mushroom Sprite.

18. Without Arms: SC 18, Sl St to beginning stitch, Ch 1 [18]

With Arms: SC 4 in body, SC 4 in the unworked stitches of the arm, SC in body, Dec x 3 in body, SC in body, SC 4 in the unworked stitches of the arm, SC 4 in body, Sl St to beginning stitch, Ch 1 [21]

When you crochet Row 18 with arms, work into the outside of the arm stitches and ignore the stitch used to connect the arm with the body from Row 17. Do not work into the "Sl St, Ch 1" join space on the arms.

19. Without Arms: SC 18, Sl St to beginning stitch, Ch 1 [18]

With Arms: (SC 5, Dec) x 3, Sl St to beginning stitch, Ch 1 [18]

Mushroom Sprite with Feet/Legs Style 10, Body Style 3, Cap Style 15

20. (SC 2, Dec, SC 2) x 3, Sl St to beginning stitch, Ch 1 [15]

21. SC 15, Sl St to beginning stitch, Ch 1 [15]

22. (SC 3, Dec) x 3, Sl St to beginning stitch, Ch 1 [12]

23–24. (2 rows of) SC 12, Sl St to beginning stitch, Ch 1 [12]

25. SC 12, Sl St to beginning stitch, Ch 1 [12]

> You can optionally use Row 25 to create a ring/annulus. If you want to create a ring/annulus (see page 69 for what this would look like), work Row 25 in the BLO and return to Row 25 in the "Optional Ring/Annulus" section to complete it.

26–32. (7 rows of) SC 12, Sl St to beginning stitch, Ch 1 [12]

> At this point, fill the bottom of the body with flat glass marble gems (or alternative weight) to balance the Mushroom Sprite and help it stand by itself. Fill the rest of the body firmly with fiberfill. It will be difficult to get gems and stuffing down past the eye posts once safety eyes are inserted.

> For a Mushroom without a ring/annulus, add 8 mm–12 mm safety eyes between Rows 23 and 24 with 2 stitch spaces between the posts, centered on the front of the body, *or* 16 mm safety eyes between Rows 23 and 24 with 3 or 4 stitch spaces between the posts (if they are sinker eyes, keep in mind that they will sink into the crochet work as you attach them).
>
> For a Mushroom with a ring/annulus, add 8 mm–12 mm safety eyes between Rows 26 and 27 with 2 stitch spaces between the posts, centered on the front of the body, *or* 16 mm safety eyes between Rows 27 and 28 with 3 or 4 stitch spaces between the posts (if they are sinker eyes, keep in mind that they will sink into the crochet work as you attach them). It is optional to trim the posts of the safety eyes—do this only if the item is not a toy intended for play, as trimming the post can marginally impact the structural integrity of the eye post. It is helpful to trim the posts of eyes that are applied to thinner Mushroom Sprite stems, which can help with stuffing and so forth. This is optional.

16 mm eyes above ring/annulus

9 mm eyes above ring/annulus

12 mm eyes above ring/annulus

8 mm eyes above ring/annulus

MUSHROOM SPRITE BODIES • 67

33. Ch 1 more, FLO [DC Inc x 12], Sl St to beginning stitch, Ch 2 [24]

You will not crochet into the Ch 2 at the end of Row 33 (and in future rows), and the Ch 2 is not counted in the stitch count.

34. (HDC Inc, FP HDC) x 12, Sl St to beginning stitch, Ch 2 [36]

35. (DC, DC Inc, FP DC) x 12, Sl St to beginning stitch, Ch 2 [48]

For a video on the "FP DC" stitch and more, go here: https://youtube.com/watch?v=DvBWZ9dCnYk&t=3s

For Cap Style 20: Picot Edge Bell, **do not** Ch 2. Fasten off with a short yarn tail, and tuck the yarn tail inside when you crochet to attach the Mushroom Cap. Proceed to Cap Style 20: Picot Bell after the Body Closure.

For Cap Style 15, 16, 17, 18, 19, 21, 22, or 23, continue to crochet the body.

36. (HDC, FP HDC) x 24, Sl St to beginning stitch, Ch 2 [48]

For Cap Style 15, 16, 17, 21, 22, or 23, **do not** Ch 2. Fasten off with a short yarn tail, and tuck the yarn tail inside when you crochet to attach the Mushroom Cap. Proceed to Cap Style 15, 16, 17, 21, 22, or 23 after the Body Closure.

For Cap Style 18 or 19, continue to crochet the body.

37. (DC, FP DC, DC Inc, FP DC, DC, FP DC) x 8, Sl St to beginning stitch [56]

Fasten off with a short yarn tail. Tuck the yarn tail inside when you crochet to attach the Mushroom Cap. Proceed to Cap Style 18 or 19 after the Body Closure.

68 • MUSHROOM SPRITE BODIES

Body Closure (Make 1)

1. SC 6 in Magic Circle, Sl St to beginning stitch, Ch 1 [6]
2. Inc x 6, Sl St to beginning stitch, Ch 1 [12]

3. Hold this piece against the top hole opening of the Mushroom Sprite body, on top of the under-cap/gills. Working through the next available stitch on the current piece and the leftover back loops from Row 32, (SC, Inc) x 6 around, connecting this piece with the Mushroom Sprite body, Sl St to beginning stitch [18]

> In Row 3, you will insert your hook first through the next available stitch on the Body Closure piece, Row 2, and then you will insert your hook through a leftover BLO stitch from Row 32 on the Mushroom Sprite Body and complete a SC.

Fasten off with a short yarn tail.

If you have not already done so, fill at least the bottom half of the legs and/or the bottom of the body with flat glass marble gems (or alternative weight) to balance the Mushroom Sprite and help it be stable and sit/stand by itself. Fill the rest of the body firmly with fiberfill.

Optional Ring/Annulus (Make 1)

> If you want the ring/annulus to point upward toward the cap, attach the yarn by inserting your hook from below the leftover FLO stitch, under the stitch, and upward toward the cap, and attaching, crocheting from there, always inserting your hook in that way to complete stitches.
>
> If you want the ring/annulus to point downward toward the feet, attach the yarn by inserting your hook from above the leftover FLO stitch, under the stitch, and downward away from the cap/toward the feet, and attaching, crocheting from there, always inserting your hook in that way to complete stitches.

1. Attach the yarn to any stitch on the back of the body of the Mushroom Sprite on the remaining FLO of Row 24.

(SC 3, Inc) x 3, Sl St to beginning stitch, Ch 1 [15]

Choose one of two options:

2. **Option 1—Chipped:** HDC 2, HDC Inc, HDC, Ch 2, Sl St 2, Ch 2, HDC, HDC Inc, HDC 2, Ch 2, Sl St 2, Ch 2, HDC Inc, HDC 2, Ch 2, Sl St in the same stitch that you worked the last HDC into [18]

Fasten off with a long enough yarn tail to weave in.

or

2. **Option 2—Ruffled:** (SC 2, Inc, SC 2) x 3, Sl St to beginning stitch, Ch 2 [18]

> Do not crochet into the Ch 2 at the end of Row 2.

3. (DC Inc, Ch 1, DC, Ch 1, DC Inc x 4) x 3, Sl St to beginning stitch [33]

Fasten off with a long enough yarn tail to weave in and proceed to a suitable cap option for this body style (see chart on page 4).

MUSHROOM SPRITE BODIES • 69

Mushroom Sprite with Arms Style 7, Feet/Legs Style 3, Body Style 3, Cap Style 18

BODY STYLE 4: MEDIUM (MAKE 1)

For use with Cap Style 5, 6, 7, or 8

Mushroom Body Color Yarn: Approximately 70 yd/64 m worsted/medium weight yarn

This body can be made with or without arms and/or feet/legs. If you are using feet/legs, select one of the twelve styles of feet/legs and make those before beginning this body.

You will be filling the base of the body with flat glass marble gems (or alternative weight) to balance the Mushroom Sprite and help it sit by itself. You will be filling the rest of the body firmly with fiberfill. You can do this as you go, or you can leave it until you have finished with the body.

Body

1. SC 6 in Magic Circle, Sl St to beginning stitch, Ch 1 [6]
2. Inc x 6, Sl St to beginning stitch, Ch 1 [12]
3. (SC, Inc) x 6, Sl St to beginning stitch, Ch 1 [18]
4. (SC, Inc, SC) x 6, Sl St to beginning stitch, Ch 1 [24]
5. (SC 3, Inc) x 6, Sl St to beginning stitch, Ch 1 [30]

> Rows 6 and 7 include instructions on how to crochet to attach feet/legs to the body. Feet/legs help balance and stabilize your Mushroom Sprite and are recommended. Without feet/legs, you'll need to carefully weight the base of your mushroom for balance. If you do not want to include feet/legs, work the rows as follows:
> Row 6: BLO [SC 30], Sl St to beginning stitch, Ch 1
> Rows 7 and 8: (2 rows of) SC 30, Sl St to beginning stitch, Ch 1, and then continue with Row 9

6. BLO [SC 10, starting in the marked stitch of the foot/leg, SC 4 in the foot/leg and the body at the same time, working in the body only, SC 6, starting in the marked stitch on the foot/leg, SC 4 in the foot/leg and the body at the same time, working in the body only, SC 6], Sl St to beginning stitch, Ch 1 [30]

> When you crochet into the foot/leg and body simultaneously, position the foot/leg piece so you are inserting your hook first into the wrong side (inside) of the foot/leg and then into the BLO of the right side of the body (as normal), and make that stitch into both pieces at the same time.

7. SC 9, Dec starting in the next available stitch on the body and ending in the next available stitch on the foot/leg, working in the foot/leg, SC, <Dec>, SC, Dec starting in the next available stitch on the foot/leg and ending in the next available stitch on the body, working in the body, SC 4, Dec starting in the next available stitch on the body and ending in the next available stitch on the foot/leg, SC, <Dec>, SC, Dec starting in the next available stitch on the foot and ending in the next available stitch on the body, SC 5, Sl St to beginning stitch, Ch 1 [28]

> All stitches in Row 7 are made into the right side of the work, working all the way around the outside edge of the body and the feet/legs. Do not crochet into the 4 SC stitches on each foot/leg used to connect the feet/legs with the body from Row 6.

> "<Dec>" is a stitch that is defined in the Glossary beginning on page 6.

8. SC 13, Inc, SC 4, Inc, SC 9, Sl St to beginning stitch, Ch 1 [30]

9. SC 30, Sl St to beginning stitch, Ch 1 [30]

10. (SC 2, Dec, SC 2) x 5, Sl St to beginning stitch, Ch 1 [25]

11. SC 10, Dec, SC 6, Dec, SC 5, Sl St to beginning stitch, Ch 1 [23]

12. SC 23, Sl St to beginning stitch, Ch 1 [23]

13. SC 10, Dec, SC 4, Dec, SC 5, Sl St to beginning stitch, Ch 1 [21]

14. SC 21, Sl St to beginning stitch, Ch 1 [21]

MUSHROOM SPRITE BODIES • 71

> In Rows 15–17, follow the instructions for either the "Without Arms" body or the "With Arms" body, based on whether you are incorporating arms. Ignore the set of instructions you do not need/are not using.

15. Without Arms: (SC 5, Dec) x 3, Sl St to beginning stitch, Ch 1 [18]

With Arms: SC 5, Dec, SC, SC in the arm and body simultaneously, SC 3, Dec, SC 4, SC in the arm and body simultaneously, Dec, Sl St to beginning stitch, Ch 1 [18]

> When you crochet into the arm and body simultaneously, position the arm piece so you are inserting your hook first into the inside of the arm to the outside of the arm and then into the right side of the body (as normal), and make that stitch into both pieces at the same time. You can work into any stitch in the arm to begin to attach each arm; aim to orient the arm's join seam to the back side of the Mushroom Sprite.

16. Without Arms: SC 18, Sl St to beginning stitch, Ch 1 [18]

With Arms: SC 2, Dec, SC 3, starting in the next available stitch on the arm, SC, Dec, SC, starting in the next available stitch on the body, SC 3, Dec, SC 3, starting in the next available stitch on the arm, SC, Dec, SC, working in the next available stitch on the body, SC, Sl St to beginning stitch, Ch 1 [20]

> When you crochet Row 16 with arms, work into the outside of the arm stitches and ignore the stitch used to connect the arm with the body from Row 15.

17. Without Arms: (SC 2, Dec, SC 2) x 3, Sl St to beginning stitch, Ch 1 [15]

With Arms: (SC, Dec, SC) x 5, Sl St to beginning stitch, Ch 1 [15]

18. SC 15, Sl St to beginning stitch, Ch 1 [15]

19. (SC 3, Dec) x 3, Sl St to beginning stitch, Ch 1 [12]

20–27. (8 rows of) SC 12, Sl St to beginning stitch, Ch 1 [12]

Mushroom Sprite with Arms Style 7, Feet/Legs Style 10, Body Style 4, Cap Style 6

72 • MUSHROOM SPRITE BODIES

Add 8 mm–12 mm safety eyes between Rows 23 and 24 with 2 stitch spaces between the posts, centered on the front of the body, **or** 16 mm safety eyes between Rows 23 and 24 with 3 or 4 stitch spaces between the posts (if they are sinker eyes, keep in mind that they will sink into the crochet work as you attach them). It is optional to trim the posts of the safety eyes—do this only if the item is not a toy intended for play, as trimming the post can marginally impact the structural integrity of the eye post. It is helpful to trim the posts of eyes that are applied to thinner Mushroom Sprite stems, which can help with stuffing and so forth. This is optional.

8 mm eyes

12 mm eyes

9 mm eyes

16 mm eyes

28. FLO [(SC 2, Inc) x 4], Sl St to beginning stitch, Ch 2 [16]

The Ch 2 at the end of Rows 28 and 29 is a join chain only; do not work into this Ch 2.

29. (DC & FP DC, DC & FP DC, DC, FP DC) x 4, Sl St to beginning stitch, Ch 2 [24]

Check the Glossary beginning on page 6 for the definition of the "FP DC" stitch and the "&" symbol. For a video on the "FP DC" stitch and the "FP DC & DC," go here: https://youtube.com/watch?v=DvBWZ9dCnYk&t=3s

Each of the repeats from Row 29 will be worked into each of the sets of "(SC 2, Inc)" from Row 28. Work the first DC as normal into the first SC. Work the first "& FP DC" around the post of the same SC you worked into with the first DC. Work the next DC as normal into the second SC from Row 28. Work the second "& FP DC" around the post of the same SC you just worked into from Row 28. Work the next DC as normal into the first SC in the Inc from Row 28. Work the last FP DC around the post of the second SC in the Inc from Row 28. Repeat these instructions around the row.

MUSHROOM SPRITE BODIES • 73

30. (DC, FP DC, DC, FP DC, DC Inc, FP DC) x 4, Sl St to beginning stitch, Ch 2 [28]

31. (DC Inc, FP DC, DC Inc, FP DC, DC 2, FP DC) x 4, Sl St to beginning stitch, Ch 2 [36]

32. (DC 2, FP DC, DC, <DC Dec>, DC, FP DC) x 6, Sl St to beginning stitch, Ch 2 [42]

> Each of the repeats from Row 30 will be worked into each of the sets of "(DC & FP DC, DC & FP DC, DC, FP DC)" from Row 29. Work the first DC as normal into the first DC. Work the first FP DC around the post of the first FP DC from Row 29. Work the next DC as normal into the next DC. Work the next FP DC around the post of the next FP DC from Row 29. Work the next DC Inc as normal into the next available DC. Work the last FP DC of the set around the post of the last FP DC of the set from Row 29. Repeat these instructions around the row.

> Each of the repeats from Row 31 will be worked into each of the sets of "(DC, FP DC, DC, FP DC, DC Inc, FP DC)" from Row 30. Work the first DC Inc as normal into the first DC. Work the first FP DC around the post of the first FP DC from Row 30. You will work the next DC Inc as normal into the next DC. Work the next FP DC around the post of the next available FP DC from Row 30. Work the next "DC 2" into the DC Inc from Row 30. Work the final FP DC around the post of the last FP DC of the set in Row 30. Repeat these instructions around the row.

> Check the Glossary beginning on page 6 for the definition of a "DC Dec," as well as what it means to make a "<Dec>" stitch.

Row 31 created sets of "(DC 2, FP DC)" all the way around the cap of the mushroom. Row 32 will work into two sets of "(DC 2, FP DC)" for each repeat of these instructions. Work the first "DC 2" into the first 2 DC stitches from Row 31 as normal. Work the next FP DC around the post of the first available FP DC. Work the next DC stitch into the next available DC stitch from Row 31. Start the next <DC Dec> into the same stitch the last DC stitch was worked into, and complete the <DC Dec> into the next available DC from Row 31. Work the next DC stitch into the same stitch that you completed the <DC Dec> into. Work the next FP DC around the post of the next available FP DC stitch from Row 31. Repeat these instructions around.

MUSHROOM SPRITE BODIES

33. (DC, <DC Dec>, DC, FP DC, DC 3, FP DC) x 6, Sl St to beginning stitch [48]

> Each of the repeats from Row 33 will be worked into each of the sets of "(DC 2, FP DC, DC, <DC Dec>, DC, FP DC)" from Row 32. Work the first DC stitch into the first available DC stitch from Row 32. Start the next <DC Dec> into the same stitch the last DC stitch was worked into and complete the <DC Dec> into the next available DC from Row 32. Work the next DC stitch into the same stitch that you completed the <DC Dec> into. Work the next FP DC around the post of the next available FP DC stitch from Row 32. Work the next "DC 3" into the next 3 available DC stitches from Row 32 as normal. Work the next FP DC around the post of the next available FP DC stitch from Row 32.

Fasten off with a short yarn tail, and tuck the yarn tail inside when you crochet to attach the Mushroom Cap.

If you have not already done so, fill at least the bottom half of the legs and/or the bottom of the body with flat glass marble gems (or alternative weight) to balance the Mushroom Sprite and help it be stable and sit/stand by itself. Fill the rest of the body firmly with fiberfill.

Body Closure (Make 1)

1. SC 6 in Magic Circle, Sl St to beginning stitch, Ch 1 [6]
2. Inc x 6, Sl St to beginning stitch, Ch 1 [12]

Mushroom Sprite with Arms Style 7, Feet/Legs Style 4, Body Style 4, Cap Style 8

3. Hold this piece against the top hole opening of the Mushroom Sprite body, on top of the under-cap/gills. Working through the next available stitch on the current piece and the leftover back loops from Row 27, (SC, Inc) x 6 around, connecting this piece with the Mushroom Sprite body, Sl St to beginning stitch [18]

> In Row 3, insert your hook first through the next available stitch on the Body Closure piece, Row 2, and then insert your hook through a leftover BLO stitch from Row 28 on the Mushroom Sprite Body, and complete a SC.

Fasten off with a short yarn tail and proceed to a cap suitable for this body style (see chart on page 4).

MUSHROOM SPRITE BODIES • 75

BODY STYLE 5: SHORT SMALL (MAKE 1)

For use with Cap Style 9, 10, 11, 12, 13, or 14

Mushroom Body Color Yarn: Approximately 30 yd/27.5 m worsted/medium weight yarn

> This body can be made with or without arms and/or feet/legs. If you are using feet/legs, select one of the twelve styles of feet/legs and make those before beginning this body.

> You will be filling the legs and base of the body with flat glass marble gems (or alternative weight) to balance the Mushroom Sprite and help it sit by itself. You will be filling the rest of the body firmly with fiberfill. You can do this as you go, or you can leave it until you have finished with the body.

Body

1. SC 6 in Magic Circle, Sl St to beginning stitch, Ch 1 [6]
2. Inc x 6, Sl St to beginning stitch, Ch 1 [12]
3. (SC, Inc) x 6, Sl St to beginning stitch, Ch 1 [18]
4. (SC, Inc, SC) x 6, Sl St to beginning stitch, Ch 1 [24]

> Rows 5 and 6 include instructions on how to crochet to attach feet/legs to the body. Feet/legs help balance and stabilize your Mushroom Sprite and are recommended. Without feet/legs, you'll need to carefully weight the base of your mushroom for balance. If you do not want to include feet/legs, work the rows as follows:
> Row 5: BLO [SC 24], Sl St to beginning stitch, Ch 1
> Rows 6–8: (3 rows of) SC 24, Sl St to beginning stitch, Ch 1, and then continue with Row 9

> In Row 6, you will work into the back loops of the body to create a flat base. When attaching the foot/leg to the body, work through both loops of the foot/leg and the back loop of the body.

5. BLO [SC 5, SC 4 in foot/leg and the BLO of the body stitches at the same time (starting in the marked stitch of the foot/leg), working in the body only, SC 6, SC 4 in foot/leg and the BLO of the body stitches at the same time (starting in the marked stitch of the foot/leg), working in the body only SC 5], Sl St to beginning stitch, Ch 1 [24]

> When you crochet into the foot/leg and the body simultaneously, position the foot/leg piece so you are inserting your hook first into the wrong side (inside) of the foot/leg and then into the BLO of the right side of the body (as normal), and make that stitch into both pieces at the same time.

> All stitches in Row 6 are made into the right side of the work, working all the way around the outside edge of the body and the feet/legs. Do not crochet into the 4 SC stitches on each foot/leg used to connect the feet/legs with the body from Row 5 or into the "Sl St, Ch 1" join.

6. SC 5, working into the first available stitch on the foot/leg, Inc, SC 2, Inc, working into the body, SC 6, working into the foot/leg, Inc, SC 2, Inc, working into the body, SC 5, Sl St to beginning stitch, Ch 1 [28]

7. SC 28, Sl St to beginning stitch, Ch 1 [28]
8. SC 8, (Dec, SC) x 2, (SC, Dec) x 2, SC 8, Sl St to beginning stitch, Ch 1 [24]
9. SC 24, Sl St to beginning stitch, Ch 1 [24]
10. SC 8, Dec x 4, SC 8, Sl St to beginning stitch, Ch 1 [20]

11. SC 20, Sl St to beginning stitch, Ch 1 [20]

12. (SC 3, Dec) x 4, Sl St to beginning stitch, Ch 1 [16]

> In Rows 13–15, follow the instructions for either the "Without Arms" body or the "With Arms" body, based on whether you are incorporating arms. Ignore the set of instructions you do not need/are not using.

13. *Without Arms:* SC 16, Sl St to beginning stitch, Ch 1 [16]

With Arms: SC 4, SC in the next available arm and body stitch at the same time, SC 8 in the body only, SC in the next available arm and body stitch at the same time, SC 2 in the body only, Sl St to beginning stitch, Ch 1 [16]

> When you crochet into the arm and body simultaneously, position the arm piece so that you are inserting your hook first into the inside of the arm to the outside of the arm and then into the right side of the body (as normal), and make that stitch into both pieces at the same time. You can use any stitch on the arm to begin attaching the arm to the body. Make sure you **do not** crochet into the "Sl St, Ch 1" join space on the arm, and aim to orient the arm's join seam to the back side of the Mushroom Sprite.

14. *Without Arms:* (SC, Dec, SC) x 4, Sl St to beginning stitch, Ch 1 [12]

With Arms: Working into the body, SC 3, start a Dec in the next available stitch, complete the Dec in the first available stitch on the first arm, SC 2 in the arm, start a Dec in the last available stitch on the arm, complete the Dec in the next available stitch on the body, working into the body, SC, Dec x 2, SC, start a Dec into the next available stitch on the body, complete the Dec into the first available stitch on the second arm, SC 2 in the arm, start a Dec in the last available stitch on the arm, complete the decrease into the next available stitch on the body, working into the body, SC, Sl St to beginning stitch, Ch 1 [16]

> When you crochet Row 14 with arms, work into the outside of the arm stitches and ignore the stitch used to connect the arm with the body from Row 13.

Mushroom Sprite with Feet/Legs Style 1, Body Style 5, Cap Style 11

MUSHROOM SPRITE BODIES • 77

15. Without Arms: SC 12, Sl St to beginning stitch, Ch 1 [12]

With Arms: (SC, Dec, SC) x 4, Sl St to beginning stitch, Ch 1 [12]

16. (SC 2, Dec, SC 2) x 2, Sl St to beginning stitch, Ch 1 [10]

17-19. (3 rows of) SC 10, Sl St to beginning stitch, Ch 1 [10]

> It is optional to repeat the "SC 10, Sl St to beginning stitch, Ch 1" instruction to create a taller mushroom, as desired.

20. FLO [(SC, Inc) x 5], Sl St to beginning stitch, Ch 2 [15]

> In Row 21, the row ends with the "Sl S to beginning stitch, Ch 2" instruction. The Ch 2 is not counted in the stitch count, and you will not crochet into it.

21. (DC & FP DC) x 15, Sl St to beginning stitch, Ch 2 [30]

> In Row 21, work each DC as normal into the next available stitch, and then work the "& FP DC" around the post of the same SC that you worked the DC stitch into. Repeat these instructions around the row. For a video on the "FP DC" stitch and the "FP DC & DC," go here: https://youtube.com/watch?v=DvBW-Z9dCnYk&t=3s

22. (DC, FP DC) x 15, Sl St to beginning stitch [30]

> In Row 22, work each DC as normal into the next available stitch (a DC from the previous row), and then work the FP DC around the post of the next available FP DC from the previous row. Repeat these instructions around the row.

Fasten off with a short yarn tail, and tuck the yarn tail inside when you crochet to attach the Mushroom Cap.

If you have not already done so, fill the legs and base of the body with flat glass marble gems (or alternative weight) to balance the Mushroom Sprite and help it sit by itself. Fill the rest of the body firmly with fiberfill.

Add 8 mm–12 mm safety eyes between Rows 16 and 17 or Rows 17 and 18 with 2 stitch spaces between the posts, centered on the front of the body, **or** 16 mm safety eyes between Rows 16 and 17 or Rows 17 and 18 with 3 or 4 stitch spaces between the posts (if they are sinker eyes, keep in mind that they will sink into the crochet work as you attach them). It is optional to trim the posts of the safety eyes—do this only if the item is not a toy intended for play, as trimming the post can marginally impact the structural integrity of the eye post. It is helpful to trim the posts of eyes that are applied to thinner Mushroom Sprite stems, which can help with stuffing and so forth. This is optional.

3. Hold this piece against the top hole opening of the Mushroom Sprite body, on top of the under-cap/gills. Working through the next available stitch on the current piece and the leftover back loops from Row 19, (SC, Inc) x 5 around, connecting this piece with the Mushroom Sprite body, Sl St to beginning stitch [15]

In Row 3, insert your hook first through the next available stitch on the Body Closure piece, Row 2, and then insert your hook through a leftover BLO stitch from Row 19 on the Mushroom Sprite Body, and complete a SC.

8 mm eyes

12 mm eyes

9 mm eyes

16 mm eyes

Body Closure (Make 1)

1. SC 5 in Magic Circle, Sl St to beginning stitch, Ch 1 [5]
2. Inc x 5, Sl St to beginning stitch, Ch 1 [10]

Fasten off with a short yarn tail and proceed to a suitable cap option for this body style (see chart on page 4).

Mushroom Sprite with Arms Style 4, Feet/Legs Style 2, Body Style 5, Cap Style 13

MUSHROOM SPRITE BODIES • 79

BODY STYLE 6: SHORT AND WIDE (MAKE 1)

For use with Cap Style 15, 16, 17, 18, 19, 20, 21, 22, or 23

Mushroom Body Color Yarn: Approximately 50 yd/45.75 m worsted/medium weight yarn

> This body can be made with or without arms and/or feet/legs. If you are using feet/legs, select one of the twelve styles of feet/legs and make those before beginning this body.

> You will be filling the base of the body with flat glass marble gems (or alternative weight) to balance the Mushroom Sprite and help it sit by itself. You will be filling the rest of the body firmly with fiberfill. You can do this as you go, or you can leave it until you have finished with the body.

Body

1. SC 6 in Magic Circle, Sl St to beginning stitch, Ch 1 [6]
2. Inc x 6, Sl St to beginning stitch, Ch 1 [12]
3. (SC, Inc) x 6, Sl St to beginning stitch, Ch 1 [18]
4. (SC, Inc, SC) x 6, Sl St to beginning stitch, Ch 1 [24]
5. (SC 3, Inc) x 6, Sl St to beginning stitch, Ch 1 [30]

> Rows 6 and 7 include instructions on how to crochet to attach feet/legs to the body. Feet/legs help balance and stabilize your Mushroom Sprite and are recommended. Without feet/legs, you'll need to carefully weight the base of your mushroom for balance. If you do not want to include feet/legs, work the rows as follows:
> Row 6: BLO [SC 30], Sl St to beginning stitch, Ch 1
> Row 7: SC 30, Sl St to beginning stitch, Ch 1, and then continue with Row 8

6. BLO [SC 8, starting in the marked stitch on the foot/leg, SC 4 in the foot/leg and body at the same time, SC 6 in the body only, starting in the marked stitch on the foot/leg, SC 4 in foot/leg and body at the same time, SC 8 in the body only], Sl St to beginning stitch, Ch 1 [30]

> When you crochet into the foot/leg and body simultaneously, position the foot/leg piece so that you are inserting your hook first into the wrong side (inside) of the foot/leg and then into the right side of the body (as normal), and make that stitch into both pieces at the same time. Make sure you **do not** crochet into the "Sl St, Ch 1" join space on the foot/leg.

7. SC 7, Dec in the next available stitch on the body and the next available stitch on the foot/leg, Inc x 2, Dec in the next available stitch on the foot/leg and the next available stitch on the body, SC 4, Dec in the next available stitch on the body and the next available stitch on the foot/leg, Inc x 2, Dec in the next available stitch on the foot/leg and the next available stitch on the body, SC 7, Sl St to beginning stitch, Ch 1 [30]

> All stitches in Row 7 are made into the right side of the work all the way around the outside edge of the body and the feet/legs. Do not crochet into the 4 SC stitches on each foot/leg used to connect the feet/legs with the body from Row 6.

80 • MUSHROOM SPRITE BODIES

8. SC 30, Sl St to beginning stitch, Ch 1 [30]

9. (SC 4, Dec, SC 4) x 3, Sl St to beginning stitch, Ch 1 [27]

10. SC 27, Sl St to beginning stitch, Ch 1 [27]

11. SC 9, Dec, SC 2, Dec, SC 2, Dec, SC 8, Sl St to beginning stitch, Ch 1 [24]

12. SC 24, Sl St to beginning stitch, Ch 1 [24]

13. SC 8, Dec, SC 2, Dec, SC 2, Dec, SC 6, Sl St to beginning stitch, Ch 1 [21]

In Rows 14–16, follow the instructions for either the "Without Arms" body or the "With Arms" body, based on whether you are incorporating arms. Ignore the set of instructions you do not need/are not using.

14. *Without Arms:* (SC 5, Dec) x 3, Sl St to beginning stitch, Ch 1 [18]

With Arms: Dec, SC 3, SC in arm and body simultaneously, SC in the body only, Dec, SC 5, Dec, SC in arm and body simultaneously, SC 4 in the body only, Sl St to beginning stitch, Ch 1 [18]

When you crochet into the arm and body simultaneously, position the arm piece so that you are inserting your hook first into the inside of the arm to the outside of the arm and then into the right side of the body (as normal), and make that stitch into both pieces at the same time. You can use any stitch on the arm to begin attaching the arm to the body. Make sure you **do not** crochet into the "Sl St, Ch 1" join space on the arm, and aim to orient the arm's join seam to the back side of the Mushroom Sprite.

15. *Without Arms:* SC 18, Sl St to beginning stitch, Ch 1 [18]

With Arms: SC 4 in body, SC 4 in arm, SC in body, Dec x 3 in body, SC in body, SC 4 in arm, SC 4 in body, Sl St to beginning stitch, Ch 1 [21]

When you crochet Row 15 with arms, work into the outside of the arm stitches and ignore the stitches used to connect the arm with the body from Row 14. **Do not** work into the "Sl St, Ch 1" join space on the arms.

16. *Without Arms:* SC 18, Sl St to beginning stitch, Ch 1 [18]

With Arms: (SC 5, Dec) x 3, Sl St to beginning stitch, Ch 1 [18]

MUSHROOM SPRITE BODIES • 81

17. (SC 2, Dec, SC 2) x 3, Sl St to beginning stitch, Ch 1 [15]

18. SC 15, Sl St to beginning stitch, Ch 1 [15]

19. (SC 3, Dec) x 3, Sl St to beginning stitch, Ch 1 [12]

20–23. (4 rows of) SC 12, Sl St to beginning stitch, Ch 1 [12]

> At this point, fill the bottom of the body with flat glass marble gems (or alternative weight) to balance the Mushroom Sprite and help it stand by itself. Fill the rest of the body firmly with fiberfill. It will be difficult to get gems and stuffing down past the eye posts once safety eyes are inserted.

For a Mushroom Sprite **without arms**, add 8 mm–12 mm safety eyes between Rows 19 and 20 with 2 stitch spaces between the posts, centered on the front of the body, **or** 15 mm–16 mm safety eyes between Rows 19 and 20 with 3 or so stitch spaces between the posts (if they are sinker eyes, keep in mind that they will sink into the crochet work as you attach them).

For a Mushroom Sprite **with arms**, add 8 mm–12 mm safety eyes between Rows 20 and 21 with 2 stitch spaces between the posts, centered on the front of the body, **or** 15 mm–16 mm safety eyes between Rows 17 and 18 with 3 or so stitch spaces between the posts (if they are sinker eyes, keep in mind that they will sink into the crochet work as you attach them). It is optional to trim the posts of the safety eyes—do this only if the item is not a toy intended for play, as trimming the post can marginally impact the structural integrity of the eye post. It is helpful to trim the posts of eyes that are applied to thinner Mushroom Sprite stems, which can help with stuffing and so forth. This is optional.

8 mm eyes

12 mm eyes

9 mm eyes

16 mm eyes

24. Ch 1 more, FLO [(DC Inc) x 12], Sl St to beginning stitch, Ch 2 [24]

> The Ch 2 in Row 24 and all following rows is just to bring you level with the first stitch of the next row; do not crochet into it.

82 • MUSHROOM SPRITE BODIES

25. (HDC Inc, FP HDC) x 12, Sl St to beginning stitch, Ch 2 [36]

26. (DC, DC Inc, FP DC) x 12, Sl St to beginning stitch, Ch 2 [48]

For a video on the "FP DC" stitch and more, go here: https://youtube.com/watch?v=DvBWZ9dCnYk&t=3s

For Cap Style 20: Picot Edge Bell, **do not** Ch 2. Fasten off with a short yarn tail, and tuck the yarn tail inside when you crochet to attach the Mushroom Sprite cap. Proceed to Cap Style 20: Picot Edge Bell.

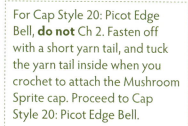

For Cap Style 15, 16, 17, 18, 19, 21, 22, or 23, continue to crochet the body.

27. (HDC, FP HDC) x 24, Sl St to beginning stitch, Ch 2 [48]

For Cap Style 15, 16, 17, 21, 22, or 23, **do not** Ch 2. Fasten off with a short yarn tail, and tuck the yarn tail inside when you crochet to attach the Mushroom Sprite cap. Proceed to Cap Style 15, 16, 17, 21, 22, or 23. For Cap Style 18 or 19, continue to crochet the body.

28. (DC, FP DC, DC Inc, FP DC, DC, FP DC) x 8, Sl St to beginning stitch [56]

Fasten off with a short yarn tail. Tuck the yarn tail inside when you crochet to attach the Mushroom Cap. Proceed to Cap Style 18 or 19.

Mushroom Sprite with Arms Style 3, Feet/Legs Style 4, Body Style 6, Cap Style 15

MUSHROOM SPRITE BODIES • 83

Body Closure (Make 1)

1. SC 6 in Magic Circle, Sl St to beginning stitch, Ch 1 [6]

2. Inc x 6, Sl St to beginning stitch, Ch 1 [12]

3. Hold this piece against the top hole opening of the Mushroom Sprite body, on top of the under-cap/gills. Working through the next available stitch on the current piece and the leftover back loops from Row 23, (SC, Inc) x 6 around, connecting this piece with the Mushroom Sprite body, Sl St to beginning stitch [18]

> In Row 3, you will insert your hook first through the next available stitch on the Body Closure piece, Row 2, and then you will insert your hook through a leftover BLO stitch from Row 23 on the Mushroom Sprite Body and complete a SC.

Fasten off with a short yarn tail and proceed to a suitable cap option for this body style (see chart on page 4).

If you have not already done so, fill at least the bottom half of the legs and/or the bottom of the body with flat glass marble gems (or alternative weight) to balance the Mushroom Sprite and help it be stable and sit/stand by itself. Fill the rest of the body firmly with fiberfill.

Mushroom Sprite with Feet/Legs Style 2, Body Style 6, Cap Style 21

84 • MUSHROOM SPRITE BODIES

BODY STYLE 7: CHANTERELLE BODY AND CAP (MAKE 1 OF EACH)

The Chanterelle Cap can be used only with the Chanterelle Body. They are paired together in this section.

Mushroom Body Color Yarn: Approximately 70 yd/64 m worsted/medium weight yarn

Mushroom Cap Color Yarn: Approximately 26 yd/23.75 m worsted/medium weight yarn

> This body can be made with or without arms and/or feet/legs. If you are using feet/legs, select one of the twelve styles of feet/legs and make those before beginning this body.

> You will be filling the legs and base of the body with flat glass marble gems (or alternative weight) to balance the Mushroom Sprite and help it sit by itself. You will be filling the rest of the body firmly with fiberfill. You can do this as you go, or you can leave it until you have finished with the body.

❶ Mushroom Sprite with Arms Style 2, Feet/Legs Style 3, Body Style 5, Cap Style 10; ❷ Mushroom Sprite with Arms Style 3, Feet/Legs Style 8, Body Style 7

Body

1. SC 6 in Magic Circle, Sl St to beginning stitch, Ch 1 [6]
2. Inc x 6, Sl St to beginning stitch, Ch 1 [12]
3. (SC, Inc) x 6, Sl St to beginning stitch, Ch 1 [18]
4. (SC, Inc, SC) x 6, Sl St to beginning stitch, Ch 1 [24]
5. (SC 3, Inc) x 6, Sl St to beginning stitch, Ch 1 [30]

> Rows 6 and 7 include instructions on how to crochet to attach feet/legs to the body. Feet/legs help balance and stabilize your Mushroom Sprite and are recommended. Without feet/legs, you'll need to carefully weight the base of your mushroom for balance. If you do not want to include feet/legs, work the rows as follows:
> Row 6: BLO [SC 30], Sl St to beginning stitch, Ch 1
> Row 7: (SC 13, Dec) x 2, Sl St to beginning stitch, Ch 1, and then continue with Row 8

MUSHROOM SPRITE BODIES • 85

6. BLO [SC 8, starting in the marked stitch of the first foot/leg, SC 4 in the foot/leg and the body at the same time; working in the body only, SC 6, starting in the marked stitch of the second foot/leg, SC 4 in the foot/leg and the body at the same time, working in the body only, SC 8], Sl St to beginning stitch, Ch 1 [30]

> When you crochet into the foot/leg and body simultaneously, position the foot/leg piece so you are inserting your hook first into the wrong side (inside) of the foot/leg and then into the BLO of the right side of the body (as normal), and make that stitch into both pieces at the same time.

7. SC 7, Dec starting in the next available stitch on the body and ending in the next available stitch on the foot/leg, working in the foot/leg only, SC, <Dec>, SC, Dec starting in the next available stitch on the foot/leg and ending in the next available stitch on the body, SC 4 in the body, Dec starting in the next available stitch on the body and ending in the next available stitch on the foot/leg, working in the foot/leg only, SC, <Dec>, SC, Dec starting in the next available stitch on the foot/leg and ending in the next available stitch on the body, SC 7 in the body, Sl St to beginning stitch, Ch 1 [28]

> All stitches in Row 7 are made into the right side of the Mushroom, working all the way around the outside edge of the body and the feet/legs. Do not crochet into the 4 SC stitches on each foot/leg used to connect the feet/legs with the body from Row 6.

> "<Dec>" is a stitch that is defined in the Glossary beginning on page 6.

8–9. (2 rows of) SC 28, Sl St to beginning stitch, Ch 1 [28]

10. (SC 6, Dec, SC 6) x 2, Sl St to beginning stitch, Ch 1 [26]

11. SC 26, Sl St to beginning stitch, Ch 1 [26]

12. (SC 11, Dec) x 2, Sl St to beginning stitch, Ch 1 [24]

13–14. (2 rows of) SC 24, Sl St to beginning stitch, Ch 1 [24]

15. SC 5, Dec, SC 10, Dec, SC 5, Sl St to beginning stitch, Ch 1 [22]

> In Rows 16–18, follow the instructions for either the "Without Arms" body or the "With Arms" body, based on whether you are incorporating arms. Ignore the set of instructions you do not need/are not using.

16. *Without Arms:* SC 22, Sl St to beginning stitch, Ch 1 [22]

With Arms: SC 7, SC in arm and body simultaneously, SC 9, SC in arm and body simultaneously, SC 4, Sl St to beginning stitch, Ch 1 [22]

> When you crochet into the arm and body simultaneously, position the arm piece so you are inserting your hook first into the inside of the arm to the outside of the arm and then into the right side of the body (as normal), and make that stitch into both pieces at the same time. You can use any stitch on the arm to begin attaching the arm to the body. Make sure you **do not** crochet into the "Sl St, Ch 1" join space on the arm, and aim to orient the arm's join seam to the back side of the Mushroom Sprite.

86 • MUSHROOM SPRITE BODIES

17. Without Arms: SC 22, Sl St to beginning stitch, Ch 1 [22]

With Arms: Working in the body, SC 5, Dec, working in the arm, SC 4, working in the body, SC, Dec, SC 5, start a Dec into the next available stitch on the body and complete the Dec into the first available stitch on the arm, working in the arm, SC 3, working in the body, SC 2, Dec, Sl St to beginning stitch, Ch 1 [24]

> When you crochet Row 17 with arms, work into the outside of the arm stitches and ignore the stitch used to connect the arm with the body from Row 16. **Do not** work into the "Sl St, Ch 1" join space on the arms.

18. Without Arms: (SC 9, Dec) x 2, Sl St to beginning stitch, Ch 1 [20]

With Arms: (SC 2, Dec, SC 2) x 4, Sl St to beginning stitch, Ch 1 [20]

19–20. (2 rows of) SC 20, Sl St to beginning stitch, Ch 1 [20]

21. (SC 4, Dec, SC 4) x 2, Sl St to beginning stitch, Ch 1 [18]

22–26. (5 rows of) SC 18, Sl St to beginning stitch, Ch 1 [18]

27. HDC 18, Sl St to beginning stitch, Ch 2 [18]

> The Ch 2 in Row 28 and all following rows is just to bring you level with the first stitch of the next row; do not crochet into it.

28. (DC, DC & FP DC) x 9, Sl St to beginning stitch, Ch 2 [27]

> For a video on the "FP DC" stitch and the "FP DC & DC," go here: https://youtube.com/watch?v=DvBWZ9dCnYk&t=3s

29. (DC & FP DC, DC, FP DC) x 9, Sl St to beginning stitch, Ch 2 [36]

30. (DC & FP DC) x 36, Sl St to beginning stitch, Ch 2 [72]

31. (DC, FP DC) x 36, Sl St to beginning stitch, Ch 1 [72]

32. SC 72, Sl St to beginning stitch [72]

Fasten off with a short yarn tail, and tuck it inside of the body when you crochet to attach the Mushroom Cap. There is no Body Closure for the Chanterelle Mushroom.

MUSHROOM SPRITE BODIES • 87

> Insert 8 mm–16 mm safety eyes between Rows 22 and 23 or Rows 23 and 24, with 2 stitch spaces between the posts.

16 mm eyes

12 mm eyes

9 mm eyes

8 mm eyes

If you have not already done so, fill the legs and the bottom of the body with flat glass marble gems (or alternative weight) to balance the Mushroom Sprite and help it stand by itself. Fill the rest of the body firmly with fiberfill.

Chanterelle Cap (Make 1)

> You will use a "Sl St to beginning stitch, Ch 1" join after each row. This approach assists with the careful shaping.

1. Ch 5, starting in the 2nd Ch from hook, SC 3, Inc, keep crocheting around to the opposite side of the original chain, SC 3, Sl St to beginning stitch, Ch 1 [8]

2. Inc x 2, HDC Inc, DC Inc, HDC & SC, SC & HDC, DC Inc, HDC & SC, Sl St to beginning stitch, Ch 1 [16]

3. SC, Inc, HDC, HDC & DC, DC, DC Inc, DC, DC & HDC, HDC Inc, Inc, SC, HDC Inc, DC, DC Triple Increase, HDC, Inc, Sl St to beginning stitch, Ch 1 [26]

> A "DC Triple Increase" is 3 DC stitches worked into the same stitch.

4. SC 2, Inc, SC 2, SC & HDC, HDC, DC, DC Triple Increase, HDC, SC, SC & HDC, DC, DC Inc, DC & HDC, SC 2, Inc, HDC, HDC & DC, DC Inc, DC & HDC, HDC & SC, SC 3, Sl St to beginning stitch, Ch 1 [38]

5. SC 3, Inc, SC 3, SC & HDC, HDC 2, DC, DC Inc x 2, DC & HDC, SC 2, SC & HDC, HDC, DC, DC Inc, DC & HDC, HDC, SC 5, HDC 2, DC Inc x 2, DC & HDC, HDC & SC, SC 5, Sl St to beginning stitch, Ch 1 [50]

6. SC, HDC, DC Inc, HDC, Inc, SC 3, HDC, HDC & DC, HDC 2, SC, SC & HDC, HDC, DC Inc, DC & HDC, SC 6, HDC Inc, DC 2, DC Inc, DC & HDC, SC 8, HDC, HDC Inc, HDC & DC, DC, DC Inc, DC & HDC, HDC 2, Inc, SC 5, Sl St to beginning stitch, Ch 1 [64]

88 • MUSHROOM SPRITE BODIES

7. SC 2, HDC, HDC Inc, SC 8, HDC Inc x 2, SC 6, HDC & DC, DC & HDC, SC 3, Dec, SC 2, HDC, HDC & DC, DC 2, DC Inc, DC & HDC, SC 5, Dec, SC 5, HDC 3, DC Inc, DC 2, DC & HDC, SC 10, Sl St to beginning stitch, Ch 1 [72]

> Stuff medium-light with fiberfill as you finish. Fill out the shape of the cap, but do not over-stuff—it's better to have it more lightly stuffed than too firm/too full.

8. SC 72 in the Mushroom Cap and the Mushroom Body at the same time, Sl St to beginning stitch [72]

> To form the first SC in Row 8, you will be inserting your hook first into the next available stitch of the Mushroom Cap and then into any stitch (I prefer the back center stitch) of the Mushroom Body, and then complete the stitch. Do not stuff the cap.

Fasten off with a 12 in/30.5 cm yarn tail and weave it in.

Mushroom Sprite with Feet/Legs Style 12, Body Style 7

MUSHROOM SPRITE BODIES • 89

BODY STYLE 8: MOREL BODY AND CAP (MAKE 1 OF EACH)

The Morel Cap can be used only with the Morel Body. They are paired together in this section.

Mushroom Body Color Yarn: Approximately 45 yd/41.25 m worsted/medium weight yarn

Accent Color Yarn for Cap: Approximately 60 yd/55 m sport/light weight yarn

This body can be made with or without arms and/or feet/legs. If you are using feet/legs, select one of the twelve styles of feet/legs and make those before beginning this body.

You will be filling the legs and base of the body with flat glass marble gems (or alternative weight) to balance the Mushroom Sprite and help it sit by itself. You will be filling the rest of the body firmly with fiberfill. You can do this as you go, or you can leave it until you have finished with the body.

Body

1. SC 6 in Magic Circle, Sl St to beginning stitch, Ch 1 [6]
2. Inc x 6, Sl St to beginning stitch, Ch 1 [12]
3. (SC, Inc) x 6, Sl St to beginning stitch, Ch 1 [18]
4. (SC, Inc, SC) x 6, Sl St to beginning stitch, Ch 1 [24]
5. (SC 3, Inc) x 6, Sl St to beginning stitch, Ch 1 [30]

Rows 6 and 7 include instructions on how to crochet to attach feet/legs to the body. Feet/legs help balance and stabilize your Mushroom Sprite and are recommended. Without feet/legs, you'll need to carefully weight the base of your mushroom for balance. If you do not want to include feet/legs, work the rows as follows:
Row 6: BLO [SC 30], Sl St to beginning stitch, Ch 1
Row 7: (SC 13, Dec) x 2, Sl St to beginning stitch, Ch 1, and then continue with Row 8

6. BLO [SC 8 in the body only, starting in the marked stitch, SC 4 in the foot/leg and the body at the same time, SC 6 in the body only, starting in the marked stitch, SC 4 in the foot/leg and the body at the same time, SC 8 in the body only], Sl St to beginning stitch, Ch 1 [30]

When you crochet into the foot/leg and body simultaneously, position the foot/leg piece so you are inserting your hook first into the wrong side (inside) of the foot/leg and then into the BLO of the right side of the body (as normal), and make that stitch into both pieces at the same time.

7. SC 7, Dec in the next available stitch on the body and the next available stitch on the foot/leg, working in the foot/leg only, SC, <Dec>, SC, Dec in the next available stitch on the foot/leg and the next available stitch on the body, working in the body only, SC 4, Dec in the next available stitch on the body and the next available stitch on the foot/leg, working in the foot/leg only, SC, <Dec>, SC, Dec in the next available stitch on the foot/leg and the next available stitch on the body, working in the body only, SC 7, Sl St to beginning stitch, Ch 1 [28]

All stitches in Row 7 are made into the right side of the Mushroom, worked all the way around the outside edge of the body and the feet/legs. Do not crochet into the 4 SC stitches on each foot/leg used to connect the feet/legs with the body from Row 6. Make sure you **do not** crochet into the "Sl St, Ch 1" join space.

"<Dec>" is a stitch that is defined in the Glossary beginning on page 6.

90 • MUSHROOM SPRITE BODIES

8–9. (2 rows of) SC 28, Sl St to beginning stitch, Ch 1 [28]

10. (SC 6, Dec, SC 6) x 2, Sl St to beginning stitch, Ch 1 [26]

11. SC 26, Sl St to beginning stitch, Ch 1 [26]

12. (SC 11, Dec) x 2, Sl St to beginning stitch, Ch 1 [24]

13–14. (2 rows of) SC 24, Sl St to beginning stitch, Ch 1 [24]

> In Rows 15–17, follow the instructions for either the "Without Arms" body or the "With Arms" body, based on whether you are incorporating arms. Ignore the set of instructions you do not need/are not using.

15. Without Arms: (SC 5, Dec, SC 5) x 2, Sl St to beginning stitch, Ch 1 [22]

With Arms: SC 5, Dec, SC in arm and body simultaneously, SC 9, Dec, SC in arm and body simultaneously, SC 4, Sl St to beginning stitch, Ch 1 [22]

> When you crochet into the arm and body simultaneously, position the arm piece so that you are inserting your hook first into the inside of the arm to the outside of the arm and then into the right side of the body (as normal), and make that stitch into both pieces at the same time. You can use any stitch on the arm to begin attaching the arm to the body, but aim to orient the arm's join seam to the back side of the Mushroom Sprite. Make sure you **do not** crochet into the "Sl St, Ch 1" join space on the arm.

16. Without Arms: SC 22, Sl St to beginning stitch, Ch 1 [22]

With Arms: SC 5, start a decrease in the next available stitch on the body and complete the decrease in the first available stitch on the arm, working in the arm, SC 3, working in the body, SC 2, Dec, SC 5, start a decrease in the next available stitch on the body and complete the decrease in the first available stitch on the arm, working in the arm, SC 3, working in the body, SC 2, Dec, Sl St to beginning stitch, Ch 1 [24]

> When you crochet Row 16 with arms, work into the outside of the arm stitches and ignore the stitches used to connect the arm with the body from Row 15. **Do not** work into the "Sl St, Ch 1" join space on the arms.

17. Without Arms: SC 22, Sl St to beginning stitch, Ch 1 [22]

With Arms: (SC 5, Dec, SC 5) x 2, Sl St to beginning stitch, Ch 1 [22]

18. (SC 9, Dec) x 2, Sl St to beginning stitch, Ch 1 [20]

19–20. (2 rows of) SC 20, Sl St to beginning stitch, Ch 1 [20]

21. (SC 4, Dec, SC 4) x 2, Sl St to beginning stitch, Ch 1 [18]

22. SC 18, Sl St to beginning stitch, Ch 1 [18]

MUSHROOM SPRITE BODIES

23. BLO [SC 18], Sl St to beginning stitch, Ch 1 [18]

> Insert 8 mm–16 mm safety eyes between Rows 19 and 20 with 2 stitch spaces between the posts. Fill the bottom half of the Mushroom Sprite with flat glass marble gems for weight and balance. Stuff the rest as you go with fiberfill.

16 mm eyes

12 mm eyes

9 mm eyes

8 mm eyes

24. *(DC into the first leftover FLO from Row 22, SC 3, DC into FLO from Row 22, SC 2, Dec) x 2, Sl St to beginning stitch, Ch 1 [16]

> Skip the stitch from Row 23 that is directly behind each FLO DC you make in Row 24. Skip the leftover front loops from Row 22 directly below the stitches you work into Row 23. You create 4 FP DC stitches in Row 24.

*Here's a detailed breakdown of Row 24: Work the first DC into the first available FLO from Row 22 (the unworked front loop left over after Row 23). Skip 1 stitch on Row 23, and then, continuing into Row 23, SC 3. Skip 3 stitches on the FLO stitches from Row 22, and then work the next DC into the next available FLO from Row 22. Skip 1 stitch on Row 23, and then, continuing into Row 23, SC 2, Dec. Skip 4 stitches on the FLO stitches from Row 22. Then repeat that set of instructions again, starting with working the next DC into the next available leftover FLO from Row 22. Repeat this full set of instructions one more time.

25. **SC 2, Half Trip into FLO from Row 22, (SC 3, Half Trip into FLO from Row 22) x 3, SC, Sl St to beginning stitch, Ch 1 [16]

**Here's a detailed breakdown of Row 25: SC in each of 2 stitches from Row 24. Then work a Half Trip into the 2nd available FLO from Row 22 (between 2 FLO DC stitches from Row 24). Skip 1 stitch on Row 24, and then, continuing into Row 24, SC 3. Then work a Half Trip into the 2nd available FLO from Row 22 (between the next 2 DC stitches from Row 24). Skip 1 stitch on Row 24, and then work SC 3 as normal into the stitches from Row 24. Then work a Half Trip into the 2nd available FLO from Row 22 (between the next 2 FLO DC stitches from Row 24). Skip 1 stitch on Row 24, and then, continuing into Row 24, SC 3. Then work a Half Trip into the 2nd available FLO from Row 22 (between the next 2 FLO DC stitches from Row 24). Skip 1 stitch on Row 24, and then, continuing into Row 24, SC, Sl St to beginning stitch, Ch 1.

> Front post stitches in Row 26 are worked into the DC stitches from Rows 24, and the front post stitches in Row 27 are worked into the Half Trip stitches from Row 25. Rows 24 and 25 create a total of 8 ridges (where you will work FP DC stitches) to anchor the ruffles of the morel cap. Each subsequent row makes 4 posts.

26. (FP DC, SC 3) x 4, Sl St to beginning stitch, Ch 1 [16]

Make each FP DC in Row 26 around the posts of the FP DC stitches in Row 24. Always skip the corresponding stitch from Row 25 behind your FP DC. "FP DC" is a stitch that is defined in the Glossary that begins on page 6.

27. Dec, (FP DC, 2 Dec in 3 SC) x 3, FP DC, SC, Sl St to beginning stitch, Ch 1 [12]

Make each FP DC in Row 27 around the Half Trip stitches in Row 25. Always skip the corresponding stitch from Row 26 behind your FP DC.

The "2 Dec in 3 SC" is a special stitch and is defined in the Glossary beginning on page 6.

28. (FP DC, SC 2) x 4, Sl St to beginning stitch, Ch 1 [12]

Make each FP DC in Row 28 around the FP DC stitches from Row 26. Always skip the corresponding stitch from Row 27 behind your FP DC.

29. SC, FP DC, (SC 2, FP DC) x 3, SC, Sl St to beginning stitch, Ch 1 [12]

Make each FP DC in Row 29 around the FP DC stitches from Row 27. Always skip the corresponding stitch from Row 28 behind your FP DC.

30. (FP DC, SC 2) x 4, Sl St to beginning stitch, Ch 1 [12]

Make each FP DC in Row 30 around the FP DC stitches from Row 28. Always skip the corresponding stitch from Row 29 behind your FP DC.

If you have not already done so, fill at least the legs and, preferably, also some of the base of the body with flat glass marble gems (or alternative weight) to balance the Mushroom Sprite and help it stand by itself. Fill the rest of the body firmly with fiberfill.

31. SC, FP DC, (SC 2, FP DC) x 3, SC, Sl St to beginning stitch, Ch 1 [12]

Make each FP DC in Row 31 around the FP DC stitches from Row 29. Always skip the corresponding stitch from Row 30 behind your FP DC.

MUSHROOM SPRITE BODIES • 93

32. (FP DC, SC 2) x 4, Sl St to beginning stitch, Ch 1 [12]

33. SC, FP DC, (SC 2, FP DC) x 3, SC, Sl St to beginning stitch, Ch 1 [12]

34. (FP DC, SC 2) x 4, Sl St to beginning stitch, Ch 1 [12]

Make each FP DC in Row 32 around the FP DC stitches from Row 30. Always skip the corresponding stitch from Row 31 behind your FP DC.

Make each FP DC in Row 33 around the FP DC stitches from Row 31. Always skip the corresponding stitch from Row 32 behind your FP DC.

Make each FP DC in Row 34 around the FP DC stitches from Row 32. Always skip the corresponding stitch from Row 33 behind your FP DC.

35. (FP DC, FP Half Trip) x 4, Sl St to beginning stitch, Ch 1 [8]

Make each FP DC in Row 35 around the FP DC stitches from Row 34. Make each FP Half Trip in Row 35 around the FP DC stitches from Row 33. Do not work into any of the SC from Row 34. Finish stuffing with fiberfill before completing the next row.

Mushroom Sprite with Arms Style 10, Feet/Legs Style 9, Body Style 8

94 • MUSHROOM SPRITE BODIES

36. Dec x 4, Sl St to beginning stitch [4]

Fasten off with a 12 in/30.5 cm yarn tail.

Morel Mushroom Cap

1. Attach the sport weight Accent Color Yarn to the top of one of the posts of a stitch in Row 35, Ch 2.

2. Make between 5 and 8 Half Trip stitches around each post stitch in the line of posts down to Row 24. The more Half Triple Crochets you make, the fuller and more ruffled the end result will be. More is better.

> You will work down and up the columns of FP stitches in these cap instructions until you get back to where you started, making ruffles of Half Triple Crochet stitches.

3. Make 2 or 3 Half Trip stitches in each of the next (1 or 2) Front Loops left over from Row 22. This will bring you to the next vertical column of Front Post stitches.

4. Make between 5 and 8 Half Trip stitches around each post in the line of Front Posts back up to Row 35.

MUSHROOM SPRITE BODIES • 95

5. Make 2 Half Trip stitches around the next closest Dec in Row 36.

6. Repeat Rows 2–5 another 3 times, Sl St to the very first Half Trip you made in this section.

Fasten off with a long enough yarn tail to weave in. Use the body's yarn tail to sew the hole shut at the top of the body of the Mushroom; weave in ends.

Mushroom Sprite with Feet/Legs Style 2, Body Style 8

Mushroom Sprite with Arms Style 9, Body Style 1, Cap Style 1, optional dots

1. **Mushroom Sprite with Feet/Legs Style 2, Body Style 8;** 2. **Mushroom Sprite with Arms Style 7, Body Style 2, Cap Style 4;** 3. **Mushroom Sprite with Arms Style 5, Feet/Legs Style 8, Body Style 3, Cap Style 16**

Mushroom Sprite Caps

Caps contribute significantly to the personality of your Mushroom Sprite. Some sprites are shy and like a cap they can hide behind; some sprites are bold and prefer a jaunty tilt to their cap. Other sprites want a clear view so they can steer their snail steed with a sure and steady hand.

OPTIONS

**Cap Style 1:
Large Round . . . 101**

Used with: Body Style 1

**Cap Style 2:
Large Pointed . . . 102**

Used with: Body Style 1

**Cap Style 3:
Large Uneven . . . 103**

Used with: Body Style 1

**Cap Style 4:
Small Cone . . . 105**

Used with: Body Style 2

Cap Style 5: Cone . . . 107

Used with: Body Style 4

**Cap Style 6:
Small Ruffle . . . 109**

Used with: Body Style 4

Cap Style 7: Round . . . 111

Used with: Body Style 4

**Cap Style 8:
Tall and Pointy . . . 113**

Used with: Body Style 4

Cap Style 9:
Gumdrop Shape . . . 115
Used with: Body Style 2 or 5

Cap Style 10:
Small Round . . . 116
Used with: Body Style 2 or 5

Cap Style 11:
Straight Pointed . . . 117
Used with: Body Style 2 or 5

Cap Style 12:
Curved Pointed . . . 119
Used with: Body Style 2 or 5

Cap Style 13: Wavy . . . 121
Used with: Body Style 2 or 5

Cap Style 14: Ruffly . . 122
Used with: Body Style 2 or 5

Cap Style 15: Fairy Cap
Spiral Curling . . . 123
Used with: Body Style 3 or 6

Cap Style 16: Fairy Cap,
Wavy and Pointing Up . . 126
Used with: Body Style 3 or 6

Cap Style 17:
Inky Cap (*Coprinopsis atramentaria*) . . . 128
Used with: Body Style 3 or 6

Cap Style 18: Fly Agaric
(*Amanita muscaria*),
Solid Color . . . 131
Used with: Body Style 3 or 6

Cap Style 19: Fly Agaric
(*Amanita muscaria*),
Two Colors . . . 132
Used with: Body Style 3 or 6

Cap Style 20:
Picot Edge Bell . . . 135
Used with: Body Style 3 or 6

Cap Style 21:
Ruffle Edge . . . 137
Used with: Body Style 3 or 6

Cap Style 22:
Wide Cap . . . 138
Used with: Body Style 3 or 6

Cap Style 23:
Wavy Edge . . . 140
Used with: Body Style 3 or 6

Optional Spots/Dots
for Caps . . . 141

MUSHROOM SPRITE CAPS

Mushroom Sprite with Arms Style 7, Body Style 1, Cap Style 1

CAP STYLE 1: LARGE ROUND (MAKE 1)

For use with Mushroom Sprite Body Style 1

Mushroom Cap Color Yarn: Approximately 62 yd/56.75 m worsted/medium weight yarn

> Where there is no join method indicated, caps can be crocheted to your preference—either worked in spiral to prevent a visible seam or using the "Sl St to beginning stitch, Ch 1" join method. The two join methods are interchangeable on simple symmetrical pieces. The join methods are **not** interchangeable on pieces with more detailed shaping, due to the shift of the stitches from a particular join method being built into the shaping.

> It is not recommended to stuff this cap with fiberfill.

1. SC 6 in Magic Circle [6]
2. Inc x 6 [12]
3. (SC, Inc) x 6 [18]
4. (SC, Inc, SC) x 6 [24]
5. (SC 3, Inc) x 6 [30]
6. (SC 2, Inc, SC 2) x 6 [36]
7. (SC 5, Inc) x 6 [42]
8. (SC 3, Inc, SC 3) x 6 [48]
9. (SC 7, Inc) x 6 [54]
10. (SC 4, Inc, SC 4) x 6 [60]
11. (SC 9, Inc) x 6 [66]
12. (SC 5, Inc, SC 5) x 6 [72]
13. (SC 11, Inc) x 6 [78]
14. (SC 6, Inc, SC 6) x 6 [84]
15. (SC 13, Inc) x 6 [90]
16. SC 90 [90]
17. (SC 7, Inc, SC 7) x 6 [96]
18–19. (2 rows of) SC 96 [96]
20. SC 96 in the Mushroom Cap and the last row of the Mushroom Body at the same time [96]

> To form the first SC in Row 20, insert your hook first into the next available stitch of the Mushroom Cap and then into any stitch (I prefer the back center stitch) of the Mushroom Body and complete the stitch.

21. SC 96 [96]
22. (SC 14, Dec) x 6, Sl St to beginning stitch [90]

Fasten off with a 12 in/30.5 cm yarn tail to weave in, and optionally position the Mushroom Cap at an angle and sew it in place.

CAP STYLE 2: LARGE POINTED (MAKE 1)

For use with Body Style 1

Mushroom Cap Color Yarn: Approximately 105 yd/96 m worsted/medium weight yarn

> Where there is no join method indicated, caps can be crocheted to your preference—either worked in spiral to prevent a visible seam or using the "Sl St to beginning stitch, Ch 1" join method. The two join methods are interchangeable on simple symmetrical pieces. The join methods are **not** interchangeable on pieces with more detailed shaping, due to the shift of the stitches from a particular join method being built into the shaping.

> It is not recommended to stuff this cap with fiberfill.

1. SC 6 in Magic Circle [6]
2. SC 6 [6]
3. Inc x 6 [12]
4. SC 12 [12]
5. (SC, Inc) x 6 [18]
6. SC 18 [18]
7. (SC, Inc, SC) x 6 [24]
8. SC 24 [24]
9. (SC 3, Inc) x 6 [30]
10. SC 30 [30]
11. (SC 2, Inc, SC 2) x 6 [36]
12. SC 36 [36]
13. (SC 5, Inc) x 6 [42]
14. SC 42 [42]
15. (SC 3, Inc, SC 3) x 6 [48]
16. (SC 7, Inc) x 6 [54]
17. SC 54 [54]
18. (SC 4, Inc, SC 4) x 6 [60]
19. (SC 9, Inc) x 6 [66]
20. SC 66 [66]
21. (SC 5, Inc, SC 5) x 6 [72]
22. (SC 11, Inc) x 6 [78]
23. (SC 6, Inc, SC 6) x 6 [84]
24. (SC 13, Inc) x 6 [90]
25. SC 90 [90]
26. (SC 7, Inc, SC 7) x 6 [96]
27-28. (2 rows of) SC 96 [96]

29. SC 96 in the Mushroom Cap and the last row of the Mushroom Body at the same time [96]

> To form the first SC in Row 29, insert your hook first into the next available stitch of the Mushroom Cap and then into any stitch (I prefer the back center stitch) of the Mushroom Body, and then complete the stitch.

30. SC 96 [96]
31. (SC 7, Dec, SC 7) x 6, Sl St to beginning stitch [90]

Fasten off with a 12 in/30.5 cm yarn tail to weave in and optionally position the Mushroom Cap at an angle and sew it in place.

Mushroom Sprite with Arms Style 8, Body Style 1, Cap Style 2

102 • MUSHROOM SPRITE CAPS

Mushroom Sprite with Body Style 1, Cap Style 2

CAP STYLE 3: LARGE UNEVEN (MAKE 1)

For use with Body Style 1

Mushroom Cap Color Yarn: Approximately 66 yd/60.5 m worsted/medium weight yarn

> Where there is no join method indicated, caps can be crocheted to your preference—either worked in spiral to prevent a visible seam or using the "Sl St to beginning stitch, Ch 1" join method. The two join methods are interchangeable on simple symmetrical pieces. The join methods are **not** interchangeable on pieces with more detailed shaping, due to the shift of the stitches from a particular join method being built into the shaping.

> It is not recommended to stuff this cap with fiberfill.

1. HDC 10 in Magic Circle [10]
2. HDC Inc x 10 [20]
3. (SC, Inc, HDC, HDC Inc) x 5 [30]

4. (SC, Inc, SC, HDC, HDC Inc, HDC) x 5 [40]
5. (SC 3, Inc, HDC 3, HDC Inc) x 5 [50]
6. (SC 2, Inc, SC 2, HDC 2, HDC Inc, HDC 2) x 5 [60]

7. (SC 5, Inc, HDC 5, Inc) x 5 [70]
8. (SC 3, Inc, SC 3, HDC 3, HDC Inc, HDC 3) x 5 [80]

MUSHROOM SPRITE CAPS • 103

9. (SC 7, Inc, HDC 7, HDC Inc) x 5 [90]

10. (SC 3, 2 Dec in 3 SC, SC 3, HDC 4, HDC Inc, HDC 4) x 5 [90]

> The "2 Dec in 3 SC" is a special stitch and is defined in the Glossary beginning on page 6.

12. (SC 2, 2 Dec in 3 SC, SC 2, HDC 3, HDC Inc, HDC 3, HDC Inc, HDC 3) x 5 [95]

13. (SC 2, Dec, SC 2, HDC 6, HDC Inc, HDC 6) x 5 [95]

> It is optional to include a flat disc (like plastic canvas cut to size, etc.) on top of the body of the Mushroom Sprite's under-cap. This helps maintain the flat under-cap when the cap is stuffed. You can also include a small amount of stuffing above this flat disc.

11. (SC 3, Dec, SC 3, HDC 5, <HDC Dec>, HDC 5) x 5 [90]

> The "<HDC Dec>" is a stitch that is defined in the Glossary beginning on page 6.

❶ **Mushroom Sprite with Arms Style 9, Body Style 1, Cap Style 3;** ❷ **Mushroom Sprite with Feet/Legs Style 10, Body Style 3, Cap Style 15**

Mushroom Sprite with Arms Style 6, Body Style 1, Cap Style 3

14. SC in the Mushroom Cap and the last row of the Mushroom Body at the same time, SC in the same stitch on the Mushroom Cap and the next available stitch on the Mushroom Body, SC 94 more in the Mushroom Cap and the last row of the Mushroom Body at the same time, Sl St to the beginning stitch [96]

Fasten off with a 12 in/30.5 cm yarn tail to weave in and optionally position the Mushroom Cap at an angle and sew it in place.

> To form the first SC in Row 14, insert your hook first into the next available stitch of the Mushroom Cap and then into any stitch (I prefer the back center stitch) of the Mushroom Body, and then complete the stitch.

CAP STYLE 4: SMALL CONE (MAKE 1 PER HEAD)

For use with Body Style 2

Mushroom Cap Color Yarn: Approximately 22 yd/20 m worsted/medium weight yarn

> Where there is no join method indicated, caps can be crocheted to your preference—either worked in spiral to prevent a visible seam or using the "Sl St to beginning stitch, Ch 1" join method. The two join methods are interchangeable on simple symmetrical pieces. The join methods are **not** interchangeable on pieces with more detailed shaping, due to the shift of the stitches from a particular join method being built into the shaping.

1. SC 5 in Magic Circle [5]
2. Inc x 5 [10]
3. SC 10 [10]
4. (SC, Inc) x 5 [15]
5. SC 15 [15]
6. (SC, Inc, SC) x 5 [20]
7. SC 20 [20]
8. (SC 3, Inc) x 5 [25]
9. (SC 2, Inc, SC 2) x 5 [30]

Mushroom Sprite with Arms Style 7, Body Style 2, Cap Style 4

MUSHROOM SPRITE CAPS • 105

10–12. (3 rows of) SC 30 [30]

13. SC 30 into the cap and body at the same time, Sl St to beginning stitch [30]

> To form the first SC in Row 13, insert your hook first into the next available stitch of the Mushroom Cap and then into any stitch (I prefer the back center stitch) of the Mushroom Body, and then complete the stitch. Optional: Stuff the cap lightly with fiberfill (the caps in the photos have not been stuffed).

Fasten off with a 12 in/30.5 cm yarn tail to weave in and optionally position the Mushroom Cap at an angle and sew it in place.

Mushroom Sprite with Body Style 2, Cap Style 4

Mushroom Sprite with Feet/Legs Style 4, Body Style 3, Cap Style 5

106 • MUSHROOM SPRITE CAPS

CAP STYLE 5: CONE (MAKE 1)

For use with Body Style 4

Mushroom Cap Color Yarn:
Approximately 43 yd/39.25 m worsted/medium weight yarn

> Where there is no join method indicated, caps can be crocheted to your preference— either worked in spiral to prevent a visible seam or using the "Sl St to beginning stitch, Ch 1" join method. The two join methods are interchangeable on simple symmetrical pieces. The join methods are **not** interchangeable on pieces with more detailed shaping, due to the shift of the stitches from a particular join method being built into the shaping.

1. SC 6 in Magic Circle [6]
2. Inc x 6 [12]
3. SC 12 [12]
4. (SC, Inc) x 6 [18]
5. (SC, Inc, SC) x 6 [24]
6. SC 24 [24]
7. (SC 3, Inc) x 6 [30]
8. (SC 2, Inc, SC 2) x 6 [36]
9. SC 36 [36]
10. (SC 5, Inc) x 6 [42]
11. (SC 3, Inc, SC 3) x 6 [48]
12. (SC 7, Inc) x 6 [54]
13. (SC 4, Inc, SC 4) x 6 [60]
14. (SC 9, Inc) x 6 [66]

> To form the SC in Row 15, insert your hook first into the next available stitch of the Mushroom Cap and then into any stitch (I recommend beginning with the back center stitch) of the Mushroom Body, and then complete the stitch. Do not stuff the cap.

15A. SC in both the next available cap and body stitch at the same time

15B. SC in both the next available cap and body stitch at the same time

15C. SC in both the next available cap stitch and the same body stitch you last crocheted into, at the same time

15D. Repeat 15A, 15B, and 15C

15E. Repeat 15A, 15B, and 15C

15F. SC in both the next available cap and body stitch at the same time

15G. SC in both the next available cap and body stitch at the same time

15H. SC in the same cap stitch you last crocheted into and the same body stitch you last crocheted into, at the same time

15I. Repeat 15A–15H 5 more times (for a total of 6 repeats around the entire edge of the Mushroom Cap) [72]

16. SC 72 [72]
17. (SC 10, Dec) x 6, Sl St to beginning stitch [66]

Fasten off with a 12 in/30.5 cm yarn tail to weave in and optionally use to position the Mushroom Cap at an angle and sew it in place.

Mushroom Sprite with Arms Style 4, Feet/Legs Style 5, Body Style 4, Cap Style 5

Top to bottom: ❶ Mushroom Sprite with Arms Style 4, Feet/Legs Style 12, Body Style 4, Cap Style 6; ❷ Mushroom Sprite with Arms Style 7, Feet/Legs Style 10, Body Style 4, Cap Style 6

If you give your Mushroom Sprite arms and legs, they will likely try to climb.

CAP STYLE 6: SMALL RUFFLE (MAKE 1)

For use with Body Style 4

Mushroom Cap Color Yarn: Approximately 50 yd/45.75 m worsted/medium weight yarn

> Where there is no join method indicated, caps can be crocheted to your preference—either worked in spiral to prevent a visible seam or using the "Sl St to beginning stitch, Ch 1" join method. The two join methods are interchangeable on simple symmetrical pieces. The join methods are **not** interchangeable on pieces with more detailed shaping, due to the shift of the stitches from a particular join method being built into the shaping.

1. SC 8 in Magic Circle [8]
2. Inc x 8 [16]
3. SC 16 [16]
4. (SC, Inc) x 8 [24]
5. SC 24 [24]
6. (SC, Inc, SC) x 8 [32]
7. SC 32 [32]
8. (SC 3, Inc) x 8 [40]
9. SC 40 [40]
10. (SC 2, Inc, SC 2) x 8 [48]
11. SC 48 [48]
12. (SC 5, Inc) x 8 [56]
13. (SC 3, Inc, SC 3) x 8 [64]
14. (SC 7, Inc) x 8 [72]
15. (SC 4, Inc, SC 4) x 8 [80]
16. (SC 2, Inc, SC 2) x 16 [96]

17. (Working into both the cap and the body at the same time, SC 2, working into the cap only, SC, Inc, SC, working into both the next available stitch on the cap and the same stitch you last crocheted into on the body at the same time, SC, and then, working in the next available stitch on both the cap and the body at the same time, SC 2) x 12, Sl St to beginning stitch [108]

> To form a SC in Row 17, insert your hook first into the next available stitch of the Mushroom Cap (inserting your hook into the right side/outside to the wrong side/inside) and then into any stitch (I prefer the back center) of the Mushroom Body (inserting your hook into the wrong side/inside to the right side/outside), and then complete the stitch. Do not stuff the cap or stuff only very lightly. **Do not** work into the "Sl St, Ch 1" join of the body.

Fasten off with a 12 in/30.5 cm yarn tail to weave in and optionally use to position the Mushroom Cap at an angle and sew it in place.

> Stuffing the cap is not necessary. However, if you choose to add stuffing, place a small amount in the tip of the cap before placing it on the Mushroom Body. You want just enough to give the very tip of the cap structure but not so much that it makes the cap stick up too far above the gills. The Mushroom Caps in the photos are not stuffed.

MUSHROOM SPRITE CAPS • 109

Mushroom Sprite with Arms Style 2, Feet/Legs Style 1, Body Style 4, Cap Style 6

CAP STYLE 7: ROUND (MAKE 1)

For use with Body Style 4

Mushroom Cap Color Yarn: Approximately 40 yd/36.5 m worsted/medium weight yarn

> Where there is no join method indicated, caps can be crocheted to your preference—either worked in spiral to prevent a visible seam or using the "Sl St to beginning stitch, Ch 1" join method. The two join methods are interchangeable on simple symmetrical pieces. The join methods are **not** interchangeable on pieces with more detailed shaping, due to the shift of the stitches from a particular join method being built into the shaping.

> The Mushroom Cap will not be stuffed with fiberfill.

1. SC 6 in Magic Circle [6]
2. Inc x 6 [12]
3. (SC, Inc) x 6 [18]
4. (SC, Inc, SC) x 6 [24]
5. (SC 3, Inc) x 6 [30]
6. (SC 2, Inc, SC 2) x 6 [36]
7. (SC 5, Inc) x 6 [42]
8. (SC 3, Inc, SC 3) x 6 [48]
9. (SC 7, Inc) x 6 [54]
10. (SC 4, Inc, SC 4) x 6 [60]
11. (SC 9, Inc) x 6 [66]
12. (SC 5, Inc, SC 5) x 6 [72]
13–14. (2 rows of) SC 72 [72]

15. Working into both the cap and the body at the same time, (SC in the next available stitch on the cap and the next available stitch on the body at the same time, SC in the next available stitch on the cap and the next available stitch on the body at the same time, SC in the next available stitch on the cap and the same stitch on the body at the same time) x 24, Sl St to beginning stitch [72]

> To form the first SC in Row 15, insert your hook first into the next available stitch of the Mushroom Cap (inserting your hook into the right side/outside to the wrong side/inside) and then into any stitch (I prefer the back center) of the Mushroom Body (inserting your hook into the wrong side/inside to the right side/outside), and then complete the stitch. **Do not** stuff the cap. Do not work into the "Sl St, Ch 1" join of the body.

Fasten off with a 12 in/30.5 cm yarn tail to weave in and optionally use to position the Mushroom Cap at an angle and sew it in place.

❶ Mushroom Sprite with Arms Style 7, Feet/Legs Style 10, Body Style 4, Cap Style 6, riding on a ❷ Giant Snail with a Pointed Shell and a saddle

MUSHROOM SPRITE CAPS • 111

Mushroom Sprite with Arms Style 6, Feet/Legs Style 2, Body Style 4, Cap Style 7

CAP STYLE 8: TALL AND POINTY (MAKE 1)

For use with Body Style 4

Mushroom Cap Color Yarn: Approximately 46 yd/42 m worsted/medium weight yarn

> Where there is no join method indicated, caps can be crocheted to your preference—either worked in spiral to prevent a visible seam or using the "Sl St to beginning stitch, Ch 1" join method. The two join methods are interchangeable on simple symmetrical pieces. The join methods are **not** interchangeable on pieces with more detailed shaping, due to the shift of the stitches from a particular join method being built into the shaping.

> The Mushroom Cap will not be stuffed with fiberfill.

1. SC 4 in Magic Circle [4]
2. SC 3, Inc [5]
3. SC 5 [5]
4. SC 2, Inc, SC 2 [6]
5. SC 6 [6]
6. SC 5, Inc [7]
7. SC 7 [7]
8. SC 3, Inc, SC 3 [8]
9. SC 8 [8]
10. SC 7, Inc [9]
11. SC 9 [9]
12. SC 4, Inc, SC 4 [10]
13. SC 10 [10]
14. (SC 2, Inc, SC 2) x 2 [12]
15. SC 12 [12]
16. (SC 3, Inc) x 3 [15]
17. SC 15 [15]
18. (SC 2, Inc, SC 2) x 3 [18]
19. SC 18 [18]
20. (SC, Inc, SC) x 6 [24]
21. SC 24 [24]
22. (SC 3, Inc) x 6 [30]
23. SC 30 [30]
24. (SC 2, Inc, SC 2) x 6 [36]
25. (SC 5, Inc) x 6 [42]
26. (SC 3, Inc, SC 3) x 6 [48]
27. (SC 7, Inc) x 6 [54]
28. (SC 4, Inc, SC 4) x 6 [60]
29. (SC 9, Inc) x 6 [66]
30. (SC 5, Inc, SC 5) x 6 [72]
31. SC 72 [72]

Mushroom Sprite with Arms Style 7, Feet/Legs Style 4, Body Style 4, Cap Style 8

32. Working into both the cap and the body at the same time, (SC in the next available stitch on the cap and the next available stitch on the body at the same time, SC in the next available stitch on the cap and the next available stitch on the body at the same time, SC in the next available stitch on the cap and the same stitch on the body at the same time) x 24, Sl St to beginning stitch [72]

> To form the first SC in Row 32, insert your hook first into the next available stitch of the Mushroom Cap (inserting your hook into the right side/outside to the wrong side/inside) and then into any stitch (I prefer the back center) of the Mushroom Body (inserting your hook into the wrong side/inside to the right side/outside), and then complete the stitch. **Do not stuff the cap. Do not work into the "Sl St, Ch 1" join of the body.**

Fasten off with a 12 in/30.5 cm yarn tail to weave in and optionally use to position the Mushroom Cap at an angle and sew it in place.

Mushroom Sprite with Arms Style 3, Feet/Legs Style 9, Body Style 4, Cap Style 8

Mushroom Sprites can be indoor creatures too. They're very quiet and very clean. They do sometimes invite friends without asking permission, but, for the most part, they're excellent roommates.

Mushroom Sprite with Arms Style 6, Feet/Legs Style 12, Body Style 4, Cap Style 8, optional dots

114 • MUSHROOM SPRITE CAPS

CAP STYLE 9: GUMDROP SHAPE (MAKE 1)

For use with Body Style 2 or 5

Mushroom Cap Color Yarn: Approximately 21 yd/19.25 m worsted/medium weight yarn

> Where there is no join method indicated, caps can be crocheted to your preference—either worked in spiral to prevent a visible seam or using the "Sl St to beginning stitch, Ch 1" join method. The two join methods are interchangeable on simple symmetrical pieces. The join methods are **not** interchangeable on pieces with more detailed shaping, due to the shift of the stitches from a particular join method being built into the shaping.

> It is optional to include a flat disc (like plastic canvas cut to size, etc.) on top of the body of the Mushroom Sprite's under-cap. This helps prevent the cap from collapsing and maintains the flat under-cap after it is stuffed. Include a small amount of stuffing above this flat disc.

1. SC 6 in Magic Circle [6]
2. Inc x 6 [12]
3. (SC 3, Inc) x 3 [15]
4. (SC 2, Inc, SC 2) x 3 [18]
5. (SC 5, Inc) x 3 [21]

6. (SC 3, Inc, SC 3) x 3 [24]
7. (SC 7, Inc) x 3 [27]
8. (SC 4, Inc, SC 4) x 3 [30]
9–12. (4 rows of) SC 30 [30]

13. SC 30 in cap and body at the same time, Sl St to beginning stitch [30]

> To form a SC in Row 13, insert your hook first into the next available stitch of the Mushroom Cap and then into any stitch (I prefer to start in the back center stitch) of the Mushroom Body, and then complete the stitch.

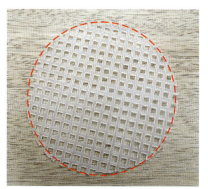

Fasten off with a 12 in/30.5 cm yarn tail to weave in and optionally use to position the Mushroom Cap at an angle and sew it in place.

MUSHROOM SPRITE CAPS · 115

Mushroom Sprite with Arms Style 2, Feet/Legs Style 6, Body Style 5, Cap Style 9

❶ Mushroom Sprite with Arms Style 4, Feet/Legs Style 1, Body Style 6, Cap Style 16; ❷ Mushroom Sprite with Arms Style 9, Body Style 2, Cap Style 10

CAP STYLE 10: SMALL ROUND (MAKE 1)

For use with Body Style 2 or 5

Mushroom Cap Color Yarn: Approximately 25 yd/22.75 m worsted/medium weight yarn

Where there is no join method indicated, caps can be crocheted to your preference—either worked in spiral to prevent a visible seam or using the "Sl St to beginning stitch, Ch 1" join method. The two join methods are interchangeable on simple symmetrical pieces. The join methods are **not** interchangeable on pieces with more detailed shaping, due to the shift of the stitches from a particular join method being built into the shaping.

1. SC 6 in Magic Circle [6]
2. Inc x 6 [12]
3. (SC, Inc) x 6 [18]
4. (SC, Inc, SC) x 6 [24]
5. (SC 3, Inc) x 6 [30]
6. (SC 2, Inc, SC 2) x 6 [36]
7–10. (4 rows of) SC 36 [36]

For a flatter round cap, you can work fewer repeats of SC 36 here. Instead of 4 rows, you can try 1 or 2 rows.

11. (SC 5, Dec, SC 5) x 3 [33]

116 • MUSHROOM SPRITE CAPS

12. In the cap and the body at the same time (SC 9, Dec [to make the Dec, insert the hook into the next available stitch on the cap and the next available stitch on the body, pull up a loop, insert the hook into the next available stitch in the cap and the same stitch on the body, pull up a second loop, and complete the Dec]) x 3, Sl St to beginning stitch [30]

> To form the first SC in Row 12, insert your hook first into the next available stitch of the Mushroom Cap and then into any stitch (I prefer the back center stitch) of the Mushroom Body, and then complete the stitch.

Fasten off with a 12 in/30.5 cm yarn tail to weave in and optionally position the Mushroom Cap at an angle and stitch it in place.

> It is optional to include a flat disc (like plastic canvas cut to size, a bottle cap, etc.) on top of the body of the Mushroom Sprite's under-cap. This helps the cap to not collapse, and it helps maintain the flat under-cap when the cap is stuffed. Include a small amount of stuffing above this flat disc.

CAP STYLE 11: STRAIGHT POINTED (MAKE 1)

For use with Body Style 2 or 5

Mushroom Cap Color Yarn: Approximately 23 yd/21 m worsted/medium weight yarn

> Where there is no join method indicated, caps can be crocheted to your preference—either worked in spiral to prevent a visible seam or using the "Sl St to beginning stitch, Ch 1" join method. The two join methods are interchangeable on simple symmetrical pieces. The join methods are **not** interchangeable on pieces with more detailed shaping, due to the shift of the stitches from a particular join method being built into the shaping. This Mushroom Cap will not be stuffed with fiberfill.

1. SC 4 in Magic Circle [4]
2. SC 3, Inc [5]
3. SC 5 [5]
4. SC 2, Inc, SC 2 [6]
5. SC 5, Inc [7]
6. SC 3, Inc, SC 3 [8]
7. SC 7, Inc [9]
8. SC 4, Inc, SC 4 [10]
9. (SC 2, Inc, SC 2) x 2 [12]
10. (SC 3, Inc) x 3 [15]
11. (SC 2, Inc, SC 2) x 3 [18]
12. (SC 5, Inc) x 3 [21]
13. (SC 3, Inc, SC 3) x 3 [24]
14. (SC 3, Inc) x 6 [30]
15. (SC 2, Inc, SC 2) x 6 [36]
16. (SC 3, Inc) x 9 [45]

MUSHROOM SPRITE CAPS • 117

To form the first SC in Row 17, insert your hook first into the next available stitch of the Mushroom Cap (inserting your hook into the right side/outside to the wrong side/inside) and then into any stitch (I prefer the back center) of the Mushroom Body (inserting your hook into the wrong side/inside to the right side/outside), and then complete the stitch. Do not stuff the cap. **Do not** work into the "Sl St, Ch 1" join of the body.

17. Working into both the cap and the body at the same time, (SC in the next available stitch on the cap and the next available stitch on the body at the same time, SC in the next available stitch on the cap and the next available stitch on the body at the same time, SC in the next available stitch on the cap and the same stitch on the body at the same time) x 15 [45]

18. (SC 4, Inc, SC 4) x 5, Sl St to beginning stitch [50]

Fasten off with a 12 in/30.5 cm yarn tail to weave in and optionally position the Mushroom Cap at an angle and stitch it in place.

Mushroom Sprite with Arms Style 6, Feet/Legs Style 10, Body Style 5, Cap Style 10

Mushroom Sprite with Arms Style 4, Feet/Legs Style 9, Body Style 5, Cap Style 11

Mushroom Sprite with Feet/Legs Style 1, Body Style 5, Cap Style 11

Mushroom Sprite with Arms Style 2, Feet/Legs Style 6, Body Style 5, Cap Style 12, optional dots (and French knot embroidery)

CAP STYLE 12: CURVED POINTED (MAKE 1)

For use with Body Style 2 or 5

Mushroom Cap Color Yarn: Approximately 28 yd/25.5 m worsted/medium weight yarn

> You will use a "Sl St to beginning stitch, Ch 1" join after each row. This approach assists in the careful shaping. This Mushroom Cap will not be stuffed with fiberfill.

1. SC 4 in Magic Circle, Sl St to beginning stitch, Ch 1 [4]
2. SC 4, Sl St to beginning stitch, Ch 1 [4]
3. Inc, SC 3, Sl St to beginning stitch, Ch 1 [5]
4. SC, Inc, SC, HDC Dec, Sl St to beginning stitch, Ch 1 [5]
5. SC, Inc, SC, HDC 2, Sl St to beginning stitch, Ch 1 [6]
6. HDC, SC, Inc, SC, HDC Dec, Sl St to beginning stitch, Ch 1 [6]
7. SC 2, Inc, SC 2, HDC, Sl St to beginning stitch, Ch 1 [7]
8. HDC, SC, Inc, SC, HDC, HDC Dec, Sl St to beginning stitch, Ch 1 [7]
9. HDC 2, SC, Inc, SC, HDC 2, Sl St to beginning stitch, Ch 1 [8]
10. SC, HDC 5, SC, Inc, Sl St to beginning stitch, Ch 1 [9]
11. SC 2, HDC 2, <HDC Dec>, HDC 2, SC 2, Inc, Sl St to beginning stitch, Ch 1 [11]
12. Inc, SC, HDC 7, SC, Inc, Sl St to beginning stitch, Ch 1 [13]
13. SC 2, Inc, SC, HDC 3, HDC Inc, HDC 3, SC, Inc, Sl St to beginning stitch, Ch 1 [16]
14. (SC 7, Inc) x 2, Sl St to beginning stitch, Ch 1 [18]
15. (SC 5, Inc) x 3, Sl St to beginning stitch, Ch 1 [21]
16. (SC 3, Inc, SC 3) x 3, Sl St to beginning stitch, Ch 1 [24]
17. (SC 3, Inc) x 6, Sl St to beginning stitch, Ch 1 [30]
18. (SC 2, Inc, SC 2) x 6, Sl St to beginning stitch, Ch 1 [36]
19. (SC 3, Inc) x 9, Sl St to beginning stitch, Ch 1 [45]

To form the first SC in Row 20, insert your hook first into the next available stitch of the Mushroom Cap (inserting your hook into the right side/outside to the wrong side/inside) and then into any stitch (I prefer the back center) of the Mushroom Body (inserting your hook into the wrong side/inside to the right side/outside), and then complete the stitch. Do not stuff the cap. Do not work into the "Sl St, Ch 1" join of the body.

20. Working into both the cap and the body at the same time, (SC in the next available stitch on the cap and the next available stitch on the body at the same time, SC in the next available stitch on the cap and the next available stitch on the body at the same time, SC in the next available stitch on the cap and the next available stitch on the body at the same time, SC in the next available stitch on the cap and the same stitch on the body at the same time) x 15, Sl St to beginning stitch, Ch 1 [45]

It is optional to fasten off after Row 20 for a slightly shorter cap.

21. (SC 4, Inc, SC 4) x 5, Sl St to beginning stitch [50]

Fasten off with a 12 in/30.5 cm yarn tail to weave in and optionally position the Mushroom Cap at an angle and stitch it in place.

Mushroom Sprite with Feet/Legs Style 3, Body Style 5, Cap Style 12

Mushroom Sprite with Arms Style 4, Feet/Legs Style 2, Body Style 5, Cap Style 13

CAP STYLE 13: WAVY (MAKE 1)

For use with Body Style 2 or 5

Mushroom Cap Color Yarn: Approximately 30 yd/27.5 m worsted/medium weight yarn

> Where there is no join method indicated, caps can be crocheted to your preference—either worked in spiral to prevent a visible seam or using the "Sl St to beginning stitch, Ch 1" join method. The two join methods are interchangeable on simple symmetrical pieces. The join methods are **not** interchangeable on pieces with more detailed shaping, due to the shift of the stitches from a particular join method being built into the shaping. This Mushroom Cap will not be stuffed with fiberfill.

1. SC 6 in Magic Circle [6]
2. (Inc, HDC Inc) x 3 [12]
3. (SC, Inc, HDC, HDC Inc) x 3 [18]
4. (SC, Inc, SC, HDC, HDC Inc, HDC) x 3 [24]
5. (SC, Dec, SC, HDC, HDC Inc x 2, HDC) x 3 [27]
6. (2 Dec in 3 SC, HDC, HDC Inc x 4, HDC) x 3 [36]

> The "2 Dec in 3 SC" is a special stitch and is defined in the Glossary beginning on page 6.

7. (Dec, HDC 3, HDC Triple Inc, HDC 2, HDC Triple Inc, HDC 3) x 3 [45]

8. Working into both the cap and the body at the same time, (HDC Inc in the next available stitch on the cap and the next available stitch on the body at the same time, HDC in the next available stitch on the cap and the next available stitch on the body at the same time, HDC in the next available stitch on the cap and the same stitch on the body at the same time) x 15 [60]

> To form the first HDC in Row 8, insert your hook first into the next available stitch of the Mushroom Cap (inserting your hook into the right side/outside to the wrong side/inside) and then into any stitch (I prefer the back center) of the Mushroom Body (inserting your hook into the wrong side/inside to the right side/outside), and then complete the stitch. Do not stuff the cap. Do not work into the "Sl St, Ch 1" join of the body.

> It is optional to fasten off here, at Row 8, for a smaller-size cap or to continue to Row 9 to complete a more ruffly, natural-looking edge.

Mushroom Sprite with Arms Style 2, Feet/Legs Style 7, Body Style 5, Cap Style 13

9. (HDC Inc, HDC, HDC Triple Inc, HDC) x 15, Sl St to beginning stitch [105]

Fasten off with a 12 in/30.5 cm yarn tail to weave in and optionally position the Mushroom Cap at an angle and stitch it in place.

CAP STYLE 14: RUFFLY (MAKE 1)

For use with Body Style 2 or 5

Mushroom Cap Color Yarn: Approximately 36 yd/33 m worsted/medium weight yarn

Where there is no join method indicated, caps can be crocheted to your preference—either worked in spiral to prevent a visible seam or using the "Sl St to beginning stitch, Ch 1" join method. The two join methods are interchangeable on simple symmetrical pieces. The join methods are **not** interchangeable on pieces with more detailed shaping, due to the shift of the stitches from a particular join method being built into the shaping. This Mushroom Cap will not be stuffed with fiberfill.

11. (Working into both the cap and the body at the same time, Inc, SC, working into the cap only, SC, Inc, SC, Inc, SC, working into both the next available stitch on the cap and the same stitch you last crocheted into on the body, SC, and then, working in the next available stitch on both the cap and the body at the same time, Inc) x 10 [130]

To form the first stitch in Row 11, insert your hook first into the next available stitch of the Mushroom Cap (inserting your hook into the right side/outside to the wrong side/inside) and then into any stitch (I prefer the center back) of the Mushroom Body (inserting your hook into the wrong side/inside to the right side/outside), and then complete the stitch. Do not stuff the cap. Do not work into the "Sl St, Ch 1" join of the body.

It is optional to Sl St to the beginning stitch and fasten off after Row 11 for a smaller-size cap, or you may continue to Row 12 to complete an even more ruffly edge.

1. SC 6 in Magic Circle [6]
2. (SC, Inc) x 3 [9]
3. (SC, Inc, SC) x 3 [12]
4. (SC 3, Inc) x 3 [15]
5. (SC 2, Inc, SC 2) x 3 [18]
6. (SC 5, Inc) x 3 [21]
7. (SC 3, Inc, SC 3) x 3 [24]
8. (SC, Inc) x 12 [36]
9. (Inc, SC, Inc) x 12 [60]
10. (SC, Inc) x 30 [90]

Mushroom Sprite with Arms Style 3, Feet/Legs Style 2, Body Style 5, Cap Style 14

12. (SC, Inc, SC 4, Inc, SC 4, Inc, SC) x 10, Sl St to beginning stitch [160]

Fasten off with a 12 in/30.5 cm yarn tail to weave in and optionally position the Mushroom Cap at an angle and stitch it in place.

Mushroom Sprite with Arms Style 3, Feet/Legs Style 4, Body Style 5, Cap Style 14

CAP STYLE 15: FAIRY CAP SPIRAL CURLING (MAKE 1)

For use with Body Style 3 or 6

Mushroom Cap Color Yarn: Approximately 66 yd/60.5 m worsted/medium weight yarn

> The Mushroom Cap will not be stuffed with fiberfill.

> You will use a "Sl St to beginning stitch, Ch 1" join after each row. This approach assists in the careful shaping.

1. SC 4 in Magic Circle, Sl St to beginning stitch, Ch 1 [4]
2. SC 4, Sl St to beginning stitch, Ch 1 [4]
3. Inc, SC 3, Sl St to beginning stitch, Ch 1 [5]
4. SC, Inc, SC, HDC Dec, Sl St to beginning stitch, Ch 1 [5]
5. SC, Inc, SC, HDC 2, Sl St to beginning stitch, Ch 1 [6]
6. HDC, SC, Inc, SC, HDC Dec, Sl St to beginning stitch, Ch 1 [6]
7. SC 2, Inc, SC 2, HDC, Sl St to beginning stitch, Ch 1 [7]
8. HDC, SC, Inc, SC, HDC, HDC Dec, Sl St to beginning stitch, Ch 1 [7]
9. HDC 2, SC, Inc, SC, HDC 2, Sl St to beginning stitch, Ch 1 [8]
10. HDC Dec, SC, Inc x 2, SC, HDC Dec, Sl St to beginning stitch, Ch 1 [8]
11. HDC 3, SC, Inc, SC, HDC 2, Sl St to beginning stitch, Ch 1 [9]
12. HDC Dec, HDC, SC 2, Inc, SC 2, HDC, Sl St to beginning stitch, Ch 1 [9]
13. HDC 3, SC, Inc x 2, SC, HDC 2, Sl St to beginning stitch, Ch 1 [11]
14. HDC 4, SC, Inc x 2, SC, HDC 3, Sl St to beginning stitch, Ch 1 [13]
15. HDC 5, SC, Inc x 2, SC, HDC 4, Sl St to beginning stitch, Ch 1 [15]
16. HDC 6, SC, Inc x 2, SC, HDC 5, Sl St to beginning stitch, Ch 1 [17]

Mushroom Sprite with Arms Style 2, Feet/Legs Style 6, Body Style 6, Cap Style 15

17. HDC 7, SC, Inc x 2, SC, HDC 6, Sl St to beginning stitch, Ch 1 [19]

18. HDC 8, SC, Inc x 2, SC, HDC 7, Sl St to beginning stitch, Ch 1 [21]

19. SC 7, HDC 5, HDC Inc, HDC 5, SC 3, Sl St to beginning stitch, Ch 1 [22]

20. Inc, SC 2, Inc, SC 2, HDC 14, SC 2, Sl St to beginning stitch, Ch 1 [24]

21. SC 24, Sl St to beginning stitch, Ch 1 [24]

22. SC, Inc, SC 3, Inc, SC 2, HDC 15, SC, Sl St to beginning stitch, Ch 1 [26]

23. SC 26, Sl St to beginning stitch, Ch 1 [26]

24. SC 2, Inc, SC 3, Inc, SC 2, HDC 17, Sl St to beginning stitch, Ch 1 [28]

25. SC 28, Sl St to beginning stitch, Ch 1 [28]

26. SC 4, Inc, SC 2, Inc, SC 4, HDC 16, Sl St to beginning stitch, Ch 1 [30]

27. (SC 7, Inc, SC 7) x 2, Sl St to beginning stitch, Ch 1 [32]

28. (SC 7, Inc) x 4, Sl St to beginning stitch, Ch 1 [36]

29. (SC 4, Inc, SC 4) x 4, Sl St to beginning stitch, Ch 1 [40]

30. (SC 9, Inc) x 4, Sl St to beginning stitch, Ch 1 [44]

31. (SC 5, Inc, SC 5) x 4, Sl St to beginning stitch, Ch 1 [48]

32. Working into both the cap and the body at the same time, (SC 7, Inc) x 6, Sl St to beginning stitch, Ch 1 [54]

> To form a SC in Row 32, insert your hook first into the next available stitch of the Mushroom Cap (inserting your hook into the right side/outside to the wrong side/inside) and then into any stitch (I prefer the back center) of the Mushroom Body (inserting your hook into the wrong side/inside to the right side/outside), and then complete the stitch. Do not stuff the cap. **Do not** work into the "Sl St, Ch 1" join of the body or the cap.

33. (SC 4, Inc, SC 4) x 6, Sl St to beginning stitch, Ch 1 [60]

34. (SC 9, Inc) x 6, Sl St to beginning stitch [66]

Fasten off with a 12 in/30.5 cm yarn tail to weave in and optionally position the spiraling Mushroom Cap at an angle and hold it in place.

124 • MUSHROOM SPRITE CAPS

Mushroom Sprite with Arms Style 3, Feet/Legs Style 4, Body Style 6, Cap Style 15

CAP STYLE 16: FAIRY CAP, WAVY AND POINTING UP (MAKE 1)

For use with Body Style 3 or 6

Mushroom Cap Color Yarn: *Approximately 48 yd/44 m worsted/medium weight yarn*

> You will use a "Sl St to beginning stitch, Ch 1" join after each row. This approach assists with the careful shaping. This Mushroom Cap will not be stuffed with fiberfill.

1. SC 4 in Magic Circle, Sl St to beginning stitch, Ch 1 [4]
2. SC 4, Sl St to beginning stitch, Ch 1 [4]
3. Inc, SC 3, Sl St to beginning stitch, Ch 1 [5]
4. SC 3, HDC 2, Sl St to beginning stitch, Ch 1 [5]
5. SC, Inc, SC, HDC 2, Sl St to beginning stitch, Ch 1 [6]
6. HDC, SC 3, HDC 2, Sl St to beginning stitch, Ch 1 [6]
7. SC 2, Inc, SC 2, HDC, Sl St to beginning stitch, Ch 1 [7]
8. SC 7, Sl St to beginning stitch, Ch 1 [7]
9. SC, HDC 4, SC, Inc, Sl St to beginning stitch, Ch 1 [8]
10. SC 2, HDC 4, SC 2, Sl St to beginning stitch, Ch 1 [8]

11. Inc, SC, HDC 5, SC, Sl St to beginning stitch, Ch 1 [9]
12. SC 3, HDC 5, SC, Sl St to beginning stitch, Ch 1 [9]
13. Inc x 2, SC, HDC 5, SC, Sl St to beginning stitch, Ch 1 [11]
14. SC, Inc x 2, SC, HDC 7, SC, Sl St to beginning stitch, Ch 1 [13]
15. SC 13, Sl St to beginning stitch, Ch 1 [13]
16. HDC 9, SC, Inc x 2, SC, Sl St to beginning stitch, Ch 1 [15]
17. HDC 10, SC, Inc x 2, SC, HDC, Sl St to beginning stitch, Ch 1 [17]
18. SC 17, Sl St to beginning stitch, Ch 1 [17]
19. HDC 12, Inc, SC 2, Inc, HDC, Sl St to beginning stitch, Ch 1 [19]
20. HDC 13, SC, Inc x 2, SC, HDC 2, Sl St to beginning stitch, Ch 1 [21]

21. SC 21, Sl St to beginning stitch, Ch 1 [21]
22. HDC 15, SC 2, Inc, SC 2, HDC, Sl St to beginning stitch, Ch 1 [22]
23. HDC 2, SC 2, Inc, SC 2, Inc, SC 2, HDC 12, Sl St to beginning stitch, Ch 1 [24]
24. SC 24, Sl St to beginning stitch, Ch 1 [24]
25. HDC 4, SC 2, Inc, SC 3, Inc, SC 2, HDC 11, Sl St to beginning stitch, Ch 1 [26]
26. SC 26, Sl St to beginning stitch, Ch 1 [26]
27. SC 5, HDC 9, SC 7, Inc, SC, Inc, SC 2, Sl St to beginning stitch, Ch 1 [28]

126 • MUSHROOM SPRITE CAPS

28. SC 28, Sl St to beginning stitch, Ch 1 [28]

29. SC 5, HDC 12, SC 6, Inc, SC 2, Inc, SC, Sl St to beginning stitch, Ch 1 [30]

30. (SC 7, Inc, SC 7) x 2, Sl St to beginning stitch, Ch 1 [32]

31. (SC 7, Inc) x 4, Sl St to beginning stitch, Ch 1 [36]

32. (SC 4, Inc, SC 4) x 4, Sl St to beginning stitch, Ch 1 [40]

33. (SC 9, Inc) x 4, Sl St to beginning stitch, Ch 1 [44]

34. (SC 5, Inc, SC 5) x 4, Sl St to beginning stitch, Ch 1 [48]

To form the first SC in Row 35, insert your hook first into the next available stitch of the Mushroom Cap (inserting your hook into the right side/outside to the wrong side/inside) and then into any stitch (I prefer the back center) of the Mushroom Body (inserting your hook into the wrong side/inside to the right side/outside), and then complete the stitch. Do not stuff the cap or stuff very lightly. It is optional to include something flat at the bottom inside of the cap, like a cut-to-size piece of plastic canvas. **Do not** work into the "Sl St, Ch 1" join of the body.

35. Working into both the cap and the body at the same time, (SC 7, Inc) x 6, Sl St to beginning stitch, Ch 1 [54]

36. (SC 4, Inc, SC 4) x 6, Sl St to beginning stitch, Ch 1 [60]

37. (SC 9, Inc) x 6, Sl St to beginning stitch [66]

Fasten off with a 12 in/30.5 cm yarn tail to weave in and optionally position the Mushroom Cap at an angle and sew it in place.

Mushroom Sprite with Arms Style 4, Feet/Legs Style 1, Body Style 6, Cap Style 16

MUSHROOM SPRITE CAPS • 127

You have almost reached the Snail instructions! Keep in mind that if your Mushroom Sprite aspires to be a Snail rider, saddle safety is paramount! Make sure your Mushroom Sprite always uses a saddle, especially going down steep inclines.

❶ Mushroom Sprite with Arms Style 6, Feet/Legs Style 11, Body Style 3, Cap Style 19, falling off a ❷ Giant Snail with a Round Shell **without a saddle!**

CAP STYLE 17: INKY CAP (COPRINOPSIS ATRAMENTARIA) (MAKE 1)

For use with Body Style 3 or 6

Mushroom Cap Color Yarn: Approximately 58 yd/53 m worsted/medium weight yarn

Where there is no join method indicated, caps can be crocheted to your preference—either worked in spiral to prevent a visible seam or using the "Sl St to beginning stitch, Ch 1" join method. The two join methods are interchangeable on simple symmetrical pieces. The join methods are **not** interchangeable on pieces with more detailed shaping, due to the shift of the stitches from a particular join method being built into the shaping.

The Mushroom Cap will be **very lightly** stuffed with fiberfill.

1. SC 6 in Magic Circle [6]
2. Inc x 6 [12]
3. (SC 3, Inc) x 3 [15]
4. (SC 2, Inc, SC 2) x 3 [18]
5. (SC 4, Inc, SC 4) x 2 [20]
6. (SC 9, Inc) x 2 [22]
7. (SC 5, Inc, SC 5) x 2 [24]
8. (SC 7, Inc) x 3 [27]
9. SC 27 [27]
10. (SC 4, Inc, SC 4) x 3 [30]
11. SC 30 [30]
12. (SC 9, Inc) x 3 [33]
13. SC 33 [33]
14. (SC 5, Inc, SC 5) x 3 [36]
15. SC 36 [36]
16. (SC 11, Inc) x 3 [39]
17. SC 39 [39]
18. (SC 6, Inc, SC 6) x 3 [42]
19. SC 42 [42]
20. (SC 13, Inc) x 3 [45]
21. SC 45 [45]

22. (SC 7, Inc, SC 7) x 3 [48]

To form a SC in Row 23, insert your hook first into the next available stitch of the Mushroom Cap (inserting your hook into the right side/outside to the wrong side/inside) and then into any stitch (I prefer the back center) of the Mushroom Body (inserting your hook into the wrong side/inside to the right side/outside), and then complete the stitch. Just before you stuff the cap, you can insert a flat, round piece (like plastic canvas cut to size) on the top of the Mushroom Body's undercap; this will help maintain a flat/secure base for the Mushroom Cap. Stuff the cap **very** lightly with fiberfill, just enough to fill out the cap. **Do not** work into the "Sl St, Ch 1" join of the body.

23. Working into both the cap and the body at the same time, (SC 5, Inc) x 8, Sl St to beginning stitch, **do not** Ch 1 [56]

If you worked in spiral for this cap up to this point, then you should still "Sl St to the beginning stitch, **do not** Ch 1" at the end of Row 23.

24A. Continue into the next available stitch on the cap, not the stitch you last slip stitched into in Row 23, Sl St 3, Ch 5, starting in the 2nd Ch from hook, SC, Sl St 2, SC

24B. Continue into the next available stitch on the cap, Sl St 4, Ch 6, starting in the 2nd Ch from hook, SC, Sl St 3, SC

24C. Continue into the next available stitch on the cap, Sl St 4, Ch 4, starting in the 2nd Ch from hook, SC, Sl St, SC

24D. Continue into the next available stitch on the cap, Sl St 4, Ch 6, starting in the 2nd Ch from hook, SC, Sl St 3, SC

24E. Continue into the next available stitch on the cap, Sl St 4, Ch 5, starting in the 2nd Ch from hook, SC, Sl St 2, SC

Mushroom Sprite with Feet/Legs Style 1, Body Style 3, Cap Style 17

MUSHROOM SPRITE CAPS • 129

24F. Continue into the next available stitch on the cap, Sl St 4, Ch 6, starting in the 2nd Ch from hook, SC, Sl St 3, SC

24G. Continue into the next available stitch on the cap, Sl St 4, Ch 4, starting in the 2nd Ch from hook, SC, Sl St, SC

24H. Continue into the next available stitch on the cap, Sl St 4, Ch 5, starting in the 2nd Ch from hook, SC, Sl St 2, SC

24I. Continue into the next available stitch on the cap, Sl St 4, Ch 4, starting in the 2nd Ch from hook, SC, Sl St, SC

24J. Continue into the next available stitch on the cap, Sl St 4, Ch 6, starting in the 2nd Ch from hook, SC, Sl St 3, SC

24K. Continue into the next available stitch on the cap, Sl St 4, Ch 5, starting in the 2nd Ch from hook, SC, Sl St 2, SC

24L. Continue into the next available stitch on the cap, Sl St 4, Ch 6, starting in the 2nd Ch from hook, SC, Sl St 3, SC

24M. Continue into the next available stitch on the cap, Sl St 4, Ch 4, starting in the 2nd Ch from hook, SC, Sl St, SC

24N. Continue into the next available stitch on the cap, Sl St 4, Ch 6, starting in the 2nd Ch from hook, SC, Sl St 3, SC, Sl St to beginning St

Fasten off with a 12 in/30.5 cm yarn tail to weave in and optionally position the Mushroom Cap at an angle and sew it in place.

It may be necessary to block/steam the "drips" into place so that they hang down nicely rather than curl upward. You can also starch them or paint the inner side of the drips with a clear-drying nontoxic glue and then pin them in place (hanging downward) until they are dry.

Starting with the last slip stitch in Row 23, in Row 24 you will work 1 slip stitch into each available stitch from Row 23 for a total of 56 stitches. The chain stitches and stitches worked into the chain stitches in each sub-row are there to create the drips and are not counted in the stitches worked into Row 23.

Mushroom Sprite with Arms Style 1, Feet/Legs Style 1, Body Style 6, Cap Style 17

130 • MUSHROOM SPRITE CAPS

CAP STYLE 18: FLY AGARIC (AMANITA MUSCARIA), SOLID COLOR (MAKE 1)

For use with Body Style 3 or 6

Mushroom Cap Color Yarn: Approximately 40 yd/36.5 m worsted/medium weight yarn

> Where there is no join method indicated, caps can be crocheted to your preference—either worked in spiral to prevent a visible seam or using the "Sl St to beginning stitch, Ch 1" join method. The two join methods are interchangeable on simple symmetrical pieces. The join methods are **not** interchangeable on pieces with more detailed shaping, due to the shift of the stitches from a particular join method being built into the shaping.

> The Mushroom Cap will not be stuffed with fiberfill.

1. SC 6 in Magic Circle [6]
2. Inc x 6 [12]
3. (SC, Inc) x 6 [18]
4. (SC, Inc, SC) x 6 [24]
5. (SC 3, Inc) x 6 [30]
6. (SC 2, Inc, SC 2) x 6 [36]
7. (SC 5, Inc) x 6 [42]
8. (SC 3, Inc, SC 3) x 6 [48]
9. (SC 11, Inc) x 4 [52]
10. (SC 6, Inc, SC 6) x 4 [56]
11–12. (2 rows of) SC 56 [56]

13. Working into both the cap and the body at the same time, SC 56 [56]

> To form the first SC in Row 13, insert your hook first into the next available stitch of the Mushroom Cap (inserting your hook into the right side/outside to the wrong side/inside) and then into any stitch (I prefer the back center) of the Mushroom Body (inserting your hook into the wrong side/inside to the right side/outside), and then complete the stitch. Do not stuff the cap. **Do not** work into the "Sl St, Ch 1" join of the body.

14. SC 56, Sl St to beginning stitch [56]

Fasten off with a 12 in/30.5 cm yarn tail to weave in and optionally position the Mushroom Cap at an angle and sew it in place.

> As an alternative to the complex colorwork in the two-color version (page 132), you can add spots by following the instructions on page 141 for the "Optional Spots/Dots for Caps."

Mushroom with Arms Style 7, Feet/Legs Style 5, Body Style 3, Cap Style 18

CAP STYLE 19: FLY AGARIC (AMANITA MUSCARIA), TWO COLORS (MAKE 1)

For use with Body Style 3 or 6

Main Mushroom Cap Color Yarn [MC]: Approximately 30 yd/27.5 m worsted/medium weight yarn

Accent Cap Color Yarn [AC]: Approximately 16 yd/14.5 m worsted/medium weight yarn

The Mushroom Cap will not be stuffed with fiberfill. The Main Color, represented by the letters "MC," will be indicated by "MC [ ]," where the stitches inside the brackets will be worked in the Main Color. The Main Color is traditionally red. The Accent Color, represented by the letters "AC," will be indicated by "AC [ ]," where the stitches inside the brackets will be worked in the Accent Color. The Accent Color is traditionally white. The way that you carry the yarn behind the work or under the stitches you make will affect the final yarn usage. The amount suggested is rounded up to ensure that you'll have enough of the indicated weight yarn with a G (4 mm) hook. This Mushroom Cap will not be stuffed with fiberfill.

In this colorwork version of the cap, it is recommended to work with the "Sl St to beginning stitch, Ch 1" join method because of the added level of difficulty and concentration required by the colorwork.

For a video on colorwork, go here: https://youtube.com/watch?v=1XReLVEjZCo

❶ **Mushroom Sprite with Arms Style 7, Feet/Legs Style 10, Body Style 8;** ❷ **Giant Snail with Round Shell**

Start considering what Snail your Mushroom Sprite would enjoy caring for! Will they prefer a Small Snail or a Giant Snail?

1. MC [SC 6] in Magic Circle, Sl St to beginning stitch, Ch 1 [6]

2. (MC [SC] & AC [SC]) x 6, Sl St to beginning stitch, Ch 1 [12]

3. (AC [SC], MC [Inc, SC, Inc]) x 3, Sl St to beginning stitch, Ch 1 [18]

4. (MC [SC, Inc], AC [SC], MC [SC], AC [Inc], MC [SC]) x 3, Sl St to beginning stitch, Ch 1 [24]

5. (MC [SC], AC [SC], MC [SC, Inc, SC 4] & AC [SC]) x 3, Sl St to beginning stitch, Ch 1 [30]

> Check the Glossary beginning on page 6 for the definition of the "&" symbol. Also note that only the last SC in MC group is combined with the AC SC in Row 5.

6. (AC [SC], MC [SC 2], & AC [SC], MC [SC 2]) x 6, Sl St to beginning stitch, Ch 1 [36]

7. (MC [SC 2], AC [SC], MC [SC 2], AC [Inc]) x 6, Sl St to beginning stitch, Ch 1 [42]

8. (AC [SC], MC [SC 2], AC [Inc], MC [SC 3]) x 6, Sl St to beginning stitch, Ch 1 [48]

9. (MC [SC 2], AC [SC], MC [SC 2], AC [SC], MC [SC], AC [SC], MC [SC 2], AC [SC], MC [Inc, SC 2], AC [SC], MC [SC 3], AC [SC], MC [SC 3], AC [SC], MC [Inc]) x 2, Sl St to beginning stitch, Ch 1 [52]

> As you continue from the end of Row 9 to the start of Row 10, there is a color change from Main Color to Accent Color. As you yarn over to make the "Sl St to the beginning stitch, Ch 1" join, change color to the AC with that yarn over for a smooth transition.

10. (AC [SC], MC [SC 3], AC [SC], MC [SC, Inc, SC 2], AC [SC], MC [SC 3]) x 4, Sl St to beginning stitch, Ch 1 [56]

MUSHROOM SPRITE CAPS • 133

11. (MC [SC 2], AC [SC], MC [SC 3], AC [SC], MC [SC 2], AC [SC], MC [SC 2], AC [SC], MC [SC]) x 4, Sl St to beginning stitch, Ch 1 [56]

12. (MC [SC], AC [SC], MC [SC 2], AC [SC], MC [SC 3], AC [SC], MC [SC 2], AC [SC], MC [SC 2]) x 4, Sl St to beginning stitch, Ch 1 [56]

To form the first SC in Row 13, insert your hook first into the next available stitch of the Mushroom Cap (inserting your hook into the right side/outside to the wrong side/inside) and then into any stitch (I prefer the back center) of the Mushroom Body (inserting your hook into the wrong side/inside to the right side/outside), and then complete the stitch. Do not stuff the cap. **Do not** work into the "Sl St, Ch 1" join of the body.

Mushroom Sprite with Arms Style 6, Feet/Legs Style 11, Body Style 3, Cap Style 19

Mushroom Sprite with Arms Style 3, Feet/Legs Style 5, Body Style 6, Cap Style 20

In Rows 13 and 14, be extra careful to keep your colorwork neat and tidy, because the back of the cap is visible. Either carry the colors behind the work in a very tidy way or crochet around the color you're not using for these last two rows.

13. Working into both the cap and the body at the same time, (MC [SC 3], AC [SC], MC [SC 2], AC [SC]) x 8, Sl St to beginning stitch, Ch 1 [56]

As you continue from the end of Row 13 to the start of Row 14, there is a color change from Accent Color to Main Color. As you yarn over to make the "Sl St to beginning stitch, Ch 1" join, change color to the Main Color with that yarn over for a smooth transition.

14. (MC [SC], AC [SC], MC [SC 5]) x 8, Sl St to beginning stitch [56]

Fasten off with a 12 in/30.5 cm yarn tail to weave in and optionally position the Mushroom Cap at an angle and sew it in place.

Mushroom Sprite with Arms Style 6, Feet/Legs Style 11, Body Style 3, Cap Style 19

CAP STYLE 20: PICOT EDGE BELL (MAKE 1)

For use with Body Style 3 or 6

Mushroom Cap Color Yarn: Approximately 50 yd/45.75 m worsted/medium weight yarn

Where there is no join method indicated, caps can be crocheted to your preference—either worked in spiral to prevent a visible seam or using the "Sl St to beginning stitch, Ch 1" join method. The two join methods are interchangeable on simple symmetrical pieces. The join methods are **not** interchangeable on pieces with more detailed shaping, due to the shift of the stitches from a particular join method being built into the shaping. This Mushroom Cap will not be stuffed with fiberfill.

1. SC 6 in Magic Circle [6]
2. Inc x 6 [12]
3. (SC, Inc) x 6 [18]
4. (SC, Inc, SC) x 6 [24]
5. (SC 3, Inc) x 6 [30]
6. SC 30 [30]
7. (SC 2, Inc, SC 2) x 6 [36]
8–9. (2 rows of) SC 36 [36]
10. (SC 5, Inc) x 6 [42]
11–13. (3 rows of) SC 42 [42]

MUSHROOM SPRITE CAPS • 135

14. (SC 3, Inc, SC 3) x 6 [48]

15–17. (3 rows of) SC 48 [48]

To form the first SC in Row 18, insert your hook first into the next available stitch of the Mushroom Cap (from the right side/outside to the wrong side/inside of the cap) and then into the next available stitch of the Mushroom Body (from the wrong side/inside to the right side/outside), and then complete the stitch. You can begin with any stitch on the body; I recommend the back center stitch on the body. Do not stuff the cap. **Do not** work into the "Sl St, Ch 1" join of the body.

18. Working into both the cap and the body at the same time, SC 48, Sl St to beginning stitch, Ch 1 [48]

19. (SC 2, Ch 2, Sl St in the 2nd Ch from hook, SC in the next available stitch from Row 18) x 16, Sl St to beginning stitch [48]

Fasten off with a 12 in/30.5 cm yarn tail to weave in and optionally position the Mushroom Cap at an angle and sew it in place.

❶ Mushroom Sprite with Arms Style 3, Feet/Legs Style 5, Body Style 6, Cap Style 20; ❷ Mushroom Sprite with Arms Style 3, Feet/Legs Style 4, Body Style 5, Cap Style 14

Mushroom Sprite with Feet/Legs Style 1, Body Style 3, Cap Style 21

CAP STYLE 21: RUFFLE EDGE (MAKE 1)

For use with Body Style 3 or 6

Mushroom Cap Color Yarn: Approximately 58 yd/53 m worsted/medium weight yarn

> The Mushroom Cap will not be stuffed with fiberfill.

> Where there is no join method indicated, caps can be crocheted to your preference—either worked in spiral to prevent a visible seam or using the "Sl St to beginning stitch, Ch 1" join method. The two join methods are interchangeable on simple symmetrical pieces. The join methods are **not** interchangeable on pieces with more detailed shaping, due to the shift of the stitches from a particular join method being built into the shaping.

1. SC 6 in Magic Circle [6]
2. (SC, Inc) x 3 [9]
3. (SC, Inc, SC) x 3 [12]
4. (SC 3, Inc) x 3 [15]
5. (SC 2, Inc, SC 2) x 3 [18]
6. (HDC 5, HDC Inc) x 3 [21]
7. (SC 3, Inc, SC 3) x 3 [24]
8. (HDC 5, HDC Inc) x 4 [28]
9. (SC 3, Inc, SC 3) x 4 [32]
10. (HDC 3, HDC Inc) x 8 [40]
11. (SC 2, Inc, SC 2) x 8 [48]
12. (SC 5, Inc) x 8 [56]
13. (SC 3, Inc) x 14 [70]
14. (SC 2, Inc, SC 2) x 14 [84]
15. (SC 2, Inc) x 28 [112]

16. Working into both the cap and the body at the same time, (SC 3, working into the cap only, SC 2, Inc, SC, Inc, SC 2, working into both the next available stitch on the cap and the same stitch you last crocheted into on the body at the same time, SC, and then, working in the next available stitch on both the cap and the body at the same time, SC 3) x 8 [128]

> To form the first SC in Row 16, insert your hook first into the next available stitch of the Mushroom Cap (from the right side/outside to the wrong side/inside of the cap) and then into the next available stitch of the Mushroom Body (from the wrong side/inside to the right side/outside), and then complete the stitch. You can begin with any stitch on the body; I recommend the back center stitch on the body. Do not stuff the cap. **Do not** work into the "Sl St, Ch 1" join of the body.

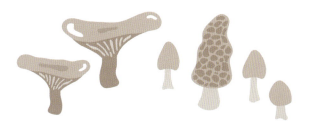

17. (SC 3, Inc) x 32 [160]
18. (SC 3, Inc) x 40, Sl St to beginning stitch [200]

Fasten off with a 12 in/30.5 cm yarn tail to weave in and optionally position the Mushroom Cap at an angle and sew it in place.

Mushroom Sprite with Feet/Legs Style 2, Body Style 6, Cap Style 21

CAP STYLE 22: WIDE CAP (MAKE 1)

For use with Body Style 3 or 6

Mushroom Cap Color Yarn: Approximately 76 yd/69.5 m worsted/medium weight yarn

> Where there is no join method indicated, caps can be crocheted to your preference—either worked in spiral to prevent a visible seam or using the "Sl St to beginning stitch, Ch 1" join method. The two join methods are interchangeable on simple symmetrical pieces. The join methods are **not** interchangeable on pieces with more detailed shaping, due to the shift of the stitches from a particular join method being built into the shaping.

> The Mushroom Cap will not be stuffed with fiberfill.

1. SC 6 in Magic Circle [6]
2. Inc x 6 [12]
3. (SC 2, Inc) x 4 [16]
4. (SC 3, Inc) x 4 [20]
5. (SC 2, Inc, SC 2) x 4 [24]
6. (SC 5, Inc) x 4 [28]
7. (SC 3, Inc, SC 3) x 4 [32]
8. (SC 7, Inc) x 4 [36]

Mushroom Sprite with Arms Style 6, Feet/Legs Style 12, Body Style 3, Cap Style 22

138 • MUSHROOM SPRITE CAPS

9. (SC 4, Inc, SC 4) x 4 [40]
10. (SC 9, Inc) x 4 [44]
11. (SC 5, Inc, SC 5) x 4 [48]
12. (SC 7, Inc) x 6 [54]
13. (SC 5, Inc) x 9 [63]
14. (SC 3, Inc, SC 3) x 9 [72]
15. (SC 7, Inc) x 9 [81]
16. (SC 4, Inc, SC 4) x 9 [90]
17. (SC 9, Inc) x 9 [99]
18–19. (2 rows of) SC 99 [99]
20. (SC 9, Dec) x 9 [90]
21. (SC 4, Dec, SC 4) x 9 [81]
22. (SC 7, Dec) x 9 [72]
23. (SC 3, Dec, SC 3) x 9 [63]
24. (SC 5, Dec) x 9 [54]
25. (SC 7, Dec) x 6 [48]

Mushroom Sprite with Feet/Legs Style 6, Body Style 6, Cap Style 22

26. Working into both the cap and the body at the same time, (SC 6, Dec) x 6, Sl St to beginning stitch [42]

> To form the first SC in Row 26, insert your hook first into the next available stitch of the Mushroom Cap (from the right side/outside to the wrong side/inside of the cap) and then into the next available stitch of the Mushroom Body (from the wrong side/inside to the right side/outside), and then complete the stitch. You can begin with any stitch on the body; I recommend the back center stitch on the body. Do not stuff the cap. **Do not** work into the "Sl St, Ch 1" join of the body.

Fasten off with a 12 in/30.5 cm yarn tail to weave in and optionally position the Mushroom Cap at an angle and sew it in place.

Mushroom Sprite with Arms Style 2, Feet/Legs Style 1, Body Style 6, Cap Style 23

MUSHROOM SPRITE CAPS • 139

CAP STYLE 23: WAVY EDGE (MAKE 1)

For use with Body Style 3 or 6

Mushroom Cap Color Yarn: Approximately 42 yd/38.5 m worsted/medium weight yarn

> Where there is no join method indicated, caps can be crocheted to your preference—either worked in spiral to prevent a visible seam or using the "Sl St to beginning stitch, Ch 1" join method. The two join methods are interchangeable on simple symmetrical pieces. The join methods are **not** interchangeable on pieces with more detailed shaping, due to the shift of the stitches from a particular join method being built into the shaping.

> The Mushroom Cap will not be stuffed with fiberfill.

1. SC 6 in Magic Circle [6]
2. Inc x 6 [12]
3. (SC 2, Inc) x 4 [16]
4. (SC 3, Inc) x 4 [20]
5. (SC 2, Inc, SC 2) x 4 [24]
6. (HDC 3, HDC Inc) x 6 [30]
7. (HDC 2, HDC Inc, HDC 2) x 6 [36]
8. (HDC 5, HDC Inc) x 6 [42]
9. (HDC 3, HDC Inc, HDC 3) x 6 [48]

10. (Working into both the cap and the body at the same time) (HDC, HDC Inc) x 24 [72]

> To form the first SC in Row 10, insert your hook first into the next available stitch of the Mushroom Cap (from the right side/outside to the wrong side/inside of the cap) and then into the next available stitch of the Mushroom Body (from the wrong side/inside to the right side/outside), and then complete the stitch. You can begin with any stitch on the body; I recommend the back center stitch on the body. Do not stuff the cap. **Do not** work into the "Sl St, Ch 1" join of the body. If you are working this cap with a "Sl St, Ch 1" join, end Row 10 with a "Ch 2" instead of a "Ch 1."

11. (DC, DC Inc, DC, DC Triple Inc) x 18, Sl St to beginning stitch [126]

> To make a "DC Triple Inc," you will work 3 DC stitches into 1 stitch.

Fasten off with a 12 in/30.5 cm yarn tail to weave in and optionally position the Mushroom Cap at an angle and sew it in place.

Mushroom Sprite with Arms Style 3, Feet/Legs Style 4, Body Style 6, Cap Style 23

OPTIONAL SPOTS/DOTS FOR CAPS (MAKE ANY NUMBER)

Mushroom Body Color Yarn: Approximately 12 yd/11 m worsted/medium weight yarn total

Dot 1: 2 yd/1.75 m worsted/medium weight yarn
Dot 2: 2 yd/1.75 m worsted/medium weight yarn
Dot 3: 2.5 yd/2.25 m worsted/medium weight yarn
Dot 4: 3 yd/2.75 m worsted/medium weight yarn
Dot 5: 3.5 yd/3.25 m worsted/medium weight yarn

There are five sizes of Dots/Spots for Mushroom Caps in this section. They are listed from smallest to largest. These are crocheted separately from the cap and sewn to attach. There are other options for creating dots/spots on a Mushroom Cap. You can paint them on with acrylic, fabric, or puff paint. You can felt them with roving and felting needles. You can embroider them on with French knots or small little lines of color using the Mushroom Body Color Yarn. You can cut small circles from felt sheets and glue them to the cap using fabric glue or sew them to attach.

Dot 1 (Smallest)

1. SC 6 in Magic Circle, Sl St to beginning stitch [6]

Fasten off with a 12 in/30.5 cm yarn tail.

Dot 2

1. HDC 8 in Magic Circle, Sl St to beginning stitch [8]

Fasten off with a 12 in/30.5 cm yarn tail.

Dot 3

1. SC 6 in Magic Circle, Sl St to beginning stitch, Ch 1 [6]
2. Inc x 6, Sl St to beginning stitch [12]

Fasten off with a 12 in/30.5 cm yarn tail.

Dot 4

1. DC 12 in Magic Circle, Sl St to beginning stitch [12]

Fasten off with a 12 in/30.5 cm yarn tail.

Dot 5 (Largest)

1. DC 12 in Magic Circle, Sl St to beginning stitch, Ch 1 [12]
2. (SC, Inc) x 6, Sl St to beginning stitch [18]

Fasten off with a 12 in/30.5 cm yarn tail.

Assembly

1. Make as many dots as desired and pin to attach to a Mushroom Cap.

2. Rearrange until you are satisfied with placement.
3. Using the yarn tails, use a whipstitch or blanket stitch to sew the edge down to attach to the Mushroom Cap, and weave in ends.

This Mushroom Sprite would like to give his snail some dots. We've never seen a snail with dots, but we wouldn't rule it out.

❶ Mushroom Sprite with Arms Style 7, Body Style 2, Cap Style 13, optional dots; ❷ Giant Snail with Round Shell

MUSHROOM SPRITE CAPS • 141

FAMILY PHOTO!

Clockwise from top left: ❶ Mushroom Sprite with Arms Style 9, Body Style 1, Cap Style 1; ❷ Mushroom Sprite with Arms Style 7, Body Style 2, Cap Style 13; ❸ Mushroom Sprite with Arms Style 2, Feet/Legs Style 6, Body Style 5, Cap Style 12; ❹ Mushroom Sprite with Arms Style 6, Feet/Legs Style 12, Body Style 4, Cap Style 8, all with optional dots

Horizontal Small Snail with Pointed Shell and Antennae Style 1

Upright Small Snail with Pointed Shell and Antennae Style 2

Horizontal Small Snail with Round Shell and Antennae Style 1

Upright Small Snail with Round Shell and Antennae Style 1

SMALL SNAILS

Small Snails are the perfect lap-sized pals for your Mushroom Sprites. They make very quiet, very slow pets, and even watching them have the zoomies is very relaxing.

Upright Small Snail with Pointed Shell and Antennae Style 2

OPTIONS

Small Snail Bodies
Horizontal

Small Snail Body Style 1: Horizontal Bottom . . . 148

Small Snail Body Style 1: Horizontal Top . . . 149

Upright

Small Snail Body Style 2: Upright Bottom . . . 152

Small Snail Body Style 2: Upright Top . . . 154

Small Snail Antennae

Small Snail Antennae Style 1 . . . 158

Small Snail Antennae Style 2 . . . 158

Small Snail Shells

Small Snail Shell Style 1: Pointed . . . 160

Small Snail Shell Style 2: Round . . . 168

SMALL SNAILS • 147

Small Snail Bodies

SMALL SNAIL BODY STYLE 1: HORIZONTAL

Horizontal Body Bottom (Make 1)

Body Bottom Color Yarn: Approximately 22 yd/20 m worsted/medium weight yarn

1. Starting with a short yarn tail, Ch 4, Turn, starting in the 2nd Ch from hook, SC, Inc, SC, Ch 1, Turn [4]

2–3. (2 rows of) SC 4, Ch 1, Turn [4]

4. SC 2, <Dec>, SC 2, Ch 1, Turn [5]

> "<Dec>" is a stitch that is defined in the Glossary beginning on page 6.

5–7. (3 rows of) SC 5, Ch 1, Turn [5]

8. SC 2, Inc, SC 2, Ch 1, Turn [6]

9–12. (4 rows of) SC 6, Ch 1, Turn [6]

13. SC 2, Dec, SC 2, Ch 1, Turn [5]

14–16. (3 rows of) SC 5, Ch 1, Turn [5]

17. SC, 2 Dec in 3 SC, SC, Ch 1, Turn [4]

> The "2 Dec in 3 SC" is a special stitch and is defined in the Glossary beginning on page 6.

18–19. (2 rows of) SC 4, Ch 1, Turn [4]

> In Row 20 and others like it, the row is broken down into sub-rows. These sub-rows all together make up an entire row. Each sub-row (20A, 20B, etc.) has its own sub-row stitch count indicated by the number preceded by a hyphen in brackets. Row 20A's sub-row stitch count is 4. The total stitch count for all of Row 20 is at the very end of the final sub-row, without the hyphen.

20A. SC, Dec, Inc [-4]

20B. Reorient work so that you will continue crocheting around the entire edge of the piece; starting with the sides of the previous rows, SC 18 along the unfinished edge [-18]

20C. Working along the opposite side of the OC, Inc, SC, Inc [-5]

20D. Reorient work so that you will continue crocheting around the entire edge of the piece; SC 18, SC in the same stitch as the first stitch of Row 20A (this creates an Inc in this corner), Sl St to the beginning stitch, Ch 2 [-19] [46]

21. Continue working around the entire edge, BLO [DC 3, (DC Inc x 3, DC) x 4, DC Inc, HDC Inc x 2, SC 5, HDC Inc x 2, DC Inc, (DC, DC Inc x 3) x 4], Sl St to beginning stitch [76]

Fasten off with a short yarn tail.

Outside

Inside

> The ridge created by the leftover front loops will be on the inside of the snail. You will hold this side against the top to crochet the pieces together. Pull the starting yarn tail through to the "inside" of the body bottom.

Horizontal Small Snail with Round Shell and Antennae Style 1

Horizontal Body Top (Make 1)

Body Top Color Yarn: *Approximately 32 yd/29.25 m worsted/medium weight yarn*

1. Starting with a short yarn tail, Ch 4, Turn, starting in the 2nd Ch from hook, Inc, SC, Inc, Ch 1, Turn [5]
2. SC, Inc, SC, Inc, SC, Ch 1, Turn [7]
3. SC 7, Ch 1, Turn [7]
4. SC, Inc, SC 3, Inc, SC, Ch 1, Turn [9]
5–7. (3 rows of) SC 9, Ch 1, Turn [9]
8. SC 2, Inc, SC 3, Inc, SC 2, Ch 1, Turn [11]
9–12. (4 rows of) SC 11, Ch 1, Turn [11]
13. SC 2, Dec, SC 3, Dec, SC 2, Ch 1, Turn [9]
14–16. (3 rows of) SC 9, Ch 1, Turn [9]
17. SC, Dec, SC 3, Dec, SC, Ch 1, Turn [7]
18. SC 7, Ch 1, Turn [7]
19. SC, Dec, SC, Dec, SC, Ch 1, Turn [5]

SMALL SNAILS • 149

In Row 20 and others like it, the row is broken down into sub-rows. These sub-rows all together make up an entire row. Each sub-row (20A, 20B, etc.) has its own sub-row stitch count indicated by the number preceded by a hyphen in brackets. Row 20A's sub-row stitch count is 3. The total stitch count for all of Row 20 is at the very end of the final sub-row, without the hyphen.

You can complete Row 22 as a straight SC row, or, for a more ruffled bottom, repeat "(SC, Inc)" across the entire edge instead of just SC. Make sure your Bobble stitches are pushed to the outside before you crochet the pieces together.

20A. Dec, SC, Dec [-3]

20C. Inc, SC, Inc [-5]

22. Hold the bottom part of the snail against the top part. Hold the wrong side of the bottom piece (with the ridge made in Row 21) against the bottom/wrong side of the top piece (with the back of the stitches from Row 21).

20B. Reorient work so that you will continue crocheting around the entire edge of the piece; starting with the sides of the previous rows, SC in the same stitch that the last Dec was crocheted into, SC 18 along the unfinished edge [-19]

20D. Reorient work so that you will continue crocheting around the entire edge of the piece; SC 18, SC in the same stitch as the start of the first Dec in Row 20A, Sl St to beginning stitch, Ch 2 [-19] [46]

21. DC 3, (DC Inc x 3, DC) x 4, HDC Inc x 2, Inc, SC, BLO [Bobble], SC, BLO [Bobble], SC, Inc, HDC Inc x 2, (DC, DC Inc x 3) x 4, Sl St to beginning stitch, Ch 1 [76]

Starting in the 1st available stitch on the top piece and the 1st stitch of the last row on the bottom piece, SC around the entire piece, working through the top piece's BLO and the bottom piece's FLO at the same time. When you are 5 stitches away from finishing this row, first pin around the border of Rows 20 and 21 of the top of the body to connect it to the border of Rows 20 and 21 of the bottom of the body, and then lightly stuff the center portion of the body—you can optionally include some flat glass marble gems for weight (you will sew around the edge of the pinned rows in order to seal the stuffing inside of that center space after you finish crocheting the body; this step is covered in the Small Snail Assembly beginning on page 170), Sl St to beginning stitch.

Fasten off with a 24 in/61 cm yarn tail.

The Bobble here is constructed as follows (and you should pop the Bobble out toward you as you make it):
YO, insert into the next available stitch, YO, pull up, YO, pull through 2 loops, YO twice, insert into the same stitch, YO, pull up, YO, pull through 2 loops, YO, pull through 2 loops, YO twice, insert into the same stitch, YO, pull up, YO, pull through 2 loops, YO, pull through 2 loops, YO, insert into the same stitch, YO, pull up, YO, pull through 2 loops, YO, pull through all 5 remaining loops

This image depicts the top/right side/outside.

This image depicts the bottom/wrong side/inside.

Next, see the Assembly section for details on using the yarn tail to sew around to seal the stuffing inside the center space of the body. This body will work well with either style of Small Snail Shell.

Horizontal Small Snail with Pointed Shell and Antennae Style 1

SMALL SNAILS • 151

SMALL SNAIL BODY STYLE 2: UPRIGHT

Upright Body Bottom (Make 1)

Body Bottom Color Yarn: *Approximately 21 yd/19.25 m worsted/medium weight yarn*

1. Starting with a short yarn tail, Ch 4, Turn, starting in the 2nd Ch from hook, SC, Inc, SC, Ch 1, Turn [4]
2-3. (2 rows of) SC 4, Ch 1, Turn [4]
4. SC 2, <Dec>, SC 2, Ch 1, Turn [5]

> "<Dec>" is a stitch that is defined in the Glossary beginning on page 6.

5-7. (3 rows of) SC 5, Ch 1, Turn [5]
8. SC 2, Inc, SC 2, Ch 1, Turn [6]
9-14. (6 rows of) SC 6, Ch 1, Turn [6]
15. SC 2, Dec, SC 2, Ch 1, Turn [5]
16-19. (4 rows of) SC 5, Ch 1, Turn [5]
20. SC, 2 Dec in 3 SC, SC, Ch 1, Turn [4]

> The "2 Dec in 3 SC" is a special stitch and is defined in the Glossary beginning on page 6.

21-23. (3 rows of) SC 4, Ch 1, Turn [4]

> In Row 24 and others like it, the row is broken down into sub-rows. These sub-rows all together make up an entire row. Each sub-row (24A, 24B, etc.) has its own sub-row stitch count indicated by the number preceded by a hyphen in brackets. Row 24A's sub-row stitch count is 4. The total stitch count for all of Row 24 is at the very end of the final sub-row, without the hyphen.

24A. SC, Dec, Inc [-4]
24B. Reorient work so that you will continue crocheting around the entire edge of the piece; starting with the sides of the previous rows, SC 22 along the unfinished edge [-22]
24C. Inc, SC, Inc [-5]
24D. Reorient work so that you will continue crocheting around the entire edge of the piece; SC 22, SC in the same stitch as the first stitch of Row 24A (this creates an Inc in this corner), Sl St to the beginning stitch, Ch 2 [-23] [54]

Upright Small Snail with Pointed Shell and Antennae Style 2

152 • SMALL SNAILS

Upright Small Snail with Pointed Shell and Antennae Style 2

25. BLO [DC 3, (DC Inc x 2, DC, DC Inc x 2) x 4, DC Inc, HDC, HDC Inc, SC 5, HDC Inc, HDC, DC Inc, (DC Inc x 2, DC, DC Inc x 2) x 4], Sl St to beginning stitch [90]

> The ridge created by the leftover front loops will be on the inside of the snail. You will hold this side against the top to crochet the pieces together.

Fasten off with a short yarn tail.

Inside

Outside

❶ Mushroom Sprite with Arms Style 6, Body Style 1, Cap Style 3, giving tiny head "scritches" to an ❷ Upright Small Snail with Pointed Shell and Antennae Style 2

SMALL SNAILS • 153

Upright Body Top (Make 1)

Body Top Color Yarn:
Approximately 31 yd/28.5 m worsted/medium weight yarn

1. Ch 4, Turn, starting in the 2nd Ch from hook, Inc, SC, Inc, Ch 1, Turn [5]
2. SC, Inc, SC, Inc, SC, Ch 1, Turn [7]
3. SC 7, Ch 1, Turn [7]
4. SC, Inc, SC 3, Inc, SC, Ch 1, Turn [9]
5-6. (2 rows of) SC 9, Ch 1, Turn [9]

In Row 7 and onward, there will be times when you do not use all of the available stitches in the row. You will come back to use them later. These create short rows. For more information on this technique, please see this YouTube video: https://www.youtube.com/watch?v=sh5T-idiwm8&t=3s

7-8. (2 rows of) SC 3, Ch 1, Turn [3]

You will start Row 9 by working across the stitches you made in Row 8 and then continue the row by working into the leftover stitches from Row 6. See the Glossary beginning on page 6 for how to work the "SC/HDC Dec" and the "&"— you will work the "& HDC" into the same stitch you finished the "SC/HDC Dec" in.

9. SC, Inc, SC/HDC Dec & HDC, SC 5, Ch 1, Turn [10]

10-11. (2 rows of) SC 3, Ch 1, Turn [3]
12. SC, Inc, SC/HDC Dec & HDC, SC 6, Ch 1, Turn [11]

13. SC 11, Ch 1, Turn [11]
14-15. (2 rows of) SC 3, Ch 1, Turn [3]

16. SC 2, SC/HDC Dec, SC 7, Ch 1, Turn [10]

17-18. (2 rows of) SC 3, Ch 1, Turn [3]

19. SC 2, SC/HDC Dec, SC 6, Ch 1, Turn [9]

20-22. (3 rows of) SC 9, Ch 1, Turn [9]
23. SC, Dec, SC 3, Dec, SC, Ch 1, Turn [7]
24-25. (2 rows of) SC 7, Ch 1, Turn [7]
26. SC, Dec, SC, Dec, SC, Ch 1, Turn [5]
27. SC 5, Ch 1, Turn [5]

154 • SMALL SNAILS

> In Row 28 and others like it, the row is broken down into sub-rows. These sub-rows all together make up an entire row. Each sub-row (28A, 28B, etc.) has its own sub-row stitch count indicated by the number preceded by a hyphen in brackets. Row 28A's sub-row stitch count is 3. The total stitch count for all of Row 28 is at the very end of the final sub-row, without the hyphen.

28A. Dec, SC, Dec [-3]

28B. Reorient work so that you will continue crocheting around the entire edge of the piece; starting with the sides of the previous rows, SC in the same stitch that the last Dec was crocheted into, SC 22 along the unfinished edge [-23]

28C. Working across the opposite side of the OC, Inc, SC, Inc [-5]

28D. Reorient work so that you will continue crocheting around the entire edge of the piece; SC 22, SC in the same stitch as the first stitch of Row 28A (this creates an Inc in this corner), Sl St to the beginning stitch, Ch 2 [-23] [54]

29. DC 3, (DC Inc x 2, DC, DC Inc x 2) x 4, DC Inc, HDC, Inc, SC, BLO [Bobble], SC, BLO [Bobble], SC, Inc, HDC, DC Inc, (DC Inc x 2, DC, DC Inc x 2) x 4, Sl St to beginning stitch, Ch 1 [90]

> The Bobble here is constructed as follows (and you should pop the Bobble out toward you as you make it): YO, insert into the next available stitch, YO, pull up, YO, pull through 2 loops, YO twice, insert into the same stitch, YO, pull up, YO, pull through 2 loops, YO, pull through 2 loops, YO twice, insert into the same stitch, YO, pull up, YO, pull through 2 loops, YO, pull through 2 loops, YO, insert into the same stitch, YO, pull up, YO, pull through 2 loops, YO, pull through all 5 remaining loops

Upright Small Snail with Round Shell and Antennae Style 1

SMALL SNAILS • 155

> You can work Row 30 as a straight SC row, or, for a more ruffled bottom, repeat "(SC, Inc)" across the entire edge instead of just SC. Make sure your Bobble stitches are pushed to the outside before you crochet the pieces together.

30. Hold the bottom part of the snail against this top part. Hold the inside of the bottom piece (with the ridge made in Row 25) against the bottom/inside of the top piece (with the back of the stitches from Row 29).

Row 30 continued

Starting in the 1st available stitch on the top piece and the 1st stitch of the last row on the bottom piece, SC around the entire piece, working through the top piece's BLO and the bottom piece's FLO at the same time. When you are 5 stitches away from finishing this row, take a moment to first pin around the border of Rows 28 and 29 of the top of the body to connect it to the border of Rows 24 and 25 of the bottom of the body, and then lightly stuff the center portion of the body—you can optionally include some flat glass marble gems, if you'd like, for weight (you will sew around the edge of the pinned rows in order to seal the stuffing inside of that center space after you finish crocheting the body; this step is covered in the Small Snail Assembly beginning on page 170), Sl St to beginning stitch.

Stitch count for Straight SC row [90]

Stitch count for (SC, Inc) row [135]

Fasten off with a 24 in/61 cm yarn tail.

> Next, see the Assembly section for details on using the yarn tail to sew around to seal the stuffing inside the center space of the body. This body will work well with either style of Small Snail Shell.

Upright Small Snail with Round Shell and Antennae Style 1

Small Snail Antennae

SMALL SNAIL ANTENNAE STYLE 1 (MAKE 2)

This antennae style can be used with either the Horizontal or the Upright Small Snail Body.

Body Top Color Yarn: Approximately 7 yd/6.5 m worsted/medium weight yarn for two antennae

> Choose **one** style of antennae to make per Snail Body. There are two options. This piece is worked in spiral. Do not "Sl St, Ch 1" to join.

Fasten off with a 12 in/30.5 cm yarn tail to use to sew to attach; weave in ends.

1. SC 4 in Magic Circle [4]

2–3. (2 rows of) SC 4 [4]

4. Inc, SC 3 [5]

5–7. (3 rows of) SC 5 [5]

Horizontal Small Snail with Round Shell and Antennae Style 1

SMALL SNAIL ANTENNAE STYLE 2 (MAKE 2)

This antennae style can be used with either the Horizontal or the Upright Small Snail Body.

Body Top Color Yarn: Approximately 5 yd/4.5 m worsted/medium weight yarn

> Choose **one** style of antennae to make per Snail Body. There are two options.

1. Start with a long enough yarn tail to weave in later, Ch 10, Turn, starting in the 2nd Ch from hook, Small Bobble, Sl St 8 [9]

> The Small Bobble is as follows (and you should pop the Bobble out toward you as you make it): YO, insert hook into next available stitch, YO, pull up, YO, pull through 2 loops, YO, insert hook into the same stitch, YO, pull up, YO, pull through 2 loops, YO, insert hook into the same stitch, YO, pull up, YO, pull through 2 loops, YO, pull through all 4 remaining loops

Fasten off with a 12 in/30.5 cm yarn tail to use to sew to attach; weave in ends.

Upright Small Snail with Round Shell and Antennae Style 2

① Upright Small Snail with Pointed Shell and Antennae Style 2; ② Upright Small Snail with Round Shell and Antennae Style 1

Small Snail Shells

SMALL SNAIL SHELL STYLE 1: POINTED (MAKE 1)

This shell style can be used with either the Horizontal or the Upright Small Snail Body.

Any Color Yarn for the Shell: Approximately 28 yd/25.5 m worsted/medium weight yarn

Any Color Yarn for the Accent: Approximately 4 yd/3.75 m worsted/medium weight yarn

The following instructions will use both Shell Color and Accent Color yarn for different rows. Accent rows are worked around the shell in a spiral, always in the same direction. Shell rows are worked back and forth to build up the outer wall of the shell, anchored to the Accent rows. The Accent Color rows are **not** optional. You **must** follow these rows with a separate strand of yarn. To make a shell in one color, use a second strand of the Shell Color for the Accent rows. Do not fasten off either color yarn until instructed to do so in the pattern.

> To change between Accent and Shell rows, remove the hook from the current color at the end of the row and insert the hook into the loop of the next color. Tighten the loop if needed.

1. **SHELL** Starting with a short yarn tail, SC 5 in Magic Circle, Ch 2, do not Turn, continue working in the same direction for Row 2 [5]

> Mark the 3rd stitch of Row 1: SHELL. This will be where you attach the Accent Color after Row 7: SHELL.

> Make sure you are working right side out as you continue your shell. The starting yarn tail should be on the inside/wrong side of this piece. You should insert your hook from the outside/right side to the inside/wrong side as you complete stitches. Here's a video on inside out versus right side out: https://www.youtube.com/watch?v=beReNFWQPAs

160 • SMALL SNAILS

2. SHELL In the 2nd Ch from hook, SC & Dec—complete the Dec into the 1st SC you made in Row 1: SHELL, Ch 1, Turn [2]

> In Row 2: SHELL, do not Turn. Continue working in the same direction, work the SC in the 2nd Ch from the hook, start a Dec in the same chain that you worked the SC into and complete the Dec into the first SC from the "SC 5 in Magic Circle" in Row 1. Four stitches remain available from Row 1. The description of exactly where to place the decrease is always included after the "—" symbol in this and all future rows.

3. SHELL Working into the stitches from Row 2, SC 2, Ch 1, Turn [2]

4. SHELL Working into the stitches from the previous row, SC, Dec—complete the Dec into the next available stitch from Row 1: SHELL, Ch 1, Turn [2]

> Row 4 uses 1 stitch from Row 1; you have 3 stitches remaining on Row 1 to crochet into.

5. SHELL Working into the stitches from the previous row, SC 2, Ch 1, Turn [2]

6. SHELL Working into the stitches from the previous row, SC, Dec—complete the Dec into the same stitch from Row 1: SHELL that you completed the last Dec into in Row 4: SHELL, Ch 1, Turn [2]

> Row 6 uses the same stitch from Row 1 that you last worked into. Three stitches remain available from Row 1.

7. SHELL Working into the stitches from the previous row, SC 2, Ch 1, Turn [2]

1. ACCENT Keeping the shell right side out, attach yarn to the BLO of the 3rd stitch you made in Row 1: SHELL, starting in the same stitch and working across the open unused stitches from Row 1, Dec, and then, working into the last available stitch from Row 1 and up the unfinished edges of the rest of the rows, make 3 more Dec stitches [4]

> Keep your Accent row Dec stitches tight; this will make the Accent rows sink into the work, creating a spiral indentation along the shell. You have 4 Accent Color stitches to work into when working with the Shell Color yarn.

8. SHELL Working into the stitches from the previous Shell row, SC, Dec—complete the Dec into the next available stitch from the Accent row, Ch 1, Turn [2]

> Row 8 uses 1 stitch from the Accent row; you have 3 stitches remaining on the Accent row to crochet into.

9. SHELL Working into the stitches from the previous row, SC 2, Ch 1, Turn [2]

10. SHELL Working into the stitches from the previous row, SC, Dec—complete the Dec into the same stitch from the Accent row that you completed the last Dec into in Row 9: SHELL, Ch 1, Turn [2]

> Row 10 uses the same stitch from the Accent row that you last worked into; 3 stitches remain available.

11. SHELL Working into the stitches from the previous row, SC 2, Ch 1, Turn [2]

12. SHELL Working into the stitches from the previous row, SC, Dec—complete the Dec into the next available stitch from the Accent row, Ch 1, Turn [2]

> Row 12 uses 1 stitch from the Accent row; you have 2 stitches remaining on the Accent row to crochet into.

SMALL SNAILS • **161**

13. SHELL Working into the stitches from the previous row, SC 2, Ch 1, Turn [2]

14. SHELL Working into the stitches from the previous row, SC, Dec—complete the Dec into the same stitch from Accent row that you completed the last Dec into in Row 12: SHELL, Ch 1, Turn [2]

> Row 14 uses the same stitch from the Accent row that you last worked into; 2 stitches remain available.

15. SHELL Working into the stitches from the previous row, SC 2, Ch 1, Turn [2]

16. SHELL Working into the stitches from the previous row, SC, Dec—complete the Dec into the next available stitch from the Accent row, Ch 1, Turn [2]

> Row 16 uses 1 stitch from the Accent row; you have 1 stitch remaining on the Accent row to crochet into.

17. SHELL Working into the stitches from the previous row, SC 2, Ch 1, Turn [2]

2. ACCENT Dec x 5 [5]

> You will continue to work these stitches along the unfinished edge/side of the rows of the shell stitches. You had 1 stitch available on the Accent row before Row 2: ACCENT. Now you have a total of 6 Accent Color stitches to work into when working with the Shell Color yarn.

18. SHELL Working into the stitches from the previous Shell row, SC, Dec—complete the Dec in the next available stitch from the Accent row, Ch 1, Turn [2]

> Row 18 uses 1 stitch from the Accent row; you have 5 stitches remaining on the Accent row to crochet into.

19. SHELL Working into the stitches from the previous row, SC 2, Ch 1, Turn [2]

20. SHELL Working into the stitches from the previous row, SC, Dec—complete the Dec into the same stitch from the Accent row that you completed the last Dec into in Row 18: SHELL, Ch 1, Turn [2]

> Row 20 uses the same stitch from the Accent row that you last worked into; 5 stitches remain available.

21. SHELL Working into the stitches from the previous row, SC 2, Ch 1, Turn [2]

22. SHELL Working into the stitches from the previous row, SC, SC & Dec—complete the Dec into the next available stitch from the Accent row, Ch 1, Turn [3]

> Row 22 uses 1 stitch from the Accent row; you have 4 stitches remaining on the Accent row to crochet into.

23. SHELL Working into the stitches from the previous row, SC 3, Ch 1, Turn [3]

24. SHELL Working into the stitches from the previous row, SC 2, Dec—complete the Dec into the same stitch from the Accent row that you completed the last Dec into in Row 22: SHELL, Ch 1, Turn [3]

> Row 24 uses the same stitch from the Accent row that you last worked into; 4 stitches remain available.

25. SHELL Working into the stitches from the previous row, SC 3, Ch 1, Turn [3]

26. SHELL Working into the stitches from the previous row, SC 2, Dec—complete the Dec into the next available stitch from the Accent row, Ch 1, Turn [3]

> Row 26 uses 1 stitch from the Accent row; you have 3 stitches remaining on the Accent row to crochet into.

27. SHELL Working into the stitches from the previous row, SC 3, Ch 1, Turn [3]

28. SHELL Working into the stitches from the previous row, SC 2, Dec—complete the Dec into the next available stitch from the Accent row, Ch 1, Turn [3]

> Row 28 uses 1 stitch from the Accent row; you have 2 stitches remaining on the Accent row to crochet into.

29. SHELL Working into the stitches from the previous row, SC 3, Ch 1, Turn [3]

30. SHELL Working into the stitches from the previous row, SC 2, Dec—complete the Dec into the same stitch from the Accent row that you completed the last Dec into in Row 28: SHELL, Ch 1, Turn [3]

> Row 30 uses the same stitch from the Accent row that you last worked into; 2 stitches remain available.

31. SHELL Working into the stitches from the previous row, SC 3, Ch 1, Turn [3]

32. SHELL Working into the stitches from the previous row, SC 2, Dec—complete the Dec into the next available stitch from the Accent row, Ch 1, Turn [3]

> Row 32 uses 1 stitch from the Accent row; you have 1 stitch remaining on the Accent row to crochet into.

33. SHELL Working into the stitches from the previous row, SC 3, Ch 1, Turn [3]

3. ACCENT Dec x 8 [8]

> You will continue to work these stitches along the unfinished edge/side of the rows of the shell stitches. You had 1 stitch available on the Accent row before Row 3: ACCENT. Now you have a total of 9 Accent Color stitches to work into when working with the Shell Color yarn.

34. SHELL Working into the stitches from the previous Shell row, SC 2, Dec—complete the Dec into the next available stitch from the Accent row, Ch 1, Turn [3]

> Row 34 uses 1 stitch from the Accent row; you have 8 stitches remaining on the Accent row to crochet into.

35. SHELL Working into the stitches from the previous row, SC 3, Ch 1, Turn [3]

36. SHELL Working into the stitches from the previous row, SC 2, Dec—complete the Dec into the same stitch from the Accent row that you completed the last Dec into in Row 34: SHELL, Ch 1, Turn [3]

> Row 36 uses the same stitch from the Accent row that you last worked into; 8 stitches remain available.

37. SHELL Working into the stitches from the previous row, SC 3, Ch 1, Turn [3]

38. SHELL Working into the stitches from the previous row, SC 2, Dec—complete the Dec into the next available stitch from the Accent row, Ch 1, Turn [3]

> Row 38 uses 1 stitch from the Accent row; you have 7 stitches remaining on the Accent row to crochet into.

39. SHELL Working into the stitches from the previous row, SC 3, Ch 1, Turn [3]

40. SHELL Working into the stitches from the previous row, SC 2, Dec—complete the Dec into the next available stitch from the Accent row, Ch 1, Turn [3]

> Row 40 uses 1 stitch from the Accent row; you have 6 stitches remaining on the Accent row to crochet into.

41. SHELL Working into the stitches from the previous row, SC 3, Ch 1, Turn [3]

42. SHELL Working into the stitches from the previous row, SC 2, Dec—complete the Dec into the same stitch from the Accent row that you completed the last Dec into in Row 40: SHELL, Ch 1, Turn [3]

> Row 42 uses the same stitch from the Accent row that you last worked into; 6 stitches remain available.

43. SHELL Working into the stitches from the previous row, SC 3, Ch 1, Turn [3]

44. SHELL Working into the stitches from the previous row, SC 2, Dec—complete the Dec into the next available stitch from the Accent row, Ch 1, Turn [3]

> Row 44 uses 1 stitch from the Accent row; you have 5 stitches remaining on the Accent row to crochet into.

45. SHELL Working into the stitches from the previous row, SC 3, Ch 1, Turn [3]

46. SHELL Working into the stitches from the previous row, SC 2, Dec—complete the Dec into the next available stitch from the Accent row, Ch 1, Turn [3]

> Row 46 uses 1 stitch from the Accent row; you have 4 stitches remaining on the Accent row to crochet into.

47. SHELL Working into the stitches from the previous row, SC 3, Ch 1, Turn [3]

48. SHELL Working into the stitches from the previous row, SC 2, Dec—complete the Dec into the same stitch from the Accent row that you completed the last Dec into in Row 46: SHELL, Ch 1, Turn [3]

> Row 48 uses the same stitch from the Accent row that you last worked into; 4 stitches remain available.

49. SHELL Working into the stitches from the previous row, SC 3, Ch 1, Turn [3]

50. SHELL Working into the stitches from the previous row, SC 2, SC & Dec—complete the Dec into the next available stitch from the Accent row, Ch 1, Turn [4]

> Row 50 uses 1 stitch from the Accent row; you have 3 stitches remaining on the Accent row to crochet into.

51. SHELL Working into the stitches from the previous row, SC 4, Ch 1, Turn [4]

52. SHELL Working into the stitches from the previous row, SC 3, Dec—complete the Dec into the next available stitch from the Accent row, Ch 1, Turn [4]

> Row 52 uses 1 stitch from the Accent row; you have 2 stitches remaining on the Accent row to crochet into.

53. SHELL Working into the stitches from the previous row, SC 4, Ch 1, Turn [4]

54. SHELL Working into the stitches from the previous row, SC 3, Dec—complete the Dec into the same stitch from the Accent row that you completed the last Dec into in Row 52: SHELL, Ch 1, Turn [3]

> Row 54 uses the same stitch from the Accent row that you last worked into; 2 stitches remain available.

55. SHELL Working into the stitches from the previous row, SC 4, Ch 1, Turn [4]

56. SHELL Working into the stitches from the previous row, SC 3, Dec—complete the Dec into the next available stitch from the Accent row, Ch 1, Turn [4]

> Row 56 uses 1 stitch from the Accent row; you have 1 stitch remaining on the Accent row to crochet into.

57. SHELL Working into the stitches from the previous row, SC 4, Ch 1, Turn [4]

4. ACCENT Dec x 5; fasten off with a short yarn tail [5]

> You will continue to work these stitches along the unfinished edge/side of the rows of the shell stitches. You had 1 stitch available on the Accent row before Row 4: ACCENT. Now you have a total of 6 Accent Color stitches to work into when working with the Shell Color yarn. This is the end of the Accent row stitches.

58. SHELL Working into the stitches from the previous Shell row, SC 3, Dec—complete the Dec into the next available stitch from the Accent row, Ch 1, Turn [4]

> Row 58 uses 1 stitch from the Accent row; you have 5 stitches remaining on the Accent row to crochet into.

59. SHELL Working into the stitches from the previous row, SC 4, Ch 1, Turn [4]

60. SHELL Working into the stitches from the previous row, SC 3, Dec—complete the Dec into the same stitch from the Accent row that you completed the last Dec into in Row 58: SHELL, Ch 1, Turn [3]

> Row 60 uses the same stitch from the Accent row that you last worked into; 5 stitches remain available.

Upright Small Snail with Pointed Shell and Antennae Style 1

SMALL SNAILS • 165

61. SHELL Working into the stitches from the previous row, SC 4, Ch 1, Turn [4]

62. SHELL Working into the stitches from the previous row, SC 3, Dec—complete the Dec into the next available stitch from the Accent row, Ch 1, Turn [4]

> Row 62 uses 1 stitch from the Accent row; you have 4 stitches remaining on the Accent row to crochet into.

63. SHELL Working into the stitches from the previous row, SC 4, Ch 1, Turn [4]

64. SHELL Working into the stitches from the previous row, SC 3, Dec—complete the Dec into the next available stitch from the Accent row, Ch 1, Turn [4]

> Row 64 uses 1 stitch from the Accent row; you have 3 stitches remaining on the Accent row to crochet into.

65. SHELL Working into the stitches from the previous row, SC 4, Ch 1, Turn [4]

66. SHELL Working into the stitches from the previous row, SC 3, Dec—complete the Dec into the same stitch from Accent row that you completed the last Dec into in Row 64: SHELL, Ch 1, Turn [3]

> Row 66 uses the same stitch from the Accent row that you last worked into; 3 stitches remain available.

67. SHELL Working into the stitches from the previous row, SC 4, Ch 1, Turn [4]

68. SHELL Working into the stitches from the previous row, SC 3, Dec—complete the Dec into the next available stitch from the Accent row, Ch 1, Turn [4]

> Row 68 uses 1 stitch from the Accent row; you have 2 stitches remaining on the Accent row to crochet into.

69. SHELL Working into the stitches from the previous row, SC 4, Ch 1, Turn [4]

70. SHELL Working into the stitches from the previous row, SC 3, Dec—complete the Dec into the next available stitch from the Accent row, Ch 1, Turn [4]

> Row 70 uses 1 stitch from the Accent row; you have 1 stitch remaining on the Accent row to crochet into.

71. SHELL Working into the stitches from the previous row, SC 4, Ch 1, Turn [4]

72. SHELL Working into the stitches from the previous row, SC 3, Dec—complete the Dec into the same stitch from Accent row that you completed the last Dec into in Row 70: SHELL, Ch 1, Turn [3]

> Row 72 uses the same stitch from the Accent row that you last worked into; 1 stitch remains available.

73. SHELL Working into the stitches from the previous row, SC 4, Ch 1, Turn [4]

74. SHELL Working into the stitches from the previous row, SC 3, Dec—complete the Dec into the next available stitch from the Accent row, Ch 1, Turn [4]

> Row 74 uses 1 stitch from the Accent row; you have 0 stitches remaining on the Accent row to crochet into.

75. SHELL Working into the stitches from the previous row, SC 4, Ch 1, Turn [4]

76. SHELL Working into the stitches from the previous row, SC 3, Dec—complete the Dec into the same stitch from Accent row that you completed the last Dec into in Row 74: SHELL, Ch 1, Turn [3]

> Row 76 uses the same stitch from the Accent row that you last worked into; you have 0 stitches remaining on the Accent row to crochet into.

77. SHELL Working into the stitches from the previous row, SC 4, Ch 1 [4]

78. SHELL Reorient your work so that you will be working back along the unfinished edge of the shell (where the Accent Color was being crocheted along). Starting around the side of the last SC you made in Row 77, SC 35, Sl St, Ch 1, Turn [36]

> It is important to end Row 78 with a total of 35 SC and a Sl St.

79. SHELL Skip the Sl St, (Dec, SC 3) x 7, Ch 1, Turn [28]

80. SHELL (SC, Dec, SC) x 6, SC, Dec, Sl St, Ch 1, Turn [21]

81. SHELL Skip the Sl St, (SC 3, Dec) x 4 [16]

Fasten off with a 24 in/61 cm yarn tail.

Stuff lightly with fiberfill. Do not change the shape of the spiral, but do your best to stuff the parts that should bulge out emphasizing the spiral, and do not warp the inset parts.

Horizontal Small Snail with Pointed Shell and Antennae Style 1

SMALL SNAILS • **167**

SMALL SNAIL SHELL STYLE 2: ROUND (MAKE 1)

This shell style can be used with either the Horizontal or the Upright Small Snail Body.

Any Color Yarn for the Shell: Approximately 30 yd/27.5 m worsted/medium weight yarn

1. Starting with a 12 in/30.5 cm yarn tail, Ch 3, starting in the 2nd Ch from hook, SC 2, Ch 1, Turn [2]
2. SC 2, Ch 1, Turn [2]
3. BLO [SC, <Dec>, SC], Ch 1, Turn [3]

> "<Dec>" is a stitch that is defined in the Glossary beginning on page 6.

4. SC 3, Ch 1, Turn [3]
5. BLO [SC, Inc, SC], Ch 1, Turn [4]
6. SC 4, Ch 1, Turn [4]
7. BLO [SC 2, <Dec>, SC 2], Ch 1, Turn [5]
8. SC 5, Ch 1, Turn [5]
9. BLO [SC 2, Inc, SC 2], Ch 1, Turn [6]
10. SC 6, Ch 1, Turn [6]

11. BLO [SC 6], Ch 1, Turn [6]
12. SC 6, Ch 1, Turn [6]
13. BLO [SC, Inc, SC 2, Inc, SC], Ch 1, Turn [8]
14. SC 8, Ch 1, Turn [8]
15. BLO [SC 8], Ch 1, Turn [8]
16. SC 8, Ch 1, Turn [8]
17. BLO [SC 8], Ch 1, Turn [8]
18. SC 2, Inc, SC 2, Inc, SC 2, Ch 1, Turn [10]
19. BLO [SC 10], Ch 1, Turn [10]

20. SC 10, Ch 1, Turn [10]

21. BLO [SC 10], Ch 1, Turn [10]
22. SC 10, Ch 1, Turn [10]
23. BLO [SC 2, Inc, SC 4, Inc, SC 2], Ch 1, Turn [12]
24. SC 12, Ch 1, Turn [12]
25. BLO [SC 12], Ch 1, Turn [12]
26. SC 12, Ch 1, Turn [12]
27. BLO [SC 12], Ch 1, Turn [12]
28. SC 3, Inc, SC 4, Inc, SC 3, Ch 1, Turn [14]
29. BLO [SC 14], Ch 1, Turn [14]
30. SC 14, Ch 1, Turn [14]

31. BLO [SC 14], Ch 1, Turn [14]
32. SC 14, Ch 1, Turn [14]
33. BLO [SC 4, Inc, SC 4, Inc, SC 4], Ch 1, Turn [16]
34. SC 16, Ch 1, Turn [16]
35. BLO [SC 16], Ch 1, Turn [16]
36. SC 16, Ch 1, Turn [16]
37. BLO [SC 16], Ch 1, Turn [16]

38. SC 16, Ch 1 [16]

39. Fold the entire long triangle in half the long way, with the visible ridges of BLO stitches on the outside.

Work through both halves of the long triangle at the same time; work one decrease for every 2 rows.

You can tell you're working only one decrease per 2 rows by placing each decrease between the BLO ridge lines, as shown.

Once you get past the midpoint of the shell, begin stuffing the shell with fiberfill. Leave the widest end unstuffed for now, concentrating on the midpoint to the thinnest end. Stuff the wider section of the shell medium-firm, stuffing more lightly as the shell tapers to a point. When in doubt, err on the side of lighter stuffing.

Finish stuffing the rest of the shell.

Fasten off the shell with a 36 in/91.5 cm yarn tail.

Upright Small Snail with Round Shell and Antennae Style 2

Assembly

1. Gently curl the shell into a spiral, starting at the thinnest end. Pin in place as you work. The very center of the spiral (where the shell is thinnest) will be stacked on top of the wider part, making a slight cone shape.

2. Once you are pleased with the shaping of the shell, use the yarn tail to sew along the spiral, securing the spiral shape in place.

3. Pin the shell to attach to the back of the snail. The front edge of the shell opening should rest at the point where the Snail Body angles upward/toward the head of the upright snail or centered on the back of the horizontal snail with slightly more space available toward the head than toward the back of the body. The back of the shell should not extend beyond the back edge of the snail "frill" (foot). Sew around the shell opening to secure the shell to the Snail Body. (This step is also covered in more detail in the Assembly section beginning on page 170.)

SMALL SNAILS • 169

Small Snail Assembly

1. The body should already be pinned with a line of pins around the edge of the snail at the border of Rows 20 and 21 for the top and bottom of the Horizontal Body or at Rows 25 and 29 for the Upright Body, trapping the stuffing inside the center of the body. Sew around the edge of the snail at the pinned row using a yarn tail. To do so without showing the color of the top part of the body through on the bottom side of the body or vice versa, you can work to capture only the bottom/inside of the stitches on the side with a different color than the yarn tail you are using. Make sure to use small stitches and catch as much of the stitch on the inside of the work as possible, without letting the needle come all the way through the work.

Horizontal Body

Upright Body

2. Pin the center of the "face" of the Snail Body down. For the Upright Small Snail, this step is more necessary to achieve the correct shaping. You can also optionally pin inward the outer-upper edges of the snail's "face" area, and you can pin down the bobbles slightly.

For the Horizontal Small Snail, it is optional to pin down the center of the face.

170 • SMALL SNAILS

3. Pin the antennae to attach to the head of the snail behind the bumps, not on the bumps.

4. Use the yarn tail from the antennae to sew the antennae to attach and to anchor the shaping of the face in place.

Top to bottom: ❶ Horizontal Small Snail with Round Shell and Antennae Style 1, ❷ Upright Small Snail with Round Shell and Antennae Style 2, ❸ Upright Small Snail with Pointed Shell and Antennae Style 1

SMALL SNAILS • 171

5. If you have not already done so, stuff the shell with fiberfill. Pin the shell in place on the body of the snail, sew in place, and weave in ends. The pins on the bodies depicted below show the edge of where the shell is positioned in the photos, without the shell pinned in place.

Body Style 1, Horizontal, with Pointed Snail Shell

Body Style 1, Horizontal, with Round Snail Shell

> The pins on the back of the snail in these photos show exactly where the edges of the shell are attached to this snail body. You can use these photos as a guide.

172 • SMALL SNAILS

Body Style 2, Upright, with Pointed Snail Shell

Body Style 2, Upright, with Round Snail Shell

> The pins on the back of the snail in these photos show exactly where the edges of the shell are attached to this snail body. You can use these photos as a guide.

SMALL SNAILS • 173

Medium Snail with Pointed Shell

Medium Snail with Pointed Shell

Medium Snail with Pointed Shell

MEDIUM SNAILS

Medium Snails are the perfect active companions for Mushroom Sprites. They can keep up with long walks and enjoy playing fetch. In between tossing a stick for them to fetch, consider teaching your Mushroom Sprite a hobby—like crochet—while they wait patiently for their snail to bring the stick back.

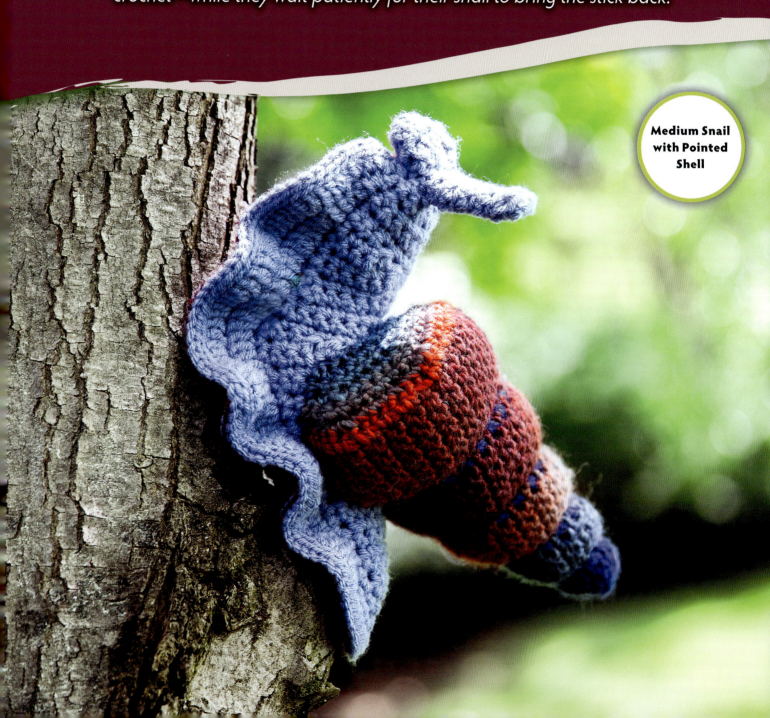

Medium Snail with Pointed Shell

OPTIONS

Medium Snail Body . . . 178

Medium Snail Antennae . . . 187

Medium Snail Shell Style 1: Pointed . . . 188

Medim Snail Shell Style 2: Round . . . 205

Medium Snail Body

MEDIUM SNAIL BODY BOTTOM (MAKE 1)

Body Bottom Color Yarn: Approximately 45 yd/41.25 m worsted/medium weight yarn

1. Starting with a short yarn tail, Ch 4, Turn, starting in the 2nd Ch from hook, SC 3, Ch 1, Turn [3]
2. Inc, SC, Inc, Ch 1, Turn [5]
3–6. (4 rows of) SC 5, Ch 1, Turn [5]
7. SC, Inc, SC, Inc, SC, Ch 1, Turn [7]
8–13. (6 rows of) SC 7, Ch 1, Turn [7]
14. SC, Inc, SC 3, Inc, SC, Ch 1, Turn [9]
15–21. (7 rows of) SC 9, Ch 1, Turn [9]
22. SC, Dec, SC 3, Dec, SC, Ch 1, Turn [7]
23–28. (6 rows of) SC 7, Ch 1, Turn [7]
29. SC, Dec, SC, Dec, SC, Ch 1, Turn [5]

30–36. (7 rows of) SC 5, Ch 1, Turn [5]
37. Dec, SC, Dec, Ch 1, Turn [3]

In Row 38 and others like it, the row is broken down into sub-rows. These sub-rows all together make up an entire row. Each sub-row (38A, 38B, etc.) has its own sub-row stitch count indicated by the number preceded by a hyphen in brackets. Row 38A's sub-row stitch count is 4. The total stitch count for all of Row 38 is at the very end of the final sub-row, without the hyphen.

38A. SC 2, Inc [-4]

38B. Reorient work so that you will continue crocheting around the entire edge of the piece; continuing along the unfinished edge of the work, SC 36 [-36]

178 • MEDIUM SNAILS

38C. Working across the OC, Inc, SC, Inc [-5]

38D. Reorient work so that you will continue crocheting around the entire edge of the piece; SC 36 (along the unfinished edge), SC in the same stitch as the first SC you made in Row 38A (this creates an Inc in this corner and shifts the seam), Sl St to beginning stitch, Ch 1 [-37] [82]

> In Row 39, the ridge created by the leftover back loops will be on the inside of the snail. You will hold this side against the top when you crochet the pieces together.

> Work all sub-rows of Row 39 in the front loop only.

39A. FLO [SC 5] [-5]
39B. FLO [Inc, HDC, HDC Inc] [-5]
39C. FLO [(DC, DC Inc) x 10] [-30]
39D. FLO [(HDC, HDC Inc) x 5] [-15]
39E. FLO [(SC, Inc) x 2] [-6]
39F. FLO [SC] [-1]

> Row 39F is the center of the front of the snail.

39G. FLO [(Inc, SC) x 2] [-6]
39H. FLO [(HDC Inc, HDC) x 5] [-15]
39I. FLO [(DC Inc, DC) x 10] [-30]
39J. FLO [HDC Inc, HDC, Inc, SC 2], Sl St to beginning stitch, Ch 1 [-7] [120]

40A. SC 5, Inc, SC [-8]
40B. (HDC, HDC Inc) x 3 [-9]
40C. (DC, DC Inc, DC, DC Inc, DC) x 4 [-28]
40D. (DC Inc, DC) x 2 [-6]
40E. (HDC, HDC Inc) x 4 [-12]
40F. (SC, Inc) x 2 [-6]
40G. (SC, Inc, SC) x 4 [-16]
40H. SC [-1]
40I. (SC, Inc, SC) x 4 [-16]
40J. (Inc, SC) x 2 [-6]
40K. (HDC Inc, HDC) x 4 [-12]
40L. (DC, DC Inc) x 2 [-6]
40M. (DC, DC Inc, DC, DC Inc, DC) x 4 [-28]
40N. (HDC Inc, HDC) x 3 [-9]
40O. SC, Inc, SC 2, Sl St to beginning stitch [-5] [168]

Fasten off with a short yarn tail.

NOTE: Mark the 5th to last stitch.
NOTE: Mark the 2nd stitch.

> The inside of the Body Bottom is the side with the ridge of leftover BLO stitches after working Row 39. This inside will be held against the inside of the Body Top to be crocheted together.

This is the outside/right side of the body bottom.

MEDIUM SNAILS • 179

Medium Snail with Round Shell

❶ Medium Snail with Pointed Shell coming to get pets from ❷ Mushroom Sprite with Arms Style 6, Body Style 2, and Cap Style 11

MEDIUM SNAIL BODY TOP (MAKE 1)

Body Top Color Yarn: Approximately 55 yd/50.25 m worsted/medium weight yarn

1. Starting with a short yarn tail, Ch 4, Turn, starting in the 2nd Ch from hook, Inc, SC, Inc, Ch 1, Turn [5]

2. SC 5, Ch 1, Turn [5]

3. Inc, SC 3, Inc, Ch 1, Turn [7]

4–5. (2 rows of) SC 7, Ch 1, Turn [7]

6. SC, Inc, SC 3, Inc, SC, Ch 1, Turn [9]

7–9. (3 rows of) SC 9, Ch 1, Turn [9]

10. SC, Inc, SC 5, Inc, SC, Ch 1, Turn [11]

11–13. (3 rows of) SC 11, Ch 1, Turn [11]

14. SC, Inc, SC 3, Inc, SC 3, Inc, SC, Ch 1, Turn [14]

> In Rows 15 and 20, and other rows like them, you will follow every lettered sub-row to create short rows of built-up stitches (for more information on this technique, please see this YouTube video: https://www.youtube.com/watch?v=sh5T-idiwm8&t=3s). These sub-rows all together make up an entire row. Each sub-row (i.e., 15A, 15B, 15C, etc.) has its own sub-row stitch count, indicated by the number preceded by a hyphen in brackets. Row 15A's sub-row stitch count is 6. The total stitch count for all of Row 15 is at the very end of the final sub-row, without the hyphen.

15A. SC 6, Ch 1, Turn [-6]
15B. SC 6, Ch 1, Turn [-6]
15C. Inc, SC 3, Ch 1, Turn [-5]
15D. SC 5, Ch 1, Turn [-5]
15E. SC 3, Ch 1, Turn [-3]
15F. SC 3, Ch 1, Turn [-3]

15G. SC 2, (SC/HDC Dec & HDC) x 3, SC 7, Ch 1, Turn [-15]

> The SC/HDC Dec is worked down the "step" created between the top row of stitches and the unworked stitches one row down. This and the "&" stitch are defined in the Glossary beginning on page 6.

15H. SC 6, Ch 1, Turn [-6]
15I. SC 6, Ch 1, Turn [-6]

15J. Inc, SC 3, Ch 1, Turn [-5]
15K. SC 5, Ch 1, Turn [-5]
15L. SC 3, Ch 1, Turn [-3]
15M. SC 3, Ch 1, Turn [-3]

15N. SC 2, (SC/HDC Dec & HDC) x 3, SC 8, Ch 1, Turn [-16] [16]

16. SC 16, Ch 1, Turn [16]

17. Dec, SC 4, Inc, SC 2, Inc, SC 4, Dec, Ch 1, Turn [16]

18. Dec, SC 12, Dec, Ch 1, Turn [14]

19. Dec, SC 3, Inc, SC 2, Inc, SC 3, Dec, Ch 1, Turn [14]

MEDIUM SNAILS • 181

20A. SC 5, Ch 1, Turn [-5]
20B. SC 5, Ch 1, Turn [-5]
20C. SC 3, Ch 1, Turn [-3]
20D. SC 3, Ch 1, Turn [-3]

20E. SC 2, SC/HDC Dec x 2, SC 8, Ch 1, Turn [-12]
20F. SC 5, Ch 1, Turn [-5]
20G. SC 5, Ch 1, Turn [-5]
20H. SC 3, Ch 1, Turn [-3]
20I. SC 3, Ch 1, Turn [-3]

20J. SC 2, SC/HDC Dec x 2, SC 6, Ch 1, Turn [-10] [10]

21. SC 10, Ch 1, Turn [10]
22. Dec, SC 2, Inc x 2, SC 2, Dec, Ch 1, Turn [10]
23. SC 10, Ch 1, Turn [10]
24. (SC, Dec) x 3, SC, Ch 1, Turn [7]

25. (SC, Dec) x 2, SC, Ch 1, Turn [5]

26A. Dec, SC, Dec [-3]
26B. Working into the same stitch as the last leg of the last Dec, SC [-1]
26C. Reorient work so that you will continue crocheting around the entire edge of the piece; continuing along the unfinished edge, SC 36 [-36]

26D. Inc (in the OC), SC, Inc [-5]

26E. Reorient work so that you will continue crocheting around the entire edge of the piece; continuing along the unfinished edge, SC 36 [-36]

26F. SC in the same stitch as where the first Dec of the row began, Sl St to the first stitch, Sl St into the next stitch, **do not** chain [-1] [82]

> The 2nd to last Sl St is a join stitch (does not add to the stitch count), and the final Sl St shifts the starting stitch of the following rows. As this is an overlapping stitch, it does not add to the stitch count.

> Stitch counts in Row 27 include Sl Sts.

27A. Skip 1 stitch, DC 6 in the next available stitch [-6]

27B. Skip 1 stitch, Sl St [-1]

27C. SC, Inc, HDC, HDC Inc [-6]

27H. (Inc, SC) x 2 [-6]

27L. Skip 1 stitch, DC 6 in the next available stitch, Skip 1 stitch, Sl St (in the same stitch you last slip stitched into in Row 26), Ch 1 [-7] [124]

> The stitch count in Row 27L includes a Sl St.

27D. (DC, DC Inc) x 9 [-27]

27I. (HDC Inc, HDC) x 5 [-15]

28A. Working in the DC sts, Inc x 6 [-12]

27E. (HDC, HDC Inc) x 5 [-15]

27J. (DC Inc, DC) x 9 [-27]

28B. Sl St in the same stitch you slip stitched into in Row 27 [-1]

27F. (SC, Inc) x 2 [-6]

27K. HDC Inc, HDC, Inc, SC, Sl St [-7]

28C. SC, Inc [-3]

27G. SC [-1]

MEDIUM SNAILS • 183

28D. (HDC, HDC Inc) x 2 [-6]

28E. (DC, DC Inc, DC, DC Inc, DC) x 4 [-28]

28F. (DC Inc, DC) x 2 [-6]

28G. (HDC, HDC Inc) x 4 [-12]

28H. (SC, Inc) x 2 [-6]

28I. (SC, Inc, SC) x 4 [-16]

28J. SC [-1]

28K. (SC, Inc, SC) x 4 [-16]

28L. (Inc, SC) x 2 [-6]

28M. (HDC Inc, HDC) x 4 [-12]

28N. (DC, DC Inc) x 2 [-6]

28O. (DC, DC Inc, DC, DC Inc, DC) x 4 [-28]

28P. (HDC Inc, HDC) x 2 [-6]

28Q. Inc, SC [-3]

184 • MEDIUM SNAILS

28R. Sl St in the same stitch you last slip stitched into in Row 27 just before the final DC 6 [-1]

28S. Inc x 6 (in the DC sts), Sl St in the same stitch you last slip stitched into in Row 27, Ch 1 [-13] [182]

The stitch count in Row 28S includes a Sl St.

Row 29 will attach the body top piece to the body bottom piece. You will hold both pieces with the insides against each other and work through the indicated stitches on both pieces at the same time, unless otherwise indicated. On the body bottom piece, the ridge created by the leftover back loops will be on the inside of the snail. You will hold this side against the inside of the top piece to crochet the pieces together.

29A. Working in the top only, Dec, HDC Dec x 4, Dec [-6]

29B. Working in both pieces, Sl St in the same stitch you slip stitched into in Row 28 (of the top) and the marked stitch (5th to last) on the bottom [-1]

29C. Working into the BLO of the body top piece and the FLO of the body bottom piece, SC 155 around the edge [-155]

29D. Working through all loops, Sl St in the next available stitch on both pieces [-1]

29E. Working along the top piece only, Dec, HDC Dec x 4, Dec [-6]

MEDIUM SNAILS • 185

29F. Working through all loops, Sl St into the same stitch you slip stitched into in Row 28 of the top and the 2nd marked stitch on the Snail bottom piece [-1] [170]

Once you have finished this row, fasten off with a 24 in/61 cm yarn tail.

Now pin around the border of Rows 26 and 27 of the top of the body to connect it to the border of Rows 38 and 39 of the bottom of the body, and then stuff the center portion of the body—you can optionally include some flat glass marble gems, if you'd like, for weight (keep the weight toward the middle and back end to help keep the snail balanced). You will sew around the edge of the pinned rows in order to seal the stuffing inside of that center space after you finish crocheting the body; this step is covered in the Assembly instructions beginning on page 209.

Inspecting this year's round up at the corral!

❶ Mushroom Sprite with Arms Style 2, Feet/Legs Style 1, Body Style 4, Cap Style 6;
❷ Two Medium Snails with Pointed Shells;
❸ Giant Snail with Round Shell

186 • MEDIUM SNAILS

Medium Snail Antennae (Make 2)

Body Top Color Yarn: Approximately 7 yd/6.5 m worsted/medium weight yarn for two antennae

> This piece is worked in spiral. Do not "Sl St, Ch 1" to join.

1. Start with a short yarn tail, SC 4 in a Magic Circle [4]
2. BLO [SC 4] [4]
3. BLO [Inc, SC 3] [5]
4. BLO [SC 5] [5]
5. BLO [Inc, SC 4] [6]
6. BLO [SC 6] [6]

Fasten off with a 12 in/30.5 cm yarn tail.

Medium Snail with Pointed Shell

Medium Snail Shells

MEDIUM SNAIL SHELL STYLE 1: POINTED (MAKE 1)

Any Color Yarn for the Shell: Approximately 62 yd/56.75 m worsted/medium weight yarn

Any Color Yarn for the Accent: Approximately 8 yd/7.25 m worsted/medium weight yarn

The following instructions will use both Shell Color and Accent Color yarn for different rows. Accent rows are worked around the shell in a spiral, always in the same direction. Shell rows are worked back and forth to build up the outer wall of the shell, anchored to the Accent rows. The Accent Color rows are **not** optional. You **must** follow these rows with a separate strand of yarn. To make a shell in one color, use a second strand of the Shell color for the Accent rows. Do not fasten off either color yarn until instructed to do so in the pattern.

> To change between Accent and Shell rows, remove the hook from the current color at the end of the row and insert the hook into the loop of the next color. Tighten the loop if needed.

1. SHELL Starting with a short yarn tail, SC 5 in Magic Circle, Ch 2, do not Turn, continue working in the same direction in the round for Row 2 [5]

> **Mark the 3rd stitch of Row 1: SHELL.** This will be where you attach the Accent color after Row 7: SHELL.

> Make sure you are working right side out as you continue your shell. The starting yarn tail should be on the inside/wrong side of this piece. You should insert your hook from the outside/right side to the inside/wrong side as you complete stitches. Here's a video on inside out versus right side out: https://www.youtube.com/watch?v=beReNFWQPAs

2. SHELL In the 2nd Ch from hook, SC & Dec—complete the Dec into the 1st SC you made in Row 1: SHELL, Ch 1, Turn [2]

> In Row 2: SHELL, do not Turn. Continue working in the same direction, work the SC in the 2nd Ch from the hook, and then start the Dec in the same chain that you worked the SC into; complete the Dec into the first SC from the "SC 5 in Magic Circle" that you worked in Row 1. You have 4 stitches remaining available on Row 1 to crochet into. The description of exactly where to place the decrease is always included after the "—" symbol in this and all future rows.

3. SHELL Working into the stitches from the previous row, SC 2, Ch 1, Turn [2]

4. SHELL Working into the stitches from the previous row, SC, Dec—complete the Dec into the next available stitch from Row 1: SHELL, Ch 1, Turn [2]

> Row 4 uses 1 stitch from Row 1; you have 3 stitches remaining on Row 1 to crochet into.

5. SHELL Working into the stitches from the previous row, SC 2, Ch 1, Turn [2]

6. SHELL Working into the stitches from the previous row, SC, Dec—complete the Dec into the same stitch from Row 1: SHELL that you completed the last Dec into in Row 4: SHELL, Ch 1, Turn [2]

> Row 6 uses the same stitch from Row 1 that you last worked into; you still have 3 stitches remaining on Row 1 to crochet into.

7. SHELL Working into the stitches from the previous row, SC 2, Ch 1, Turn [2]

1. ACCENT Keeping the shell right side out, attach yarn to the BLO of the 3rd (marked) stitch you made in Row 1: SHELL, starting in the same stitch and working across the open unused stitches from Row 1, BLO [Dec], and then, working into the last available stitch (in the BLO) from Row 1 and up the unfinished edges of the rest of the rows, make 3 more Dec stitches [4]

> Keep your Accent row Dec stitches tight; this will make the Accent rows sink into the work, creating a spiral indentation along the shell. At the end of Row 1: ACCENT, you have 4 Accent Color stitches to work into when working with the Shell Color yarn.

❶ **Medium Snail with Pointed Shell being cuddled by** ❷ **Mushroom Sprite with Arms Style 4, Feet/Legs Style 5, Body Style 4, Cap Style 5**

8. SHELL Working into the stitches from the previous Shell row, SC, Dec—complete the Dec into the next (first) available stitch from the Accent row, Ch 1, Turn [2]

Row 8 uses 1 stitch from the Accent row; you have 3 stitches remaining on the Accent row to crochet into.

9. SHELL Working into the stitches from the previous row, SC 2, Ch 1, Turn [2]

10. SHELL Working into the stitches from the previous row, SC, Dec—complete the Dec into the same stitch from the Accent row that you completed the last Dec into in Row 8: SHELL, Ch 1, Turn [2]

Row 10 uses the same stitch from the Accent row that you last worked into; 3 stitches remain available.

11. SHELL Working into the stitches from the previous row, SC 2, Ch 1, Turn [2]

12. SHELL Working into the stitches from the previous row, SC, Dec—complete the Dec into the next available stitch from the Accent row, Ch 1, Turn [2]

Row 12 uses 1 stitch from the Accent row; you have 2 stitches remaining on the Accent row to crochet into.

13. SHELL Working into the stitches from the previous row, SC 2, Ch 1, Turn [2]

14. SHELL Working into the stitches from the previous row, SC, Dec—complete the Dec into the same stitch from Accent row that you completed the last Dec into in Row 12: SHELL, Ch 1, Turn [2]

Row 14 uses the same stitch from the Accent row that you last worked into; 2 stitches remain available.

15. SHELL Working into the stitches from the previous row, SC 2, Ch 1, Turn [2]

16. SHELL Working into the stitches from the previous row, SC, Dec—complete the Dec into the next available stitch from the Accent row, Ch 1, Turn [2]

Row 16 uses 1 stitch from the Accent row; you have 1 stitch remaining on the Accent row to crochet into.

17. SHELL Working into the stitches from the previous row, SC 2, Ch 1, Turn [2]

2. ACCENT Dec x 5 [5]

You will continue to work these stitches along the unfinished edge/side of the rows of the shell stitches. You had 1 stitch available on the Accent row before Row 2: ACCENT. Now you have a total of 6 Accent Color stitches to work into when working with the Shell Color yarn.

18. SHELL Working into the stitches from the previous Shell row, SC, SC & Dec—complete the Dec into the next available stitch from the Accent row, Ch 1, Turn [3]

Row 18 uses 1 stitch from the Accent row; you have 5 stitches remaining on the Accent row to crochet into.

19. SHELL Working into the stitches from the previous row, SC 3, Ch 1, Turn [3]

20. SHELL Working into the stitches from the previous row, SC 2, Dec—complete the Dec into the same stitch from the Accent row that you completed the last Dec into in Row 18: SHELL, Ch 1, Turn [3]

> Row 20 uses the same stitch from the Accent row that you last worked into; 5 stitches remain available.

21. SHELL Working into the stitches from the previous row, SC 3, Ch 1, Turn [3]

22. SHELL Working into the stitches from the previous row, SC 2, Dec—complete the Dec into the next available stitch from the Accent row, Ch 1, Turn [3]

> Row 22 uses 1 stitch from the Accent row; you have 4 stitches remaining on the Accent row to crochet into.

23. SHELL Working into the stitches from the previous row, SC 3, Ch 1, Turn [3]

24. SHELL Working into the stitches from the previous row, SC 2, Dec—complete the Dec into the next available stitch from the Accent row, Ch 1, Turn [3]

> Row 24 uses 1 stitch from the Accent row; you have 3 stitches remaining on the Accent row to crochet into.

25. SHELL Working into the stitches from the previous row, SC 3, Ch 1, Turn [3]

26. SHELL Working into the stitches from the previous row, SC 2, Dec—complete the Dec into the same stitch from Accent row that you completed the last Dec into in Row 24: SHELL, Ch 1, Turn [3]

> Row 26 uses the same stitch from the Accent row that you last worked into; 3 stitches remain available.

27. SHELL Working into the stitches from the previous row, SC 3, Ch 1, Turn [3]

28. SHELL Working into the stitches from the previous row, SC 2, Dec—complete the Dec into the next available stitch from the Accent row, Ch 1, Turn [3]

> Row 28 uses 1 stitch from the Accent row; you have 2 stitches remaining on the Accent row to crochet into.

29. SHELL Working into the stitches from the previous row, SC 3, Ch 1, Turn [3]

30. SHELL Working into the stitches from the previous row, SC 2, Dec—complete the Dec into the next available stitch from the Accent row, Ch 1, Turn [3]

> Row 30 uses 1 stitch from the Accent row; you have 1 stitch remaining on the Accent row to crochet into.

31. SHELL Working into the stitches from the previous row, SC 3, Ch 1, Turn [3]

32. SHELL Working into the stitches from the previous row, SC 2, Dec—complete the Dec into the same stitch from Accent row that you completed the last Dec into in Row 30: SHELL, Ch 1, Turn [3]

> Row 32 uses the same stitch from the Accent row that you last worked into; 1 stitch remains available.

33. SHELL Working into the stitches from the previous row, SC 3, Ch 1, Turn [3]

MEDIUM SNAILS • 191

3. ACCENT Dec x 8 [8]

You will continue to work these stitches along the unfinished edge/side of the rows of the shell stitches. You had 1 stitch available on the Accent row before Row 3: ACCENT. Now you have a total of 9 Accent Color stitches to work into when working with the Shell Color yarn.

34. SHELL Working into the stitches from the previous Shell row, SC 2, Dec—complete the Dec into the next available stitch from the Accent row, Ch 1, Turn [3]

Row 34 uses 1 stitch from the Accent row; you have 8 stitches remaining on the Accent row to crochet into.

35. SHELL Working into the stitches from the previous row, SC 3, Ch 1, Turn [3]

36. SHELL Working into the stitches from the previous row, SC 2, Dec—complete the Dec into the next available stitch from the Accent row, Ch 1, Turn [3]

Row 36 uses 1 stitch from the Accent row; you have 7 stitches remaining on the Accent row to crochet into.

37. SHELL Working into the stitches from the previous row, SC 3, Ch 1, Turn [3]

38. SHELL Working into the stitches from the previous row, SC 2, Dec—complete the Dec into the same stitch from Accent row that you completed the last Dec into in Row 36: SHELL, Ch 1, Turn [3]

Row 38 uses the same stitch from the Accent row that you last worked into; 7 stitches remain available.

39. SHELL Working into the stitches from the previous row, SC 3, Ch 1, Turn [3]

40. SHELL Working into the stitches from the previous row, SC 2, Dec—complete the Dec into the next available stitch from the Accent row, Ch 1, Turn [3]

Row 40 uses 1 stitch from the Accent row; you have 6 stitches remaining on the Accent row to crochet into.

41. SHELL Working into the stitches from the previous row, SC 3, Ch 1, Turn [3]

42. SHELL Working into the stitches from the previous row, SC 2, Dec—complete the Dec into the next available stitch from the Accent row, Ch 1, Turn [3]

Row 42 uses 1 stitch from the Accent row; you have 5 stitches remaining on the Accent row to crochet into.

43. SHELL Working into the stitches from the previous row, SC 3, Ch 1, Turn [3]

44. SHELL Working into the stitches from the previous row, SC 2, Dec—complete the Dec into the same stitch from Accent row that you completed the last Dec into in Row 42: SHELL, Ch 1, Turn [3]

Row 44 uses the same stitch from the Accent row that you last worked into; 5 stitches remain available.

45. SHELL Working into the stitches from the previous row, SC 3, Ch 1, Turn [3]

46. SHELL Working into the stitches from the previous row, SC 2, SC & Dec—complete the Dec into the next available stitch from the Accent row, Ch 1, Turn [4]

Row 46 uses 1 stitch from the Accent row; you have 4 stitches remaining on the Accent row to crochet into.

47. SHELL Working into the stitches from the previous row, SC 4, Ch 1, Turn [4]

48. SHELL Working into the stitches from the previous row, SC 3, Dec—complete the Dec into the next available stitch from the Accent row, Ch 1, Turn [4]

Row 48 uses 1 stitch from the Accent row; you have 3 stitches remaining on the Accent row to crochet into.

49. SHELL Working into the stitches from the previous row, SC 4, Ch 1, Turn [4]

50. SHELL Working into the stitches from the previous row, SC 3, Dec—complete the Dec into the same stitch from Accent row that you completed the last Dec into in Row 48: SHELL, Ch 1, Turn [4]

Row 50 uses the same stitch from the Accent row that you last worked into; 3 stitches remain available.

51. SHELL Working into the stitches from the previous row, SC 4, Ch 1, Turn [4]

52. SHELL Working into the stitches from the previous row, SC 3, Dec—complete the Dec into the next available stitch from the Accent row, Ch 1, Turn [4]

Row 52 uses 1 stitch from the Accent row; you have 2 stitches remaining on the Accent row to crochet into.

53. SHELL Working into the stitches from the previous row, SC 4, Ch 1, Turn [4]

4. ACCENT Dec x 10 [10]

You will continue to work these stitches along the unfinished edge/side of the rows of the shell stitches. You had 2 stitches available on the Accent row before Row 4: ACCENT. Now you have a total of 12 Accent Color stitches to work into when working with the Shell Color yarn.

MEDIUM SNAILS • 193

54. SHELL Working into the stitches from the previous Shell row, SC 3, Dec—complete the Dec into the next available stitch from the Accent row, Ch 1, Turn [4]

> Row 54 uses 1 stitch from the Accent row; you have 11 stitches remaining on the Accent row to crochet into.

55. SHELL Working into the stitches from the previous row, SC 4, Ch 1, Turn [4]

56. SHELL Working into the stitches from the previous row, SC 3, Dec—complete the Dec into the next available stitch from the Accent row, Ch 1, Turn [4]

> Row 56 uses 1 stitch from the Accent row; you have 10 stitches remaining on the Accent row to crochet into.

57. SHELL Working into the stitches from the previous row, SC 4, Ch 1, Turn [4]

58. SHELL Working into the stitches from the previous row, SC 3, Dec—complete the Dec into the same stitch from Accent row that you completed the last Dec into in Row 56: SHELL, Ch 1, Turn [4]

> Row 58 uses the same stitch from the Accent row that you last worked into; 10 stitches remain available.

59. SHELL Working into the stitches from the previous row, SC 4, Ch 1, Turn [4]

60. SHELL Working into the stitches from the previous row, SC 3, Dec—complete the Dec into the next available stitch from the Accent row, Ch 1, Turn [4]

> Row 60 uses 1 stitch from the Accent row; you have 9 stitches remaining on the Accent row to crochet into.

61. SHELL Working into the stitches from the previous row, SC 4, Ch 1, Turn [4]

62. SHELL Working into the stitches from the previous row, SC 3, Dec—complete the Dec into the next available stitch from the Accent row, Ch 1, Turn [4]

> Row 62 uses 1 stitch from the Accent row; you have 8 stitches remaining on the Accent row to crochet into.

63. SHELL Working into the stitches from the previous row, SC 4, Ch 1, Turn [4]

64. SHELL Working into the stitches from the previous row, SC 3, Dec—complete the Dec into the next available stitch from the Accent row, Ch 1, Turn [4]

> Row 64 uses 1 stitch from the Accent row; you have 7 stitches remaining on the Accent row to crochet into.

65. SHELL Working into the stitches from the previous row, SC 4, Ch 1, Turn [4]

66. SHELL Working into the stitches from the previous row, SC 3, Dec—complete the Dec into the same stitch from Accent row that you completed the last Dec into in Row 64: SHELL, Ch 1, Turn [4]

> Row 66 uses the same stitch from the Accent row that you last worked into; 7 stitches remain available.

67. SHELL Working into the stitches from the previous row, SC 4, Ch 1, Turn [4]

68. SHELL Working into the stitches from the previous row, SC 3, Dec—complete the Dec into the next available stitch from the Accent row, Ch 1, Turn [4]

> Row 68 uses 1 stitch from the Accent row; you have 6 stitches remaining on the Accent row to crochet into.

69. SHELL Working into the stitches from the previous row, SC 4, Ch 1, Turn [4]

70. SHELL Working into the stitches from the previous row, SC 3, Dec—complete the Dec into the next available stitch from the Accent row, Ch 1, Turn [4]

> Row 70 uses 1 stitch from the Accent row; you have 5 stitches remaining on the Accent row to crochet into.

71. SHELL Working into the stitches from the previous row, SC 4, Ch 1, Turn [4]

72. SHELL Working into the stitches from the previous row, SC 3, Dec—complete the Dec into the next available stitch from the Accent row, Ch 1, Turn [4]

> Row 72 uses 1 stitch from the Accent row; you have 4 stitches remaining on the Accent row to crochet into.

73. SHELL Working into the stitches from the previous row, SC 4, Ch 1, Turn [4]

74. SHELL Working into the stitches from the previous row, SC 3, Dec—complete the Dec into the same stitch from Accent row that you completed the last Dec into in Row 72: SHELL, Ch 1, Turn [4]

> Row 74 uses the same stitch from the Accent row that you last worked into; 4 stitches remain available.

75. SHELL Working into the stitches from the previous row, SC 4, Ch 1, Turn [4]

76. SHELL Working into the stitches from the previous row, SC 3, Dec—complete the Dec into the next available stitch from the Accent row, Ch 1, Turn [4]

> Row 76 uses 1 stitch from the Accent row; you have 3 stitches remaining on the Accent row to crochet into.

77. SHELL Working into the stitches from the previous row, SC 4, Ch 1, Turn [4]

Medium Snail with Pointed Shell

MEDIUM SNAILS • 195

5. ACCENT Dec x 12 [12]

> You will continue to work these stitches along the unfinished edge/side of the rows of the shell stitches. You had 3 stitches available on the Accent row before Row 5: ACCENT; now you have a total of 15 Accent Color stitches to work into when working with the Shell Color yarn.

78. SHELL Working into the stitches from the previous Shell row, SC 3, Dec—complete the Dec into the next available stitch from the Accent row, Ch 1, Turn [4]

> Row 78 uses 1 stitch from the Accent row; you have 14 stitches remaining on the Accent row to crochet into.

79. SHELL Working into the stitches from the previous row, SC 4, Ch 1, Turn [4]

80. SHELL Working into the stitches from the previous row, SC 3, Dec—complete the Dec into the next available stitch from the Accent row, Ch 1, Turn [4]

> Row 80 uses 1 stitch from the Accent row; you have 13 stitches remaining on the Accent row to crochet into.

81. SHELL Working into the stitches from the previous row, SC 4, Ch 1, Turn [4]

82. SHELL Working into the stitches from the previous row, SC 3, Dec—complete the Dec into the same stitch from Accent row that you completed the last Dec into in Row 80: SHELL, Ch 1, Turn [4]

> Row 82 uses the same stitch from the Accent row that you last worked into; 13 stitches remain available.

83. SHELL Working into the stitches from the previous row, SC 4, Ch 1, Turn [4]

84. SHELL Working into the stitches from the previous row, SC 3, Dec—complete the Dec into the next available stitch from the Accent row, Ch 1, Turn [4]

> Row 84 uses 1 stitch from the Accent row; you have 12 stitches remaining on the Accent row to crochet into.

85. SHELL Working into the stitches from the previous row, SC 4, Ch 1, Turn [4]

86. SHELL Working into the stitches from the previous row, SC 3, SC & Dec—complete the Dec into the next available stitch from the Accent row, Ch 1, Turn [5]

> Row 86 uses 1 stitch from the Accent row; you have 11 stitches remaining on the Accent row to crochet into.

87. SHELL Working into the stitches from the previous row, SC 5, Ch 1, Turn [5]

88. SHELL Working into the stitches from the previous row, SC 4, Dec—complete the Dec into the next available stitch from the Accent row, Ch 1, Turn [5]

> Row 88 uses 1 stitch from the Accent row; you have 10 stitches remaining on the Accent row to crochet into.

89. SHELL Working into the stitches from the previous row, SC 5, Ch 1, Turn [5]

90. SHELL Working into the stitches from the previous row, SC 4, Dec—complete the Dec into the same stitch from the Accent row that you completed the last Dec into in Row 88: SHELL, Ch 1, Turn [5]

> Row 90 uses the same stitch from the Accent row that you last worked into; 10 stitches remain available.

91. SHELL Working into the stitches from the previous row, SC 5, Ch 1, Turn [5]

92. SHELL Working into the stitches from the previous row, SC 4, Dec—complete the Dec into the next available stitch from the Accent row, Ch 1, Turn [5]

> Row 92 uses 1 stitch from the Accent row; you have 9 stitches remaining on the Accent row to crochet into.

93. SHELL Working into the stitches from the previous row, SC 5, Ch 1, Turn [5]

94. SHELL Working into the stitches from the previous row, SC 4, Dec—complete the Dec into the next available stitch from the Accent row, Ch 1, Turn [5]

> Row 94 uses 1 stitch from the Accent row; you have 8 stitches remaining on the Accent row to crochet into.

95. SHELL Working into the stitches from the previous row, SC 5, Ch 1, Turn [5]

96. SHELL Working into the stitches from the previous row, SC 4, Dec—complete the Dec into the next available stitch from the Accent row, Ch 1, Turn [5]

> Row 96 uses 1 stitch from the Accent row; you have 7 stitches remaining on the Accent row to crochet into.

Medium Snail with Pointed Shell

97. SHELL Working into the stitches from the previous row, SC 5, Ch 1, Turn [5]

98. SHELL Working into the stitches from the previous row, SC 4, Dec—complete the Dec into the same stitch from the Accent row that you completed the last Dec into in Row 96: SHELL, Ch 1, Turn [5]

> Row 98 uses the same stitch from the Accent row that you last worked into; 7 stitches remain available.

99. SHELL Working into the stitches from the previous row, SC 5, Ch 1, Turn [5]

100. SHELL Working into the stitches from the previous row, SC 4, Dec—complete the Dec into the next available stitch from the Accent row, Ch 1, Turn [5]

> Row 100 uses 1 stitch from the Accent row; you have 6 stitches remaining on the Accent row to crochet into.

101. SHELL Working into the stitches from the previous row, SC 5, Ch 1, Turn [5]

102. SHELL Working into the stitches from the previous row, SC 4, Dec—complete the Dec into the next available stitch from the Accent row, Ch 1, Turn [5]

> Row 102 uses 1 stitch from the Accent row; you have 5 stitches remaining on the Accent row to crochet into.

103. SHELL Working into the stitches from the previous row, SC 5, Ch 1, Turn [5]

104. SHELL Working into the stitches from the previous row, SC 4, Dec—complete the Dec into the next available stitch from the Accent row, Ch 1, Turn [5]

> Row 104 uses 1 stitch from the Accent row; you have 4 stitches remaining on the Accent row to crochet into.

105. SHELL Working into the stitches from the previous row, SC 5, Ch 1, Turn [5]

106. SHELL Working into the stitches from the previous row, SC 4, Dec—complete the Dec into the same stitch from the Accent row that you completed the last Dec into in Row 104: SHELL, Ch 1, Turn [5]

> Row 106 uses the same stitch from the Accent row that you last worked into; 4 stitches remain available.

107. SHELL Working into the stitches from the previous row, SC 5, Ch 1, Turn [5]

108. SHELL Working into the stitches from the previous row, SC 4, Dec—complete the Dec into the next available stitch from the Accent row, Ch 1, Turn [5]

> Row 108 uses 1 stitch from the Accent row; you have 3 stitches remaining on the Accent row to crochet into.

198 • MEDIUM SNAILS

109. SHELL Working into the stitches from the previous row, SC 5, Ch 1, Turn [5]

6. ACCENT Dec x 16; fasten off with a short yarn tail [16]

> You will continue to work Row 6's stitches along the unfinished edge/side of the rows of the shell stitches. You had 3 stitches available on the Accent row before Row 6: ACCENT; now you have a total of 19 Accent Color stitches to work into when working with the Shell Color yarn. You will not crochet more Accent Color stitches.

110. SHELL Working into the stitches from the previous Shell row, SC 4, Dec—complete the Dec into the next available stitch from the Accent row, Ch 1, Turn [5]

> Row 110 uses 1 stitch from the Accent row; you have 18 stitches remaining on the Accent row to crochet into.

111. SHELL Working into the stitches from the previous row, SC 5, Ch 1, Turn [5]

112. SHELL Working into the stitches from the previous row, SC 4, Dec—complete the Dec into the next available stitch from the Accent row, Ch 1, Turn [5]

> Row 112 uses 1 stitch from the Accent row; you have 17 stitches remaining on the Accent row to crochet into.

113. SHELL Working into the stitches from the previous row, SC 5, Ch 1, Turn [5]

114. SHELL Working into the stitches from the previous row, SC 4, Dec—complete the Dec into the same stitch from the Accent row that you completed the last Dec into in Row 112: SHELL, Ch 1, Turn [5]

> Row 114 uses the same stitch from the Accent row that you last worked into; 17 stitches remain available.

115. SHELL Working into the stitches from the previous row, SC 5, Ch 1, Turn [5]

116. SHELL Working into the stitches from the previous row, SC 4, Dec—complete the Dec into the next available stitch from the Accent row, Ch 1, Turn [5]

> Row 116 uses 1 stitch from the Accent row; you have 16 stitches remaining on the Accent row to crochet into.

117. SHELL Working into the stitches from the previous row, SC 5, Ch 1, Turn [5]

MEDIUM SNAILS • **199**

118. SHELL Working into the stitches from the previous row, SC 4, Dec—complete the Dec into the next available stitch from the Accent row, Ch 1, Turn [5]

> Row 118 uses 1 stitch from the Accent row; you have 15 stitches remaining on the Accent row to crochet into.

119. SHELL Working into the stitches from the previous row, SC 5, Ch 1, Turn [5]

120. SHELL Working into the stitches from the previous row, SC 4, Dec—complete the Dec into the next available stitch from the Accent row, Ch 1, Turn [5]

> Row 120 uses 1 stitch from the Accent row; you have 14 stitches remaining on the Accent row to crochet into.

121. SHELL Working into the stitches from the previous row, SC 5, Ch 1, Turn [5]

122. SHELL Working into the stitches from the previous row, SC 4, Dec—complete the Dec into the same stitch from the Accent row that you completed the last Dec into in Row 120: SHELL, Ch 1, Turn [5]

> Row 122 uses the same stitch from the Accent row that you last worked into; 14 stitches remain available.

123. SHELL Working into the stitches from the previous row, SC 5, Ch 1, Turn [5]

124. SHELL Working into the stitches from the previous row, SC 4, Dec—complete the Dec into the next available stitch from the Accent row, Ch 1, Turn [5]

> Row 124 uses 1 stitch from the Accent row; you have 13 stitches remaining on the Accent row to crochet into.

125. SHELL Working into the stitches from the previous row, SC 5, Ch 1, Turn [5]

126. SHELL Working into the stitches from the previous row, SC 4, Dec—complete the Dec into the next available stitch from the Accent row, Ch 1, Turn [5]

> Row 126 uses 1 stitch from the Accent row; you have 12 stitches remaining on the Accent row to crochet into.

127. SHELL Working into the stitches from the previous row, SC 5, Ch 1, Turn [5]

128. SHELL Working into the stitches from the previous row, SC 4, Dec—complete the Dec into the next available stitch from the Accent row, Ch 1, Turn [5]

> Row 128 uses 1 stitch from the Accent row; you have 11 stitches remaining on the Accent row to crochet into.

129. SHELL Working into the stitches from the previous row, SC 5, Ch 1, Turn [5]

130. SHELL Working into the stitches from the previous row, SC 4, Dec—complete the Dec into the same stitch from the Accent row that you completed the last Dec into in Row 128: SHELL, Ch 1, Turn [5]

Row 130 uses the same stitch from the Accent row that you last worked into; 11 stitches remain available.

131. SHELL Working into the stitches from the previous row, SC 5, Ch 1, Turn [5]

132. SHELL Working into the stitches from the previous row, SC 4, Dec—complete the Dec into the next available stitch from the Accent row, Ch 1, Turn [5]

Row 132 uses 1 stitch from the Accent row; you have 10 stitches remaining on the Accent row to crochet into.

133. SHELL Working into the stitches from the previous row, SC 5, Ch 1, Turn [5]

134. SHELL Working into the stitches from the previous row, SC 4, SC & Dec—complete the Dec into the next available stitch from the Accent row, Ch 1, Turn [6]

Row 134 uses 1 stitch from the Accent row; you have 9 stitches remaining on the Accent row to crochet into.

135. SHELL Working into the stitches from the previous row, SC 6, Ch 1, Turn [6]

136. SHELL Working into the stitches from the previous row, SC 5, Dec—complete the Dec into the next available stitch from the Accent row, Ch 1, Turn [6]

Row 136 uses 1 stitch from the Accent row; you have 8 stitches remaining on the Accent row to crochet into.

137. SHELL Working into the stitches from the previous row, SC 6, Ch 1, Turn [6]

138. SHELL Working into the stitches from the previous row, SC 5, Dec—complete the Dec into the same stitch from the Accent row that you completed the last Dec into in Row 136: SHELL, Ch 1, Turn [6]

Row 138 uses the same stitch from the Accent row that you last worked into; 8 stitches remain available.

139. SHELL Working into the stitches from the previous row, SC 6, Ch 1, Turn [6]

140. SHELL Working into the stitches from the previous row, SC 5, Dec—complete the Dec into the next available stitch from the Accent row, Ch 1, Turn [6]

Row 140 uses 1 stitch from the Accent row; you have 7 stitches remaining on the Accent row to crochet into.

141. SHELL Working into the stitches from the previous row, SC 6, Ch 1, Turn [6]

MEDIUM SNAILS • **201**

142. SHELL Working into the stitches from the previous row, SC 5, Dec—complete the Dec into the next available stitch from the Accent row, Ch 1, Turn [6]

> Row 142 uses 1 stitch from the Accent row; you have 6 stitches remaining on the Accent row to crochet into.

143. SHELL Working into the stitches from the previous row, SC 6, Ch 1, Turn [6]

144. SHELL Working into the stitches from the previous row, SC 5, Dec—complete the Dec into the next available stitch from the Accent row, Ch 1, Turn [6]

> Row 144 uses 1 stitch from the Accent row; you have 5 stitches remaining on the Accent row to crochet into.

145. SHELL Working into the stitches from the previous row, SC 6, Ch 1, Turn [6]

146. SHELL Working into the stitches from the previous row, SC 5, Dec—complete the Dec into the same stitch from the Accent row that you completed the last Dec into in Row 144: SHELL, Ch 1, Turn [6]

> Row 146 uses the same stitch from the Accent row that you last worked into; 5 stitches remain available.

147. SHELL Working into the stitches from the previous row, SC 6, Ch 1, Turn [6]

148. SHELL Working into the stitches from the previous row, SC 5, Dec—complete the Dec into the next available stitch from the Accent row, Ch 1, Turn [6]

> Row 148 uses 1 stitch from the Accent row; you have 4 stitches remaining on the Accent row to crochet into.

149. SHELL Working into the stitches from the previous row, SC 6, Ch 1, Turn [6]

150. SHELL Working into the stitches from the previous row, SC 5, Dec—complete the Dec into the next available stitch from the Accent row, Ch 1, Turn [6]

> Row 150 uses 1 stitch from the Accent row; you have 3 stitches remaining on the Accent row to crochet into.

151. SHELL Working into the stitches from the previous row, SC 6, Ch 1, Turn [6]

152. SHELL Working into the stitches from the previous row, SC 5, Dec—complete the Dec into the next available stitch from the Accent row, Ch 1, Turn [6]

> Row 152 uses 1 stitch from the Accent row; you have 2 stitches remaining on the Accent row to crochet into.

153. SHELL Working into the stitches from the previous row, SC 6, Ch 1, Turn [6]

154. SHELL Working into the stitches from the previous row, SC 5, Dec—complete the Dec into the same stitch from the Accent row that you completed the last Dec into in Row 152: SHELL, Ch 1, Turn [6]

> Row 154 uses the same stitch from the Accent row that you last worked into; 2 stitches remain available.

155. SHELL Working into the stitches from the previous row, SC 6, Ch 1, Turn [6]

156. SHELL Working into the stitches from the previous row, SC 5, Dec—complete the Dec into the next available stitch from the Accent row, Ch 1, Turn [6]

> Row 156 uses 1 stitch from the Accent row; you have 1 stitch remaining on the Accent row to crochet into.

157. SHELL Working into the stitches from the previous row, SC 6, Ch 1, Turn [6]

158. SHELL Working into the stitches from the previous row, SC 5, Dec—complete the Dec into the next available stitch from the Accent row, Ch 1, Turn [6]

> Row 158 uses 1 stitch from the Accent row; you have 0 stitches remaining on the Accent row to crochet into.

159. SHELL Working into the stitches from the previous row, SC 6, Ch 1, Turn [6]

160. SHELL Working into the stitches from the previous row, SC 5, Dec—complete the Dec into the same stitch from the Accent row that you completed the last Dec into in Row 158: SHELL, Ch 1, Turn [6]

> Row 160 uses the same stitch from the Accent row that you last worked into; 0 stitches remain available.

161. SHELL Working into the stitches from the previous row, SC 6, Ch 1 [6]

162. SHELL Reorient your work so that you will be working back along the unfinished edge of the shell; starting around the side of the last SC you made in Row 161, SC 52, Sl St, Ch 1, Turn [53]

163. SHELL Skip the Sl St, Dec, (SC 3, Dec) x 10, Ch 1, Turn [41]

164. SHELL (SC, Dec, SC) x 10, Sl St, Ch 1, Turn [31]

165. SHELL Skip the Sl St, (SC 2, Dec, SC 2) x 5, Ch 1, Turn [25]

166. SHELL (SC, Dec, SC) x 4, Sl St, Ch 1, Turn [12]

167. SHELL Skip the Sl St, (SC, Dec, SC) x 3 [9]

Fasten off with a 24 in/61 cm yarn tail.

204 • MEDIUM SNAILS

Stuff lightly with fiberfill; do not change the shape of the spiral, but do your best to stuff the parts that should bulge out, emphasizing the spiral, and do not warp the inset parts.

MEDIUM SNAIL SHELL STYLE 2: ROUND (MAKE 1)

Any Color Yarn for the Shell: Approximately 54 yd/49.5 m worsted/medium weight yarn

1. Starting with a long enough yarn tail to weave in later, Ch 3, starting in the 2nd Ch from hook, SC 2, Ch 1, Turn [2]
2. SC 2, Ch 1, Turn [2]
3. BLO [SC, <Dec>, SC], Ch 1, Turn [3]

> "<Dec>" is a stitch that is defined in the Glossary beginning on page 6.

4. SC 3, Ch 1, Turn [3]
5. BLO [SC, Inc, SC], Ch 1, Turn [4]
6. SC 4, Ch 1, Turn [4]
7. BLO [SC 2, <Dec>, SC 2], Ch 1, Turn [5]
8. SC 5, Ch 1, Turn [5]
9. BLO [SC 2, Inc, SC 2], Ch 1, Turn [6]
10. SC 6, Ch 1, Turn [6]
11. BLO [SC 6], Ch 1, Turn [6]
12. SC 6, Ch 1, Turn [6]
13. BLO [SC, Inc, SC 2, Inc, SC], Ch 1, Turn [8]
14. SC 8, Ch 1, Turn [8]
15. BLO [SC 8], Ch 1, Turn [8]
16. SC 8, Ch 1, Turn [8]
17. BLO [SC 2, Inc, SC 2, Inc, SC 2], Ch 1, Turn [10]
18. SC 10, Ch 1, Turn [10]
19. BLO [SC 10], Ch 1, Turn [10]
20. SC 10, Ch 1, Turn [10]

MEDIUM SNAILS • 205

21. BLO [SC 2, Inc, SC 4, Inc, SC 2], Ch 1, Turn [12]
22. SC 12, Ch 1, Turn [12]
23. BLO [SC 12], Ch 1, Turn [12]
24. SC 12, Ch 1, Turn [12]
25. BLO [SC 3, Inc, SC 4, Inc, SC 3], Ch 1, Turn [14]
26. SC 14, Ch 1, Turn [14]
27. BLO [SC 14], Ch 1, Turn [14]
28. SC 14, Ch 1, Turn [14]
29. BLO [SC 4, Inc, SC 4, Inc, SC 4], Ch 1, Turn [16]
30. SC 16, Ch 1, Turn [16]

31. BLO [SC 16], Ch 1, Turn [16]
32. SC 16, Ch 1, Turn [16]
33. BLO [(SC 4, <Dec>, SC 4) x 2], Ch 1, Turn [18]
34. SC 18, Ch 1, Turn [18]
35. BLO [SC 18], Ch 1, Turn [18]
36. SC 18, Ch 1, Turn [18]

In the following rows, you will follow every lettered sub-row to create short rows of built-up stitches (for more information on this technique, please see this YouTube video: https://www.youtube.com/watch?v=sh5T-idiwm8&t=3s). Each sub-row (i.e., 37A, 37B, 37C, etc.) has its own sub-row stitch count indicated by the number preceded by a hyphen in brackets. Row 37A's sub-row stitch count is 14. The total stitch count for all of Row 37 is at the very end of the final sub-row, without the hyphen.

37A. BLO [(SC 3, <Dec>, SC 3) x 2], Ch 1, Turn [-14]
37B. SC 7, Ch 1, Turn [-7]
37C. SC 6, SC/BLO [HDC Dec & HDC, SC 2, <Dec>, SC 3], Ch 1, Turn [-14] [21]

In Rows 37C, 41C, and 45C, the "SC/BLO [HDC Dec & HDC]" stitch is just a "SC/HDC Dec & HDC," in which the latter part of the "Dec" and the "& HDC" are worked into the BLO. The "SC/HDC Dec" and the "&" are defined in the Glossary beginning on page 6 and demonstrated on the Crafty Intentions YouTube channel.

38. SC 13, SC/HDC Dec & HDC, SC 6, Ch 1, Turn [21]
39. BLO [SC 21], Ch 1, Turn [21]
40. SC 21, Ch 1, Turn [21]

41A. BLO [SC 17], Ch 1, Turn [-17]
41B. SC 13, Ch 1, Turn [-13]
41C. SC 12, SC/BLO [HDC Dec & HDC, SC 3], Ch 1, Turn [-17] [21]
42. SC 16, SC/HDC Dec & HDC, SC 3, Ch 1, Turn [21]
43. BLO [(SC 3, Inc, SC 3) x 3], Ch 1, Turn [24]
44. SC 24, Ch 1, Turn [24]
45A. BLO [SC 18], Ch 1, Turn [-18]
45B. SC 12, Ch 1, Turn [-12]
45C. SC 11, SC/BLO [HDC Dec & HDC, SC 5], Ch 1, Turn [-18] [24]

Medium Snail with Round Shell

206 • MEDIUM SNAILS

Medium Snail with Round Shell

46. SC 17, SC/HDC Dec & HDC, SC 5, Ch 1, Turn [24]

47. BLO [(SC 3, <Dec>, SC 3) x 4], Ch 1, Turn [28]

48. SC 28, Ch 1, Turn [28]

49. BLO [SC 28], Ch 1, Turn [28]

50. SC 28, Ch 1, Turn [28]

51. In this row, you will Dec along the entire unfinished edge, working through both sides at once to make a long, thin cone shape.

Fold the entire long triangle in half the long way, with the visible ridges of BLO stitches on the outside.

You will be working through both halves of the long triangle at the same time, working one Dec for every 2 rows.

You can tell you're working only one Dec per 2 rows by placing each Dec between the BLO ridge lines, as shown.

Once you get past the midpoint of the shell, begin stuffing the shell with fiberfill. Leave the widest end unstuffed for now, concentrating on the midpoint to the thinnest end. Stuff the wider section of the shell medium-firm, stuffing more lightly as the shell tapers to a point.

Finish stuffing the rest of the shell. Fasten off the shell with a 36 in/91.5 cm yarn tail.

Gently curl the shell into a spiral, starting at the thinnest end. Pin in place as you work. The very center of the spiral (where the shell is thinnest) will be stacked on top of the wider part, making a slight cone shape.

The bottommost edge of the shell should fold in on itself a little bit, and you can use it to help shape the shell to fit against the back of the snail. Once you are pleased with the shaping of the shell, use the yarn tail to sew along the spiral, securing the spiral shape in place.

MEDIUM SNAILS • 207

Pin the shell to attach to the back of the snail. The front edge of the shell opening should rest at the point where the Snail Body angles upward. The back of the shell should not extend beyond the back edge of the snail "frill" (foot). Sew around the shell opening to secure the shell to the Snail Body. (This step is also covered in the Assembly section beginning on the next page.)

Medium Snail with Round Shell

MEDIUM ROUND SNAIL SHELL OPTIONAL CLOSURE (MAKE 1)

Any Color Yarn for the Shell: Approximately 8 yd/7.25 m worsted/medium weight yarn

> Use these instructions to close the Medium Snail Shell option without attaching it to the Medium Snail Body. This is just used to make a single shell without the snail.

1. SC 6 in Magic Circle, Sl St to beginning stitch, Ch 1 [6]
2. Inc x 6, Sl St to beginning stitch, Ch 1 [12]
3. (SC, Inc) x 6, Sl St to beginning stitch, Ch 1 [18]
4. (SC, Inc, SC) x 6, Sl St to beginning stitch, Ch 1 [24]
5. (SC 3, Inc) x 6, Sl St to beginning stitch, Ch 1 [30]
6. FLO [SC 30], Sl St to beginning stitch [30]

Fasten off with a 24 in/61 cm yarn tail.

Insert the disk into the wide shell opening. The disk should be slightly inset into the shell. Pin in place. Use the yarn tail to sew in place. If your shell is made with variegated yarn, take care to catch only the parts of the stitches that are inside the shell as you sew. Weave in ends.

Medium Snail with Round Shell

Medium Snail Assembly

1. If you have not already done so, pin around the border of Rows 26 and 27 of the top of the body to connect it to the border of Rows 38 and 39 of the bottom of the body, and then stuff the center portion of the body—you can optionally include some flat glass marble gems, if you'd like, for weight. Keep the weight toward the middle and back end to help keep the snail balanced. You will sew around the edge of the pinned rows in order to seal the stuffing inside of that center space after you finish crocheting the body.

Sew around the edge of the snail at the pinned row using a yarn tail. To do so without showing the color of the top part of the body through on the bottom side of the body, or vice versa, you can work to capture only the bottom/inside of the stitches on the side with a different color than the yarn tail you are using. Make sure to use small stitches and catch as much of the stitch on the inside of the work as possible without letting the needle come all the way through the work.

2. Shape and close the top of the head. Tuck the bottom body piece into the top body piece.

Once this piece is pinned, you can insert flat glass marble gems or alternative weights inside the body, placing most of the weight toward the middle and back end to help keep the snail balanced. Then stuff the rest of the center of the body with fiberfill.

Pin the center of the head down over the bottom part of the body.

It is optional to put a small amount of fiberfill inside each bump on the head.

Pinch both sides of the head, just below the bumps, in toward the center and pin them in place.. Pin the bumps down so that you'll sew their open side closed and attached to the body.

Use a yarn tail or separate piece of yarn to sew the head in place, securing the openings underneath those two bump-shaped pieces at the top.

The round bobbles should be pulled together close and then anchored down against the bottom center of the body.

3. Pin the antennae in place, as shown on the head of the Medium Snail, centered on the head, just before each of the two rounded parts at the front of the head. Sew to attach; weave in ends.

210 • MEDIUM SNAILS

4. Pin the shell in place on the back—see photos to orient it. Stitch in place around the entire edge of the shell that touches the snail's body using small whipstitches and the yarn tail from the shell; weave in ends. The pins on the bodies show the edge of where the shell should be positioned, without the shell pinned in place.

Pinning to Attach Pointed Shell to Medium Snail Body

The pins on the back of the snail in these photos show exactly where the edges of the pointed shell are attached to this snail body. You can use these photos as a guide.

MEDIUM SNAILS • 211

For the Round Snail Shell: Pin the shell to attach to the back of the snail. The front edge of the shell opening should rest at the point where the Snail Body angles upward. The back of the shell should not extend beyond the back edge of the snail "frill" (foot). Sew around the shell opening to secure the shell to the Snail Body.

Pinning to Attach Round Shell to Medium Snail Body

The pins on the back of the snail in these photos show exactly where the edges of the round shell are attached to this snail body. You can use these photos as a guide.

212 • MEDIUM SNAILS

Medium Snail with Pointed Shell

Medium Snail with Round Shell

Giant Snail with Pointed Shell

Giant Snail with Pointed Shell

Giant Snail with Pointed Shell

Giant Snail with Pointed Shell

Giant Snail with Round Shell

Giant Snail with Pointed Shell

Giant Snail with Pointed Shell

GIANT SNAILS

This is the start of the Giant Snail pattern! Your Mushroom Sprite may be clamoring for a Giant Snail of their very own to ride (very slowly) off into the sunset . . .

Giant Snail with Round Shell

. . . but don't let them ride without a saddle! Saddle safety is **very** important, as you can see here (don't try this at home—no Mushroom Sprites or Giant Snails were harmed in the making of this book). Saddle instructions can be found starting on page 274.

OPTIONS

Giant Snail Body . . . 219

Short Giant Snail Antennae . . . 232

Long Giant Snail Antennae . . . 232

Giant Snail Shell Style 1: Pointed . . . 233

Giant Snail Shell Style 2: Round . . . 254

❶ Mushroom Sprite with Arms Style 6, Feet/Legs Style 9, Body Style 5, Cap Style 10, "riding"
❷ Giant Snail with Round Shell

Giant Snail Body

GIANT SNAIL BODY BOTTOM (MAKE 1)

Giant Snail Body Bottom Color Yarn: Approximately 110 yd/ 100.5 m worsted/medium weight yarn

1. Starting with a short yarn tail, Ch 5, Turn, starting in the 2nd Ch from hook, Inc, SC 2, Inc, Ch 1, Turn [6]
2. SC 6, Ch 1, Turn [6]
3. Inc, SC 4, Inc, Ch 1, Turn [8]
4-11. (8 rows of) SC 8, Ch 1, Turn [8]
12. SC, Inc, SC 4, Inc, SC, Ch 1, Turn [10]
13-20. (8 rows of) SC 10, Ch 1, Turn [10]
21. SC, Inc, SC 6, Inc, SC, Ch 1, Turn [12]
22-29. (8 rows of) SC 12, Ch 1, Turn [12]
30. SC, Inc, SC 8, Inc, SC, Ch 1, Turn [14]
31-39. (9 rows of) SC 14, Ch 1, Turn [14]
40. SC, Dec, SC 8, Dec, SC, Ch 1, Turn [12]
41-48. (8 rows of) SC 12, Ch 1, Turn [12]
49. SC, Dec, SC 6, Dec, SC, Ch 1, Turn [10]
50-57. (8 rows of) SC 10, Ch 1, Turn [10]
58. SC, Dec, SC 4, Dec, SC, Ch 1, Turn [8]
59-66. (8 rows of) SC 8, Ch 1, Turn [8]
67. Dec, SC 4, Dec, Ch 1, Turn [6]
68. SC 6, Ch 1, Turn [6]

In Row 69 and others like it, the row is broken down into sub-rows. These sub-rows all together make up an entire row. Each sub-row (69A, 69B, etc.) has its own sub-row stitch count indicated by the number preceded by a hyphen in brackets. Row 69A's sub-row stitch count is 4. The total stitch count for all of Row 69 is at the very end of the final sub-row, without the hyphen.

69A. Dec, SC 2, Dec [-4]

GIANT SNAILS • 219

69B. SC in the same stitch as where you completed your last Dec [-1]

69C. Reorient work so that you will continue crocheting around the entire edge of the piece; continuing to work along the unfinished edge of the piece, SC 67 along the edge of the previous rows [-67]

69D. Working across the OC, Inc, SC 2, Inc [-6]

69E. Reorient work so that you will continue crocheting around the entire edge of the piece; continuing to work along the unfinished edge back toward where Row 69A began, SC 67 along the edge of the previous rows [-67]

69F. SC in the same stitch as the first leg of the first Dec of Row 69A, Sl St to the beginning stitch, Ch 1 [-1] [146]

70A. Starting in the same stitch as last row's Sl St (as usual), BLO [SC 4, Inc, SC, Inc, HDC 2, HDC Inc [-13]

> All of Row 70 is worked in the Back Loop Only. The end bracket, marking the end of the stitches worked in the BLO, is at the end of 70G.

70B. (DC 3, DC Inc) x 14 [-70]

70C. HDC 2, HDC Inc, SC 3, Inc [-9]

70D. Sl St 4 [-4]

70E. Inc, SC 3, HDC Inc, HDC 2 [-9]

70F. (DC Inc, DC 3) x 14 [-70]

70G. HDC Inc, HDC 2, Inc, SC, Inc], Sl St to beginning stitch, Ch 1 [-9] [184]

> Place a stitch marker in ANY of the leftover front loops in Row 70.

71. HDC 88, SC 4, SC 4 around the Sl Sts you made in Row 70 and into the stitches the Sl Sts were worked into, SC 4, HDC 84, Sl St to beginning stitch, Ch 1 [184]

> The technique of working a SC around a previous row's Sl St is demonstrated in this YouTube video: https://www.youtube.com/watch?v=khed-Ni_AjM&t=2s

72. HDC 6, HDC Inc, (HDC 9, HDC Inc) x 8, SC 4, Inc, Sl St 6, Inc, SC 4, (HDC Inc, HDC 9) x 8, HDC Inc, Sl St to beginning stitch, Ch 1 [204]

220 • GIANT SNAILS

73A. HDC 6, (HDC, HDC Inc, HDC) x 2, [-14]

73B. (DC 5, DC Inc) x 12, DC 2, [-86]

73C. HDC 2, HDC Inc, HDC 4, HDC Inc, [-10]

73D. SC 3, Inc, SC 4, working around the Sl Sts from Row 72 (SC 6), SC 4, Inc, SC 3 (**Note:** Insert a stitch marker into the first of these 3 SC stitches) [-24]

73E. HDC Inc, HDC 4, HDC Inc, HDC 2 [-10]

73F. DC 2, (DC Inc, DC 5) x12 [86]

73G. (HDC, HDC Inc, HDC) x 2, Sl St to beginning stitch [-8] [238]

Fasten off with a short yarn tail you will tuck inside of the work once attached to the Giant Snail Body top.

The side of the Giant Snail Body bottom with the stitch marker you placed at the end of Row 70 is the inside or wrong side, and it will be on the inside of the body of the Giant Snail. This marked loop side will be held against the back side of the Giant Snail Body top to be crocheted together.

Giant Snail with Round Shell

❶ **Mushroom Sprite with Arms Style 7, Body Style 1, Cap Style 1, trying to lasso a ❷ Giant Snail with a Pointed Shell**

Giant Snail with Round Shell

GIANT SNAIL BODY TOP (MAKE 1)

Giant Snail Body Top Color Yarn: Approximately 175 yd/160 m worsted/medium weight yarn

1. Starting with a short yarn tail, Ch 5, starting in the 2nd Ch from hook, Inc, SC 2, Inc, Ch 1, Turn [6]
2. SC, Inc, SC 2, Inc, SC, Ch 1, Turn [8]
3. SC, Inc x 2, SC 2, Inc x 2, SC, Ch 1, Turn [12]
4–5. (2 rows of) SC 12, Ch 1, Turn [12]
6. SC 3, Inc, SC 4, Inc, SC 3, Ch 1, Turn [14]
7. SC 14, Ch 1, Turn [14]
8. SC 4, Inc, SC 4, Inc, SC 4, Ch 1, Turn [16]
9–10. (2 rows of) SC 16, Ch 1, Turn [16]
11. SC 4, Inc, SC 6, Inc, SC 4, Ch 1, Turn [18]
12–13. (2 rows of) SC 18, Ch 1, Turn [18]
14. Inc, SC 16, Inc, Ch 1, Turn [20]
15–16. (2 rows of) SC 20, Ch 1, Turn [20]
17. SC 8, Inc, SC 2, Inc, SC 8, Ch 1, Turn [22]
18–20. (3 rows of) SC 22, Ch 1, Turn [22]
21. SC 6, Inc, SC 8, Inc, SC 6, Ch 1, Turn [24]
22–24. (3 rows of) SC 24, Ch 1, Turn [24]
25. SC 7, Inc, SC 8, Inc, SC 7, Ch 1, Turn [26]
26–28. (3 rows of) SC 26, Ch 1, Turn [26]

> In Row 29 and others like it, you will follow every lettered sub-row to create short rows of built-up stitches (for more information on this technique, please see this YouTube video: https://www.youtube.com/watch?v=sh5T-idiwm8&t=3s). Each sub-row (i.e., 29A, 29B, 29C, etc.) has its own sub-row stitch count indicated by the number preceded by a hyphen in brackets. Row 29A's sub-row stitch count is 12. The total stitch count for all of Row 29 is at the very end of the final sub-row, without the hyphen.

29A. SC 12, Ch 1, Turn [-12]

> After Row 29A, you should have 14 unworked stitches from Row 28 remaining.

29B. SC 12, Ch 1, Turn [-12]
29C. Inc, SC 9, Ch 1, Turn [-11]

> After Row 29C, you should have 2 stitches unworked from Row 29B, in addition to 14 stitches still unworked from Row 28.

29D. SC 11, Ch 1, Turn [-11]
29E. SC 9, Ch 1, Turn [-9]

> After Row 29E, you should have 2 stitches unworked from Row 29D, in addition to 2 stitches unworked from Row 29B and 14 stitches unworked from Row 28.

29F. SC 9, Ch 1, Turn [-9]
29G. SC 7, Ch 1, Turn [-7]

> After Row 29G, you should have 2 stitches unworked from Row 29F, in addition to 2 stitches unworked from Row 29D, 2 stitches unworked from Row 29B, and 14 stitches unworked from Row 28.

29H. SC 7, Ch 1, Turn [-7]

29I. SC 5, Ch 1, Turn [-5]

> After Row 29I, you should have 2 stitches unworked from Row 29H, in addition to 2 stitches unworked from Row 29F, 2 stitches unworked from Row 29D, 2 stitches unworked from Row 29B, and 14 stitches unworked from Row 28.

29J. SC 5, Ch 1, Turn [-5]
29K. SC 3, Ch 1, Turn [-3]

> After Row 29K, you should have 2 stitches unworked from Row 29J, in addition to 2 stitches unworked from Row 29H, 2 stitches unworked from Row 29F, 2 stitches unworked from Row 29D, 2 stitches unworked from Row 29B, and 14 stitches unworked from Row 28.

29L. SC 3, Ch 1, Turn [-3]

GIANT SNAILS • 223

29M. SC 2, (SC/HDC Dec & HDC) x 6, SC 13, Ch 1, Turn [-27] [27]

In Row 29M, you will work into all previously unworked stitches. Check the Glossary beginning on page 6 for a definition of the stitch "SC/HDC Dec" and the "&" symbol.

30A. SC 12, Ch 1, Turn [-12]

After Row 30A, you should have 15 unworked stitches from Row 29M remaining.

30B. SC 12, Ch 1, Turn [-12]
30C. Inc, SC 9, Ch 1, Turn [-11]

After Row 30C, you should have 2 stitches unworked from Row 30B, in addition to 15 stitches still unworked from Row 29M.

30D. SC 11, Ch 1, Turn [-11]
30E. SC 9, Ch 1, Turn [-9]

After Row 30E, you should have 2 stitches unworked from Row 30D, in addition to 2 stitches unworked from Row 30B and 15 stitches unworked from Row 29M.

30F. SC 9, Ch 1, Turn [-9]

30G. SC 7, Ch 1, Turn [-7]

After Row 30G, you should have 2 stitches unworked from Row 30F, in addition to 2 stitches unworked from Row 30D, 2 stitches unworked from Row 30B, and 15 stitches unworked from Row 29M.

30H. SC 7, Ch 1, Turn [-7]
30I. SC 5, Ch 1, Turn [-5]

After Row 30I, you should have 2 stitches unworked from Row 30H, in addition to 2 stitches unworked from Row 30F, 2 stitches unworked from Row 30D, 2 stitches unworked from Row 30B, and 15 stitches unworked from Row 29M.

30J. SC 5, Ch 1, Turn [-5]
30K. SC 3, Ch 1, Turn [-3]

After Row 30K, you should have 2 stitches unworked from Row 30J, in addition to 2 stitches unworked from Row 30H, 2 stitches unworked from Row 30F, 2 stitches unworked from Row 30D, 2 stitches unworked from Row 30B, and 15 stitches unworked from Row 29M.

30L. SC 3, Ch 1, Turn [-3]

30M. SC 2, (SC/HDC Dec & HDC) x 6, SC 14, Ch 1, Turn [-28] [28]

In Row 30M, you will work into all previously unworked stitches.

31. SC 28, Ch 1, Turn [28]
32A. SC 12, Ch 1, Turn [-12]

After Row 32A, you should have 16 stitches unworked from Row 31.

32B. SC 12, Ch 1, Turn [-12]
32C. SC 9, Ch 1, Turn [-9]

After Row 32C, you should have 3 stitches unworked from Row 32B, in addition to 16 stitches unworked from Row 31.

32D. SC 9, Ch 1, Turn [-9]
32E. SC 6, Ch 1, Turn [-6]

After Row 32E, you should have 3 stitches unworked from Row 32D, in addition to 3 stitches unworked from Row 32B and 16 stitches unworked from Row 31.

32F. SC 6, Ch 1, Turn [-6]

32G. SC 3, Ch 1, Turn [-3]

> After Row 32G, you should have 3 stitches unworked from Row 32F, in addition to 3 stitches unworked from Row 32D, 3 stitches unworked from Row 32B, and 16 stitches unworked from Row 31.

32H. SC 3, Ch 1, Turn [-3]

32I. SC 2, (SC/HDC Dec & HDC, SC) x 4, SC 14, Ch 1, Turn [-28] [28]

> In Row 32I, you will work into all previously unworked stitches.

33A. SC 12, Ch 1, Turn [-12]

> After Row 33A, you should have 16 stitches unworked from Row 32I.

33B. SC 12, Ch 1, Turn [-12]
33C. SC 9, Ch 1, Turn [-9]

> After Row 33C, you should have 3 stitches unworked from Row 33B, in addition to 16 stitches unworked from Row 32I.

33D. SC 9, Ch 1, Turn [-9]
33E. SC 6, Ch 1, Turn [-6]

> After Row 33E, you should have 3 stitches unworked from Row 33D, in addition to 3 stitches unworked from Row 33B and 16 stitches unworked from Row 32I.

33F. SC 6, Ch 1, Turn [-6]
33G. SC 3, Ch 1, Turn [-3]

> After Row 33G, you should have 3 stitches unworked from Row 33F, in addition to 3 stitches unworked from Row 33D, 3 stitches unworked from Row 33B, and 16 stitches unworked from Row 32I.

33H. SC 3, Ch 1, Turn [-3]

33I. SC 2, (SC/HDC Dec & HDC, SC) x 4, SC 14, Ch 1, Turn [-28] [28]

> In Row 33I, you will work into all previously unworked stitches.

34–35. (2 rows of) SC 28, Ch 1, Turn [28]

36. SC 3, Dec, SC 18, Dec, SC 3, Ch 1, Turn [26]

37–38. (2 rows of) SC 26, Ch 1, Turn [26]

39. SC 5, Dec, SC 12, Dec, SC 5, Ch 1, Turn [24]

40. SC 24, Ch 1, Turn [24]

41. SC 4, Dec, SC 12, Dec, SC 4, Ch 1, Turn [22]

42. SC 22, Ch 1, Turn [22]

43. SC 3, Dec, SC 2, Dec, SC 4, Dec, SC 2, Dec, SC 3, Ch 1, Turn [18]

44. SC 18, Ch 1, Turn [18]

45. (SC 2, Dec, SC 2) x 3, Ch 1, Turn [15]

46. SC 15, Ch 1, Turn [15]

47. (SC, Dec) x 5, Ch 1, Turn [10]

48. (Dec, SC 2) x 2, Dec, Ch 1, Turn [7]

GIANT SNAILS • 225

49. Dec, 2 Dec in 3 SC, Dec, Ch 1, Turn [4]

> The "2 Dec in 3 SC" is a special stitch and is defined in the Glossary beginning on page 6.

> The side that is facing up in the photos (with your hook oriented to the right side of the row at the end of Row 49) is the right side; the underside is the back side—for reference later when assembling with the bottom.

> In Row 50 and others like it, the row is broken down into sub-rows. These sub-rows all together make up an entire row. Each sub-row (50A, 50B, etc.) has its own sub-row stitch count indicated by the number preceded by a hyphen in brackets. Row 50A's sub-row stitch count is 5. The total stitch count for all of Row 50 is at the very end of the final sub-row, without the hyphen.

50A. SC 3, Inc [-5]

50B. Then tilt the work/reorient, continuing along the unfinished edge, SC 68 [-68]

50C. Working across the OC, SC 4 [-4]

50D. SC 68 back up the edge of the previous rows to the start of this Row 50A [-68]

50E. SC in the same stitch as the first SC in Row 50A, Sl St to beginning stitch, Ch 1 [-1] [146]

> Make sure you Sl St to the beginning stitch (from Row 50A) at the end of Row 50E.

51A. SC 4, Inc, SC 3, HDC Inc, HDC 2 [-13]

51B. (DC Inc, DC 3) x 14 [-70]

51C. HDC Inc, HDC 2, Inc, SC, Inc, SC 4, Inc, SC, Inc, HDC 2, HDC Inc [-22]

51D. (DC 3, DC Inc) x 14 [-70]

51E. HDC 2, HDC Inc, SC 3, Inc, Sl St to beginning stitch and put a stitch marker into the same stitch you slip stitched into [-9]

51F. Sl St 3 more beyond where the row started [184 + 3 Sl Sts]

52A. Skip 1 stitch, DC 6 in the next available stitch, Skip 1 stitch, Sl St [-7]

52B. SC 2, HDC 168, SC 2 [-172]

52C. Sl St, Skip 1 stitch, DC 6 in next available stitch, Skip 1 stitch, Sl St into the marked stitch from Row 51 (and remove the stitch marker) [-8]

52D. Ch 1, Dec around the next two available Sl Sts from Row 51, and into the stitches they were slip stitched into, skip the last Sl St that was worked in Row 51 [-1] [188]

When you crochet into a stitch that has a Sl St in it, work into the **same** stitch that the Sl St was worked into. For a video on this technique, go here: https://www.youtube.com/watch?v=khed-Ni_AjM&t=4s

❶ **Mushroom Sprite with Arms Style 8, Body Style 1, Cap Style 2**, hugging their very best buddy, a ❷ **Giant Snail with a Pointed Shell**

53A. Starting in the 1st available DC stitch from Row 52, (HDC Inc) x 6 [-12]

53B. Skip the Sl St, Sl St in the 1st available SC stitch, SC, Dec, HDC Inc, HDC 8 [-13]

53C. (HDC Inc, HDC 9) x 7 [-77]
53D. HDC Inc, HDC 6, HDC Inc [-10]
53E. (HDC 9, HDC Inc) x 7 [-77]

53F. HDC 8, HDC Inc, Inc, Sl St in the next stitch [-13]

53G. Skip the Sl St, starting in the 1st available DC stitch (HDC Inc) x 6, Sl St into the final Dec stitch from Row 52, Ch 1 [-13] [215]

54A. Starting in the first available HDC stitch, HDC 12 [-12]

54B. Sl St into the same stitch you slip stitched into in the previous row [-1]

54C. SC [-1]

NOTE: Place a stitch marker in this SC stitch.

54D. Inc, SC, HDC 3, HDC Inc, HDC 2, DC 3 [-13]

54E. (DC Inc, DC 5) x 12 [-84]

54F. HDC [-1]

54G. (HDC, HDC Inc, HDC) x 2 [-8]

54H. HDC 6 [-6]

54I. (HDC, HDC Inc, HDC) x 2 [-8]

228 • GIANT SNAILS

54J. HDC [-1]

54K. (DC 5, DC Inc) x 12 [-84]

54L. DC 3, HDC 2, HDC Inc, HDC 3, SC, Inc, SC [-14]

54M. Sl St into the same stitch you slip stitched into in the previous row, Ch 1 [-1]

54N. HDC 12, Sl St into the same stitch you slip stitched into in the previous row, Ch 1 [-13] [247]

55. Starting in the first available HDC stitch, HDC 12, Sl St into the same (next stitch) you slip stitched into in the previous row, Ch 1, Turn [13]

56. (HDC, HDC Dec) x 4, Sl St into the same Dec stitch (from Row 52) you slip stitched into in the last several rows, Ch 1, starting in the first available HDC Stitch, HDC 12, Sl St into the same (next) stitch you slip stitched into in Row 54, Ch 1, Turn [22]

57. (HDC, HDC Dec) x 4, Sl St into the same Dec stitch (from Row 52) you slip stitched into in the previous row [9]

> Pull the final Sl St as tight as possible.

Fasten off with a 24 in/61 cm yarn tail to use for sewing/soft sculpting later.

Giant Snail with Round Shell

GIANT SNAILS • 229

Hold the bottom of the snail (inside) against the top of the snail (inside). Reattach the yarn (this can be an accent color or the same color as the top of the body), working into the BLO of the top of the snail and the FLO of the bottom of the snail, starting in the marked stitches on both.

> You are using the loops that are closest to each other and sandwiching them together using SC stitches. Tuck the yarn tails inside the snail as you crochet Row 58. Do not work into the "Sl St to beginning stitch, Ch 1" join.

58. SC around, ending at the start of the bumps on the head (leave this part open) [220]

Giant Snail with Pointed Shell

Fasten off with a 36 in/91.5 cm yarn tail. This yarn tail will be used to sew around the top and the bottom.

You have two options for stuffing the body of the snail. You can wait until you have completed Row 58 and have pinned the body shut, and then insert flat glass marble gems/weight and fiberfill, **or**, when you get three-quarters of the way around the edge of the snail, you can include some flat glass marble gems or alternative weight inside the body of the snail, all the way to the end of the tail, to give the body some weight and help with balance, and then stuff with fiberfill as you go. When you end the row, there will still be a hole at the head available for you to insert stuffing through, but it will be difficult to reach the very end of the inside of the body/tail, so it is recommended to use a tool like hemostats/forceps to grip and insert stuffing deep inside the work. Even with the difficulty of reaching into the body to stuff it, it is recommended to wait to stuff until after crocheting the whole piece and pinning the body.

Once Row 58 is complete, it is recommended to pin shut the line around the body where you will be sewing—this is the border between Rows 50 and 51 on the top of the body and the border between Rows 69 and 70 on the bottom of the body. Pinning makes sewing easier.

After you pin the body: If you have not already done so, stuff the body with fiberfill and optionally insert flat glass marble gems/weight. Keep the weight toward the middle and back end to help keep the snail balanced. You will sew around the edge of the pinned rows in order to seal the stuffing inside of that center space after you finish crocheting the body.

Sew around the edge of the snail at the pinned row using a yarn tail. To do so without showing the color of the top part of the body through on the bottom side of the body, or vice versa, you can work to capture only the bottom/inside of the stitches on the side with a different color than the yarn tail you are using. Make sure to use small stitches, and catch as much of the stitch on the inside of the work as possible without letting the needle come all the way through the work.

If you catch a small amount of the fiberfill stuffing ever so slightly inside the outer edges as you sew, that is okay. **Do not** catch a flat glass marble gem in the outer edges as you sew. **Do not** sew the top head area shut yet—leave it open.

For the rest of the instructions on the Giant Snail Body, see Assembly on page 261.

GIANT SNAILS • 231

Giant Snail Antennae

GIANT SNAIL SHORT ANTENNAE (MAKE 2)

Giant Snail Body Top Color Yarn: Approximately 4 yd/3.75 m worsted/medium weight yarn for two antennae

> This piece will be made in spiral/in the round; there is no "Sl St, Ch 1" join.

1. SC 4 in Magic Circle [4]
2–3. (2 rows of) SC 4 [4]
4. Inc, SC 3 [5]
5. SC 5

Fasten off with a 12 in/30.5 cm yarn tail to use to sew to attach.

Giant Snail with Pointed Shell

Giant Snail with Round Shell

Giant Snail with Round Shell

GIANT SNAIL LONG ANTENNAE (MAKE 2)

Giant Snail Body Top Color Yarn: Approximately 9 yd/8.25 m worsted/medium weight yarn for two antennae

> This piece will be made in spiral/in the round, there is no "Sl St, Ch 1" join.

1. SC 5 in Magic Circle [5]
2–5. (4 rows of) SC 5 [5]
6. Inc, SC 4 [6]
7–8. (2 rows of) SC 6 [6]
9. Inc, SC 5 [7]
10–11. (2 rows of) SC 7 [7]
12. Inc, SC 6 [8]
13–14. (2 rows of) SC 8 [8]
15. Inc, SC 7 [9]
16. SC 9 [9]

Fasten off with a 12 in/30.5 cm yarn tail to use to sew to attach.

232 • GIANT SNAILS

Giant Snail Shells

GIANT SNAIL SHELL STYLE 1: POINTED (MAKE 1)

Any Color Yarn for the Shell: Approximately 125 yd/114.25 m worsted/medium weight yarn

Any Color Yarn for the Accent: Approximately 6 yd/5.5 m worsted/medium weight yarn

The following instructions will use both Shell Color and Accent Color yarn for different rows. You will start with the Shell Color yarn, and all Shell Color rows will be labeled "1. SHELL," and so forth. Before an Accent Color row labeled "ACCENT," you should drop your Shell Color yarn (remove your hook from the final loop). Then pick up the Accent Color yarn (insert your hook into the available Accent yarn loop) and work the Accent row with the Accent Color. When you finish with the Accent row, drop your Accent Color yarn and insert your hook back into the Shell Color loop you dropped (you may need to tighten the loop if it has become loose). The Accent rows are worked around the shell in a spiral, always in the same direction. The Shell rows are worked back and forth to build up the outer wall of the shell. Do not fasten off either color yarn until the very end.

1. **SHELL** Starting with a short yarn tail, SC 8 in Magic Circle, Ch 2, do not Turn, continue working in the same direction for Row 2 [8]

Mark the 4th stitch of Row 1: SHELL. This will be where you attach the Accent Color after Row 9: SHELL.

The Accent Color rows are **not** optional. You **must** follow these rows with a separate strand of yarn. You do not have to use an actual Accent Color. If you want your shell to be all one color, you can use the same color yarn for the Accent Color rows that you are using for the Shell Color rows, but you must use two separate pieces of yarn for the Shell and the Accent.

GIANT SNAILS • 233

Make sure you are working right side out as you continue your shell. The starting yarn tail should be on the inside/wrong side of this piece. You should insert your hook from the outside/right side to the inside/wrong side as you complete stitches. Here's a video on inside out versus right side out: https://www.youtube.com/watch?v=beReNFWQPAs

2. SHELL In the 2nd Ch from hook, SC & Dec—complete the Dec into the 1st SC you made in Row 1: SHELL, Ch 1, Turn [2]

In Row 2: SHELL, you will be working the SC in the 2nd Ch from the hook, and then you will start the Dec in the same chain that you worked the SC into and you will complete the decrease into the first SC from the "SC 8 in Magic Circle" that you worked in Row 1. You have 7 stitches remaining on Row 1 to crochet into. The description of exactly where to place the decrease is always included after the "—" symbol in this and all future rows.

3. SHELL Working into the stitches from the previous row, SC 2, Ch 1, Turn [2]

4. SHELL Working into the stitches from the previous row, SC, SC & Dec—complete the Dec into the next available stitch from Row 1: SHELL, Ch 1, Turn [3]

Row 4 uses 1 stitch from Row 1; you have 6 stitches remaining on Row 1 to crochet into.

5. SHELL Working into the stitches from the previous row, SC 3, Ch 1, Turn [3]

6. SHELL Working into the stitches from the previous row, SC 2, Dec—complete the Dec into the same stitch from Row 1: SHELL that you completed the last Dec into in Row 4: SHELL, Ch 1, Turn [3]

Row 6 uses the same stitch from Row 1 that you last worked into; you still have 6 stitches remaining on Row 1 to crochet into.

7. SHELL Working into the stitches from the previous row, SC 3, Ch 1, Turn [3]

8. SHELL Working into the stitches from the previous row, SC 2, SC & Dec—complete the Dec into the next available stitch from Row 1: SHELL, Ch 1, Turn [4]

Row 8 uses 1 stitch from Row 1; you have 5 stitches remaining on Row 1 to crochet into.

9. SHELL Working into the stitches from the previous row, SC 4, Ch 1, Turn [4]

1. ACCENT Keeping the shell right side out, attach yarn to the BLO of the 4th stitch you made in Row 1: SHELL, starting in the same stitch and working across the open unused stitches from Row 1, BLO [Dec x 2], and then, working into the last available stitch (in the BLO) from Row 1 and up the unfinished edges of the rest of the rows, make 4 more Dec stitches [6]

Keep your Accent row Dec stitches tight; this will make the Accent rows sink into the work, creating a spiral indentation along the shell. You have 6 Accent Color stitches to work into when working with the Shell Color yarn. Double-check that you are working right side out. Pop the point of the shell (the magic circle) out so that the outside is pointing toward you.

234 • GIANT SNAILS

10. SHELL Working into the stitches from the previous Row 9: SHELL, SC 3, Dec—complete the Dec into the first available stitch on the Accent row, Ch 1, Turn [4]

> Row 10 uses 1 stitch from the Accent row; 5 stitches remain available.

11. SHELL Working into the stitches from the previous row, SC 4, Ch 1, Turn [4]

12. SHELL Working into the stitches from the previous row, SC 3, Dec—complete the Dec into the next available stitch on the Accent row, Ch 1, Turn [4]

> Row 12 uses 1 stitch from the Accent row; 4 stitches remain available.

13. SHELL Working into the stitches from the previous row, SC 4, Ch 1, Turn [4]

14. SHELL Working into the stitches from the previous row, SC 3, Dec—complete the Dec into the same stitch on the Accent row that you finished the last decrease into, Ch 1, Turn [4]

> Row 14 uses the same stitch from Row 1: ACCENT that you last worked into; 4 stitches remain available.

15. SHELL Working into the stitches from the previous row, SC 4, Ch 1, Turn [4]

16. SHELL Working into the stitches from the previous row, SC 3, Dec—complete the Dec into the next available stitch on the Accent row, Ch 1, Turn [4]

> Row 16 uses 1 stitch from the Accent row; 3 stitches remain available.

17. SHELL Working into the stitches from the previous row, SC 4, Ch 1, Turn [4]

18. SHELL Working into the stitches from the previous row, SC 3, Dec—complete the Dec into the next available stitch on the Accent row, Ch 1, Turn [4]

> Row 18 uses 1 stitch from the Accent row; 2 stitches remain available.

19. SHELL Working into the stitches from the previous row, SC 4, Ch 1, Turn [4]

20. SHELL Working into the stitches from the previous row, SC 3, SC & Dec—complete the Dec into the next available stitch on the Accent row, Ch 1, Turn [5]

> Check the Glossary beginning on page 6 for the definition of the "&" symbol.

> Row 20 uses 1 stitch from the Accent row; 1 stitch remains available.

Giant Snail with Pointed Shell

GIANT SNAILS • 235

21. SHELL Working into the stitches from the previous row, SC 5, Ch 1, Turn [5]

2. ACCENT Dec x 6 [6]

> You will continue to work these stitches along the unfinished edge/side of the rows of the shell stitches. You had 1 stitch available on the Accent row before Row 2: ACCENT. At the end of Row 2: ACCENT, you will have a total of 7 Accent Color stitches to work into when working with the Shell Color yarn.

22. SHELL Working into the stitches from the previous Shell row, Dec, SC 2, SC & Dec—complete the Dec into the next available stitch on the Accent row, Ch 1, Turn [5]

> Row 22 uses 1 stitch from the Accent row; 6 stitches remain available.

23. SHELL Working into the stitches from the previous row, SC 5, Ch 1, Turn [5]

24. SHELL Working into the stitches from the previous row, SC 4, Dec—complete the Dec into the same stitch on the Accent row that you finished the last Dec into, Ch 1, Turn [5]

> Row 24 uses the same stitch from the Accent row that you last worked into; 6 stitches remain available.

25. SHELL Working into the stitches from the previous row, SC 5, Ch 1, Turn [5]

26. SHELL Working into the stitches from the previous row, SC 4, Dec—complete the Dec into the next available stitch on the Accent row, Ch 1, Turn [5]

> Row 26 uses 1 stitch from the Accent row; 5 stitches remain available.

27. SHELL Working into the stitches from the previous row, SC 5, Ch 1, Turn [5]

28. SHELL Working into the stitches from the previous row, SC 4, Dec—complete the Dec into the next available stitch on the Accent row, Ch 1, Turn [5]

> Row 28 uses 1 stitch from the Accent row; 4 stitches remain available.

29. SHELL Working into the stitches from the previous row, SC 5, Ch 1, Turn [5]

30. SHELL Working into the stitches from the previous row, SC 4, Dec—complete the Dec into the same stitch on the Accent row that you finished the last decrease into, Ch 1, Turn [5]

> Row 30 uses the same stitch from the Accent row that you last worked into; 4 stitches remain available.

31. SHELL Working into the stitches from the previous row, SC 5, Ch 1, Turn [5]

32. SHELL Working into the stitches from the previous row, SC 4, SC & Dec—complete the Dec into the next available stitch on the Accent row, Ch 1, Turn [6]

> Row 32 uses 1 stitch from the Accent row; 3 stitches remain available.

33. SHELL Working into the stitches from the previous row, SC 6, Ch 1, Turn [6]

34. SHELL Working into the stitches from the previous row, Dec, SC 3, SC & Dec—complete Dec into the same stitch on the Accent row that you finished the last decrease into, Ch 1, Turn [6]

> Row 34 uses the same stitch from the Accent row that you last worked into; 3 stitches remain available.

35. SHELL Working into the stitches from the previous row, SC 6, Ch 1, Turn [6]

3. ACCENT Dec x 7 [7]

> You will continue to work these stitches along the unfinished edge/side of the rows of the Shell stitches. You had 3 stitches available on the Accent row before Row 3: ACCENT. At the end of Row 3: ACCENT, you will have a total of 10 Accent Color stitches to work into when working with the Shell Color yarn.

36. SHELL Working into the stitches from the previous Shell row, SC 5, Dec—complete the Dec into the next available stitch on the Accent row, Ch 1, Turn [6]

> Row 36 uses 1 stitch from the Accent row; 9 stitches remain available.

37. SHELL Working into the stitches from the previous row, SC 6, Ch 1, Turn [6]

38. SHELL Working into the stitches from the previous row, SC 5, Dec—complete the Dec into the next available stitch on the Accent row, Ch 1, Turn [6]

> Row 38 uses 1 stitch from the Accent row; 8 stitches remain available.

39. SHELL Working into the stitches from the previous row, SC 6, Ch 1, Turn [6]

40. SHELL Working into the stitches from the previous row, SC 5, Dec—complete the Dec into the same stitch on the Accent row that you finished the last decrease into, Ch 1, Turn [6]

> Row 40 uses the same stitch from the Accent row that you last worked into; 8 stitches remain available.

41. SHELL Working into the stitches from the previous row, SC 6, Ch 1, Turn [6]

42. SHELL Working into the stitches from the previous row, SC 5, Dec—complete the Dec into the next available stitch on the Accent row, Ch 1, Turn [6]

> Row 42 uses 1 stitch from the Accent row; 7 stitches remain available.

43. SHELL Working into the stitches from the previous row, SC 6, Ch 1, Turn [6]

44. Working into the stitches from the previous row, SC 5, Dec—complete the Dec into the next available stitch on the Accent row, Ch 1, Turn [6]

> Row 44 uses 1 stitch from the Accent row; 6 stitches remain available.

45. Working into the stitches from the previous row, SC 6, Ch 1, Turn [6]

46. SHELL Working into the stitches from the previous row, SC 5, Dec—complete the Dec into the same stitch on the Accent row that you finished the last decrease into, Ch 1, Turn [6]

> Row 46 uses the same stitch from the Accent row that you last worked into; 6 stitches remain available.

47. SHELL Working into the stitches from the previous row, SC 6, Ch 1, Turn [6]

48. SHELL Working into the stitches from the previous row, SC 5, SC & Dec—complete the Dec into the next available stitch on the Accent row, Ch 1, Turn [7]

> Row 48 uses 1 stitch from the Accent row; 5 stitches remain available.

49. SHELL Working into the stitches from the previous row, SC 7, Ch 1, Turn [7]

50. SHELL Working into the stitches from the previous row, Dec, SC 4, SC & Dec—complete Dec into the same stitch on the Accent row that you finished the last Dec into, Ch 1, Turn [7]

> Row 50 uses the same stitch from the Accent row that you last worked into; 5 stitches remain available.

51. SHELL Working into the stitches from the previous row, SC 7, Ch 1, Turn [7]

52. SHELL Working into the stitches from the previous row, SC 6, Dec—complete the Dec into the next available stitch on the Accent row, Ch 1, Turn [7]

> Row 52 uses 1 stitch from the Accent row; 4 stitches remain available.

53. SHELL Working into the stitches from the previous row, SC 7, Ch 1, Turn [7]

54. SHELL Working into the stitches from the previous row, SC 6, Dec—complete the Dec into the next available stitch on the Accent row, Ch 1, Turn [7]

> Row 54 uses 1 stitch from the Accent row; 3 stitches remain available.

55. SHELL Working into the stitches from the previous row, SC 7, Ch 1, Turn [7]

4. ACCENT Dec x 10 [10]

> You will continue to work these stitches along the unfinished edge/side of the rows of the shell stitches. You had 3 stitches available on the Accent row before Row 4: ACCENT. At the end of Row 4: ACCENT, you will have a total of 13 Accent Color stitches to work into when working with the Shell Color yarn.

56. SHELL Working into the stitches from the previous Shell row, SC 6, Dec—complete the Dec into the next available stitch on the Accent row, Ch 1, Turn [7]

> Row 56 uses 1 stitch from the Accent row; 12 stitches remain available.

57. SHELL Working into the stitches from the previous row, SC 7, Ch 1, Turn [7]

58. SHELL Working into the stitches from the previous row, SC 6, Dec—complete the Dec into the same stitch on the Accent row that you finished the last decrease into, Ch 1, Turn [7]

> Row 58 uses the same stitch from the Accent row that you last worked into; 12 stitches remain available.

59. SHELL Working into the stitches from the previous row, SC 7, Ch 1, Turn [7]

60. SHELL Working into the stitches from the previous row, SC 6, Dec—complete the Dec into the next available stitch on the Accent row, Ch 1, Turn [7]

> Row 60 uses 1 stitch from the Accent row; 11 stitches remain available.

61. SHELL Working into the stitches from the previous row, SC 7, Ch 1, Turn [7]

62. SHELL Working into the stitches from the previous row, SC 6, Dec—complete the Dec into the next available stitch on the Accent row, Ch 1, Turn [7]

> Row 62 uses 1 stitch from the Accent row; 10 stitches remain available.

63. SHELL Working into the stitches from the previous row, SC 7, Ch 1, Turn [7]

64. SHELL Working into the stitches from the previous row, SC 6, Dec—complete the Dec into the same stitch on the Accent row that you finished the last decrease into, Ch 1, Turn [7]

> Row 64 uses the same stitch from the Accent row that you last worked into; 10 stitches remain available.

65. SHELL Working into the stitches from the previous row, SC 7, Ch 1, Turn [7]

66. SHELL Working into the stitches from the previous row, SC 6, Dec—complete the Dec into the next available stitch on the Accent row, Ch 1, Turn [7]

> Row 66 uses 1 stitch from the Accent row; 9 stitches remain available.

67. SHELL Working into the stitches from the previous row, SC 7, Ch 1, Turn [7]

68. SHELL Working into the stitches from the previous row, SC 6, Dec—complete the Dec into the next available stitch on the Accent row, Ch 1, Turn [7]

> Row 68 uses 1 stitch from the Accent row; 8 stitches remain available.

69. SHELL Working into the stitches from the previous row, SC 7, Ch 1, Turn [7]

70. SHELL Working into the stitches from the previous row, SC 6, Dec—complete the Dec into the same stitch on the Accent row that you finished the last Dec into, Ch 1, Turn [7]

> Row 70 uses the same stitch from the Accent row that you last worked into; 8 stitches remain available.

71. SHELL Working into the stitches from the previous row, SC 7, Ch 1, Turn [7]

72. SHELL Working into the stitches from the previous row, SC 6, SC & Dec—complete the Dec into the next available stitch on the Accent row, Ch 1, Turn [8]

> Row 72 uses 1 stitch from the Accent row; 7 stitches remain available.

73. SHELL Working into the stitches from the previous row, SC 8, Ch 1, Turn [8]

74. SHELL Working into the stitches from the previous row, Dec, SC 5, SC & Dec—complete the Dec into the next available stitch on the Accent row, Ch 1, Turn [8]

> Row 74 uses 1 stitch from the Accent row; 6 stitches remain available.

75. SHELL Working into the stitches from the previous row, SC 8, Ch 1, Turn [8]

76. SHELL Working into the stitches from the previous row, SC 7, Dec—complete the Dec into the same stitch on the Accent row that you finished the last decrease into, Ch 1, Turn [8]

> Row 76 uses the same stitch from the Accent row that you last worked into; 6 stitches remain available.

77. SHELL Working into the stitches from the previous row, SC 8, Ch 1, Turn [8]

78. SHELL Working into the stitches from the previous row, SC 7, Dec—complete the Dec into the next available stitch on the Accent row, Ch 1, Turn [8]

> Row 78 uses 1 stitch from the Accent row; 5 stitches remain available.

79. SHELL Working into the stitches from the previous row, SC 8, Ch 1, Turn [8]

80. SHELL Working into the stitches from the previous row, SC 7, Dec—complete the Dec into the next available stitch on the Accent row, Ch 1, Turn [8]

> Row 80 uses 1 stitch from the Accent row; 4 stitches remain available.

81. SHELL Working into the stitches from the previous row, SC 8, Ch 1, Turn [8]

82. SHELL Working into the stitches from the previous row, SC 7, Dec—complete the Dec into the same stitch on the Accent row that you finished the last decrease into, Ch 1, Turn [8]

> Row 82 uses the same stitch from the Accent row that you last worked into; 4 stitches remain available.

83. SHELL Working into the stitches from the previous row, SC 8, Ch 1, Turn [8]

84. SHELL Working into the stitches from the previous row, SC 7, Dec—complete the Dec into the next available stitch on the Accent row, Ch 1, Turn [8]

> Row 84 uses 1 stitch from the Accent row; 3 stitches remain available.

85. SHELL Working into the stitches from the previous row, SC 8, Ch 1, Turn [8]

86. SHELL Working into the stitches from the previous row, SC 7, Dec—complete the Dec into the next available stitch on the Accent row, Ch 1, Turn [8]

> Row 86 uses 1 stitch from the Accent row; 2 stitches remain available.

87. SHELL Working into the stitches from the previous row, SC 8, Ch 1, Turn [8]

88. SHELL Working into the stitches from the previous row, Dec, SC 5, SC & Dec—complete the Dec into the same stitch on the Accent row that you finished the last Dec into, Ch 1, Turn [8]

> Row 88 uses the same stitch from the Accent row that you last worked into; 2 stitches remain available.

89. SHELL Working into the stitches from the previous row, SC 8, Ch 1, Turn [8]

GIANT SNAILS · 241

5. ACCENT Dec x 17 [17]

> You will continue to work these stitches along the unfinished edge/side of the rows of the shell stitches. You had 2 stitches available on the Accent row before Row 5: ACCENT. At the end of Row 5: ACCENT, you will have a total of 19 Accent Color stitches to work into when working with the Shell Color yarn.

90. SHELL Working into the stitches from the previous row, SC 7, Dec—complete the Dec into the next available stitch on the Accent row, Ch 1, Turn [8]

> Row 90 uses 1 stitch from the Accent row; 18 stitches remain available.

91. SHELL Working into the stitches from the previous row, SC 8, Ch 1, Turn [8]

92. SHELL Working into the stitches from the previous row, SC 7, Dec—complete the Dec into the next available stitch on the Accent row, Ch 1, Turn [8]

> Row 92 uses 1 stitch from the Accent row; 17 stitches remain available.

93. SHELL Working into the stitches from the previous row, SC 8, Ch 1, Turn [8]

94. SHELL Working into the stitches from the previous row, SC 7, Dec—complete the Dec into the same stitch on the Accent row that you finished the last Dec into, Ch 1, Turn [8]

> Row 94 uses the same stitch from the Accent row that you last worked into; 17 stitches remain available.

95. SHELL Working into the stitches from the previous row, SC 8, Ch 1, Turn [8]

96. SHELL Working into the stitches from the previous row, SC 7, SC & Dec—complete the Dec into the next available stitch on the Accent row, Ch 1, Turn [9]

> Row 96 uses 1 stitch from the Accent row; 16 stitches remain available.

97. SHELL Working into the stitches from the previous row, SC 9, Ch 1, Turn [9]

98. SHELL Working into the stitches from the previous row, SC 8, Dec—complete the Dec into the next available stitch on the Accent row, Ch 1, Turn [9]

> Row 98 uses 1 stitch from the Accent row; 15 stitches remain available.

99. SHELL Working into the stitches from the previous row, SC 9, Ch 1, Turn [9]

100. SHELL Working into the stitches from the previous row, SC 8, Dec—complete the Dec into the same stitch on the Accent row that you finished the last Dec into, Ch 1, Turn [9]

> Row 100 uses the same stitch from the Accent row that you last worked into; 15 stitches remain available.

101. SHELL Working into the stitches from the previous row, SC 9, Ch 1, Turn [9]

102. SHELL Working into the stitches from the previous row, Dec, SC 6, SC & Dec—complete the Dec into the next available stitch on the Accent row, Ch 1, Turn [9]

> Row 102 uses 1 stitch from the Accent row; 14 stitches remain available.

103. SHELL Working into the stitches from the previous row, SC 9, Ch 1, Turn [9]

104. SHELL Working into the stitches from the previous row, SC 8, Dec—complete the Dec into the next available stitch on the Accent row, Ch 1, Turn [9]

> Row 104 uses 1 stitch from the Accent row; 13 stitches remain available.

105. SHELL Working into the stitches from the previous row, SC 9, Ch 1, Turn [9]

106. SHELL Working into the stitches from the previous row, SC 8, Dec—complete the Dec into the same stitch on the Accent row that you finished the last decrease into, Ch 1, Turn [9]

> Row 106 uses the same stitch from the Accent row that you last worked into; 13 stitches remain available.

107. SHELL Working into the stitches from the previous row, SC 9, Ch 1, Turn [9]

108. SHELL Working into the stitches from the previous row, SC 8, Dec—complete the Dec into the next available stitch on the Accent row, Ch 1, Turn [9]

> Row 108 uses 1 stitch from the Accent row; 12 stitches remain available.

109. SHELL Working into the stitches from the previous row, SC 9, Ch 1, Turn [9]

110. SHELL Working into the stitches from the previous row, SC 8, Dec—complete the Dec into the same stitch on the Accent row that you finished the last Dec into, Ch 1, Turn [9]

> Row 110 uses the same stitch from the Accent row that you last worked into; 12 stitches remain available.

111. SHELL Working into the stitches from the previous row, SC 9, Ch 1, Turn [9]

112. SHELL Working into the stitches from the previous row, SC 8, Dec—complete the Dec into the next available stitch on the Accent row, Ch 1, Turn [9]

> Row 112 uses 1 stitch from the Accent row; 11 stitches remain available.

113. SHELL Working into the stitches from the previous row, SC 9, Ch 1, Turn [9]

117. SHELL Working into the stitches from the previous row, SC 9, Ch 1, Turn [9]

121. SHELL Working into the stitches from the previous row, SC 9, Ch 1, Turn [9]

114. SHELL Working into the stitches from the previous row, SC 8, Dec—complete the Dec into the next available stitch on the Accent row, Ch 1, Turn [9]

> Row 114 uses 1 stitch from the Accent row; 10 stitches remain available.

115. SHELL Working into the stitches from the previous row, SC 9, Ch 1, Turn [9]

116. SHELL Working into the stitches from the previous row, Dec, SC 6, SC & Dec—complete the Dec into the same stitch on the Accent row that you finished the last decrease into, Ch 1, Turn [9]

> Row 116 uses the same stitch from the Accent row that you last worked into; 10 stitches remain available.

118. SHELL Working into the stitches from the previous row, SC 8, Dec—complete the Dec into the next available stitch on the Accent row, Ch 1, Turn [9]

> Row 118 uses 1 stitch from the Accent row; 9 stitches remain available.

119. SHELL Working into the stitches from the previous row, SC 9, Ch 1, Turn [9]

120. SHELL Working into the stitches from the previous row, SC 8, Dec—complete the Dec into the next available stitch on the Accent row, Ch 1, Turn [9]

> Row 120 uses 1 stitch from the Accent row; 8 stitches remain available.

122. SHELL Working into the stitches from the previous row, SC 8, Dec—complete the Dec into the same stitch on the Accent row that you finished the last Dec into, Ch 1, Turn [9]

> Row 122 uses the same stitch from the Accent row that you last worked into; 8 stitches remain available.

123. SHELL Working into the stitches from the previous row, SC 9, Ch 1, Turn [9]

6. ACCENT Dec x 17 [17]

> You will continue to work these stitches along the unfinished edge/side of the rows of the shell stitches. You had 8 stitches available on the Accent row before Row 6: ACCENT. At the end of Row 6: ACCENT, you will have a total of 25 Accent Color stitches to work into when working with the Shell Color yarn.

124. SHELL Working into the stitches from the previous row, SC 8, SC & Dec—complete the Dec into the next available stitch on the Accent row, Ch 1, Turn [10]

> Row 124 uses 1 stitch from the Accent row; 24 stitches remain available.

125. SHELL Working into the stitches from the previous row, SC 10, Ch 1, Turn [10]

126. SHELL Working into the stitches from the previous row, Dec, SC 7, SC & Dec—complete the Dec into the same stitch on the Accent row that you finished the last Dec into, Ch 1, Turn [10]

> Row 126 uses the same stitch from the Accent row that you last worked into; 24 stitches remain available.

127. SHELL Working into the stitches from the previous row, SC 10, Ch 1, Turn [10]

128. SHELL Working into the stitches from the previous row, SC 9, Dec—complete the Dec into the next available stitch on the Accent row, Ch 1, Turn [10]

> Row 128 uses 1 stitch from the Accent row; 23 stitches remain available.

129. SHELL Working into the stitches from the previous row, SC 10, Ch 1, Turn [10]

130. SHELL Working into the stitches from the previous row, SC 9, Dec—complete the Dec into the next available stitch on the Accent row, Ch 1, Turn [10]

> Row 130 uses 1 stitch from the Accent row; 22 stitches remain available.

131. SHELL Working into the stitches from the previous row, SC 10, Ch 1, Turn [10]

132. SHELL Working into the stitches from the previous row, SC 9, Dec—complete the Dec into the next available stitch on the Accent row, Ch 1, Turn [10]

> Row 132 uses 1 stitch from the Accent row; 21 stitches remain available.

133. SHELL Working into the stitches from the previous row, SC 10, Ch 1, Turn [10]

134. SHELL Working into the stitches from the previous row, SC 9, Dec—complete the Dec into the same stitch on the Accent row that you finished the last Dec into, Ch 1, Turn [10]

> Row 134 uses the same stitch from the Accent row that you last worked into; 21 stitches remain available.

GIANT SNAILS • 245

135. SHELL Working into the stitches from the previous row, SC 10, Ch 1, Turn [10]

136. SHELL Working into the stitches from the previous row, SC 9, Dec—complete the Dec into the next available stitch on the Accent row, Ch 1, Turn [10]

> Row 136 uses 1 stitch from the Accent row; 20 stitches remain available.

137. SHELL Working into the stitches from the previous row, SC 10, Ch 1, Turn [10]

138. SHELL Working into the stitches from the previous row, SC 9, Dec—complete the Dec into the next available stitch on the Accent row, Ch 1, Turn [10]

> Row 138 uses 1 stitch from the Accent row; 19 stitches remain available.

139. SHELL Working into the stitches from the previous row, SC 10, Ch 1, Turn [10]

140. SHELL Working into the stitches from the previous row, SC 9, Dec—complete the Dec into the same stitch on the Accent row that you finished the last decrease into, Ch 1, Turn [10]

> Row 140 uses the same stitch from the Accent row that you last worked into; 19 stitches remain available.

141. SHELL Working into the stitches from the previous row, SC 10, Ch 1, Turn [10]

142. SHELL Working into the stitches from the previous row, Dec, SC 7, SC & Dec—complete the Dec into the next available stitch on the Accent row, Ch 1, Turn [10]

> Row 142 uses 1 stitch from the Accent row; 18 stitches remain available.

143. SHELL Working into the stitches from the previous row, SC 10, Ch 1, Turn [10]

144. SHELL Working into the stitches from the previous row, SC 9, Dec—complete the Dec into the next available stitch on the Accent row, Ch 1, Turn [10]

> Row 144 uses 1 stitch from the Accent row; 17 stitches remain available.

145. SHELL Working into the stitches from the previous row, SC 10, Ch 1, Turn [10]

146. SHELL Working into the stitches from the previous row, SC 9, Dec—complete the Dec into the same stitch on the Accent row that you finished the last Dec into, Ch 1, Turn [10]

> Row 146 uses the same stitch from the Accent row that you last worked into; 17 stitches remain available.

147. SHELL Working into the stitches from the previous row, SC 10, Ch 1, Turn [10]

148. SHELL Working into the stitches from the previous row, SC 9, Dec—complete the Dec into the next available stitch on the Accent row, Ch 1, Turn [10]

> Row 148 uses 1 stitch from the Accent row; 16 stitches remain available.

149. SHELL Working into the stitches from the previous row, SC 10, Ch 1, Turn [10]

150. SHELL Working into the stitches from the previous row, SC 9, Dec—complete the Dec into the next available stitch on the Accent row, Ch 1, Turn [10]

> Row 150 uses 1 stitch from the Accent row; 15 stitches remain available.

151. SHELL Working into the stitches from the previous row, SC 10, Ch 1, Turn [10]

152. SHELL Working into the stitches from the previous row, SC 9, Dec—complete the Dec into the same stitch on the Accent row that you finished the last decrease into, Ch 1, Turn [10]

> Row 152 uses the same stitch from the Accent row that you last worked into; 15 stitches remain available.

153. SHELL Working into the stitches from the previous row, SC 10, Ch 1, Turn [10]

154. SHELL Working into the stitches from the previous row, SC 9, Dec—complete the Dec into the next available stitch on the Accent row, Ch 1, Turn [10]

> Row 154 uses 1 stitch from the Accent row; 14 stitches remain available.

155. SHELL Working into the stitches from the previous row, SC 10, Ch 1, Turn [10]

156. SHELL Working into the stitches from the previous row, SC 9, Dec—complete the Dec into the next available stitch on the Accent row, Ch 1, Turn [10]

> Row 156 uses 1 stitch from the Accent row; 13 stitches remain available.

157. SHELL Working into the stitches from the previous row, SC 10, Ch 1, Turn [10]

158. SHELL Working into the stitches from the previous row, SC 9, Dec—complete the Dec into the same stitch on the Accent row that you finished the last decrease into, Ch 1, Turn [10]

> Row 158 uses the same stitch from the Accent row that you last worked into; 13 stitches remain available.

Giant Snail with Pointed Shell

159. SHELL Working into the stitches from the previous row, SC 10, Ch 1, Turn [10]

7. ACCENT Dec; fasten off with a short yarn tail that you will tuck inside the work when you sew to attach [1]

> You will continue to work these stitches along the unfinished edge/side of the rows of the shell stitches. You had 13 stitches available on the Accent row before Row 7: ACCENT. At the end of Row 7: ACCENT, you will have a total of 14 Accent Color stitches to work into when working with the Shell Color yarn. Do not make any more Accent stitches.

160. SHELL Working into the stitches from the previous row, SC 9, SC & Dec—complete the Dec into the next available stitch on the Accent row, Ch 1, Turn [11]

> Row 160 uses 1 stitch from the Accent row; 13 stitches remain available.

161. SHELL Working into the stitches from the previous row, SC 11, Ch 1, Turn [11]

162. SHELL Working into the stitches from the previous row, SC 10, Dec—complete the Dec into the next available stitch on the Accent row, Ch 1, Turn [11]

> Row 162 uses 1 stitch from the Accent row; 12 stitches remain available.

163. SHELL Working into the stitches from the previous row, SC 11, Ch 1, Turn [11]

164. SHELL Working into the stitches from the previous row, SC 10, Dec—complete the Dec into the same stitch on the Accent row that you finished the last Dec into, Ch 1, Turn [11]

> Row 164 uses the same stitch from the Accent row that you last worked into; 12 stitches remain available.

165. SHELL Working into the stitches from the previous row, SC 11, Ch 1, Turn [11]

166. SHELL Working into the stitches from the previous row, Dec, SC 8, SC & Dec—complete the Dec into the next available stitch on the Accent row, Ch 1, Turn [11]

> Row 166 uses 1 stitch from the Accent row; 11 stitches remain available.

167. SHELL Working into the stitches from the previous row, SC 11, Ch 1, Turn [11]

168. SHELL Working into the stitches from the previous row, SC 10, Dec—complete the Dec into the next available stitch on the Accent row, Ch 1, Turn [11]

> Row 168 uses 1 stitch from the Accent row; 10 stitches remain available.

169. SHELL Working into the stitches from the previous row, SC 11, Ch 1, Turn [11]

170. SHELL Working into the stitches from the previous row, SC 10, Dec—complete the Dec into the same stitch on the Accent row that you finished the last Dec into, Ch 1, Turn [11]

> Row 170 uses the same stitch from the Accent row that you last worked into; 10 stitches remain available.

171. SHELL Working into the stitches from the previous row, SC 11, Ch 1, Turn [11]

GIANT SNAILS • 249

172. SHELL Working into the stitches from the previous row, SC 10, Dec—complete the Dec into the next available stitch on the Accent row, Ch 1, Turn [11]

> Row 172 uses 1 stitch from the Accent row; 9 stitches remain available.

173. SHELL Working into the stitches from the previous row, SC 11, Ch 1, Turn [11]

174. SHELL Working into the stitches from the previous row, SC 10, Dec—complete the Dec into the next available stitch on the Accent row, Ch 1, Turn [11]

> Row 174 uses 1 stitch from the Accent row; 8 stitches remain available.

175. SHELL Working into the stitches from the previous row, SC 11, Ch 1, Turn [11]

176. SHELL Working into the stitches from the previous row, SC 10, Dec—complete the Dec into the same stitch on the Accent row that you finished the last Dec into, Ch 1, Turn [11]

> Row 176 uses the same stitch from the Accent row that you last worked into; 8 stitches remain available.

177. SHELL Working into the stitches from the previous row, SC 11, Ch 1, Turn [11]

178. SHELL Working into the stitches from the previous row, Dec, SC 8, SC & Dec—complete the Dec into the next available stitch on the Accent row, Ch 1, Turn [11]

> Row 178 uses 1 stitch from the Accent row; 7 stitches remain available.

179. SHELL Working into the stitches from the previous row, SC 11, Ch 1, Turn [11]

180. SHELL Working into the stitches from the previous row, SC 10, Dec—complete the Dec into the next available stitch on the Accent row, Ch 1, Turn [11]

> Row 180 uses 1 stitch from the Accent row; 6 stitches remain available.

181. SHELL Working into the stitches from the previous row, SC 11, Ch 1, Turn [11]

182. SHELL Working into the stitches from the previous row, SC 10, Dec—complete the Dec into the same stitch on the Accent row that you finished the last Dec into, Ch 1, Turn [11]

> Row 182 uses the same stitch from the Accent row that you last worked into; 6 stitches remain available.

183. SHELL Working into the stitches from the previous row, SC 11, Ch 1, Turn [11]

184. SHELL Working into the stitches from the previous row, SC 10, Dec—complete the Dec into the next available stitch on the Accent row, Ch 1, Turn [11]

> Row 184 uses 1 stitch from the Accent row; 5 stitches remain available.

185. SHELL Working into the stitches from the previous row, SC 11, Ch 1, Turn [11]

186. SHELL Working into the stitches from the previous row, SC 10, Dec—complete the Dec into the next available stitch on the Accent row, Ch 1, Turn [11]

> Row 186 uses 1 stitch from the Accent row; 4 stitches remain available.

187. SHELL Working into the stitches from the previous row, SC 11, Ch 1, Turn [11]

188. SHELL Working into the stitches from the previous row, SC 10, Dec—complete the Dec into the same stitch on the Accent row that you finished the last Dec into, Ch 1, Turn [11]

> Row 188 uses the same stitch from the Accent row that you last worked into; 4 stitches remain available.

189. SHELL Working into the stitches from the previous row, SC 11, Ch 1, Turn [11]

190. SHELL Working into the stitches from the previous row, SC 10, Dec—complete the Dec into the next available stitch on the Accent row, Ch 1, Turn [11]

> Row 190 uses 1 stitch from the Accent row; 3 stitches remain available.

191. SHELL Working into the stitches from the previous row, SC 11, Ch 1, Turn [11]

192. SHELL Working into the stitches from the previous row, SC 10, Dec—complete the Dec into the next available stitch on the Accent row, Ch 1, Turn [11]

> Row 192 uses 1 stitch from the Accent row; 2 stitches remain available.

193. SHELL Working into the stitches from the previous row, SC 11, Ch 1, Turn [11]

194. SHELL Working into the stitches from the previous row, Dec, SC 8, SC & Dec—complete the Dec into the same stitch on the Accent row that you finished the last Dec into, Ch 1, Turn [11]

> Row 194 uses the same stitch from the Accent row that you last worked into; 2 stitches remain available.

195. SHELL Working into the stitches from the previous row, SC 11, Ch 1, Turn [11]

196. SHELL Working into the stitches from the previous row, SC 10, Dec—complete the Dec into the next available stitch on the Accent row, Ch 1, Turn [11]

> Row 196 uses 1 stitch from the Accent row; 1 stitch remains available.

197. SHELL Working into the stitches from the previous row, SC 11, Ch 1, Turn [11]

198. SHELL Working into the stitches from the previous row, SC 10, Dec—complete the Dec into the next available stitch on the Accent row, Ch 1, Turn [11]

> Row 198 uses 1 stitch from the Accent row; 0 stitches remain available.

199. SHELL Working into the stitches from the previous row, SC 11, Ch 1, Turn [11]

200. SHELL Working into the stitches from the previous row, SC 10, Dec—complete the Dec into the same stitch on the Accent row that you finished the last Dec into, Ch 1, Turn [11]

> Row 200 uses the same stitch from the Accent row that you last worked into; 0 stitches remain available.

201. SHELL Working into the stitches from the previous row, SC 11, Ch 1 [11]

202. SHELL Reorient your work so that you will be working back along the unfinished edge of the shell (see arrow in above photo); starting around the side of the last SC you made in Row 201, SC 76, Sl St, Ch 1, Turn [77]

203. SHELL Skip the Sl St, Dec, SC 74, Ch 1, Turn [75]

204. SHELL (SC, Dec) x 24, SC 2, Sl St, Ch 1, Turn [51]

205. SHELL Skip the Sl St, Dec, SC 48, Ch 1, Turn [49]

206. SHELL (SC, Dec) x 16, Sl St, Ch 1, Turn [33]

252 • GIANT SNAILS

207. SHELL Skip the Sl St, Dec, SC 28, Dec, Ch 1, Turn [30]

208. SHELL SC 29, Sl St, Ch 1, Turn [30]

209. SHELL Skip the Sl St, Dec, SC 25, Dec, Ch 1, Turn [27]

210. SHELL SC 21, Sl St, Ch 1, Turn [22]

> Five stitches remain unworked from Row 209 after completing Row 210.

211. SHELL Skip the Sl St, Dec, SC 16, Dec [18]

> There will be 1 unworked stitch left from Row 210 after completing Row 211.

Fasten off with a 24 in/61 cm yarn tail.

Stuff lightly with fiberfill, and do not change the shape of the spiral; do your best to stuff the parts that should bulge out emphasizing the spiral, and do not warp the inset parts (the Accent stitches). See the Assembly section starting on page 261 for how to pin to attach.

Giant Snail with Pointed Shell

GIANT SNAILS • 253

GIANT SNAIL SHELL STYLE 2: ROUND (MAKE 1)

Any Color Yarn for the Shell: Approximately 150 yd/137.25 m worsted/medium weight yarn

1. Starting with a long enough yarn tail to weave in later, Ch 3, starting in the 2nd Ch from hook, SC 2, Ch 1, Turn [2]
2. SC 2, Ch 1, Turn [2]
3. BLO [SC, <Dec>, SC], Ch 1, Turn [3]

> "<Dec>" is a stitch that is defined in the Glossary beginning on page 6.

4. SC 3, Ch 1, Turn [3]
5. BLO [SC, Inc, SC], Ch 1, Turn [4]
6. SC 4, Ch 1, Turn [4]
7. BLO [SC 2, <Dec>, SC 2], Ch 1, Turn [5]
8. SC 5, Ch 1, Turn [5]
9. BLO [SC 2, Inc, SC 2], Ch 1, Turn [6]
10. SC 6, Ch 1, Turn [6]

11. BLO [SC 6], Ch 1, Turn [6]
12. SC 6, Ch 1, Turn [6]
13. BLO [SC, Inc, SC 2, Inc, SC], Ch 1, Turn [8]
14. SC 8, Ch 1, Turn [8]
15. BLO [SC 8], Ch 1, Turn [8]
16. SC 8, Ch 1, Turn [8]
17. BLO [SC 2, Inc, SC 2, Inc, SC 2], Ch 1, Turn [10]
18. SC 10, Ch 1, Turn [10]
19. BLO [SC 10], Ch 1, Turn [10]
20. SC 10, Ch 1, Turn [10]

21. BLO [SC 2, Inc, SC 4, Inc, SC 2], Ch 1, Turn [12]
22. SC 12, Ch 1, Turn [12]
23. BLO [SC 12], Ch 1, Turn [12]
24. SC 12, Ch 1, Turn [12]
25. BLO [SC 3, Inc, SC 4, Inc, SC 3], Ch 1, Turn [14]
26. SC 14, Ch 1, Turn [14]
27. BLO [SC 14], Ch 1, Turn [14]
28. SC 14, Ch 1, Turn [14]
29. BLO [SC 4, Inc, SC 4, Inc, SC 4], Ch 1, Turn [16]
30. SC 16, Ch 1, Turn [16]

31. BLO [SC 16], Ch 1, Turn [16]
32. SC 16, Ch 1, Turn [16]
33. BLO [(SC 4, <Dec>, SC 4) x 2], Ch 1, Turn [18]
34. SC 18, Ch 1, Turn [18]
35. BLO [SC 18], Ch 1, Turn [18]
36. SC 18, Ch 1, Turn [18]

> In the following rows, you will follow every lettered sub-row to create short rows of built-up stitches (for more information on this technique, please see this YouTube video: https://www.youtube.com/watch?v=sh5T-idiwm8&t=3s). Each sub-row (i.e., 37A, 37B, 37C, etc.) has its own sub-row stitch count, indicated by the number preceded by a hyphen in brackets. Row 37A's sub-row stitch count is 14. The total stitch count for all of Row 37 is at the very end of the final sub-row, without the hyphen.

37A. BLO [(SC 3, <Dec>, SC 3) x 2], Ch 1, Turn [-14]
37B. SC 7, Ch 1, Turn [-7]
37C. SC 6, SC/BLO [HDC Dec & HDC, SC 2, <Dec>, SC 3], Ch 1, Turn [-14] [21]

> In Row 37C, the "SC/BLO [HDC Dec & HDC]" stitch is just a "SC/HDC Dec & HDC" in which the latter part of the "Dec" and the "& HDC" are worked into the BLO. The SC/HDC Dec and the "&" are defined in the Glossary beginning on page 6.

38. SC 13, SC/HDC Dec & HDC, SC 6, Ch 1, Turn [21]
39. BLO [SC 21], Ch 1, Turn [21]

40. SC 21, Ch 1, Turn [21]

41A. BLO [SC 17], Ch 1, Turn [-17]
41B. SC 13, Ch 1, Turn [-13]
41C. SC 12, SC/BLO [HDC Dec & HDC, SC 3], Ch 1, Turn [-17] [21]
42. SC 16, SC/HDC Dec & HDC, SC 3, Ch 1, Turn [21]
43. BLO [(SC 3, Inc, SC 3) x 3], Ch 1, Turn [24]
44. SC 24, Ch 1, Turn [24]
45A. BLO [SC 18], Ch 1, Turn [-18]
45B. SC 12, Ch 1, Turn [-12]
45C. SC 11, SC/BLO [HDC Dec & HDC, SC 5], Ch 1, Turn [-18] [24]
46. SC 17, SC/HDC Dec & HDC, SC 5, Ch 1, Turn [24]
47. BLO [SC 24], Ch 1, Turn [24]
48. SC 24, Ch 1, Turn [24]
49A. BLO [(SC 4, <Dec>, SC 4) x 2], Ch 1, Turn [-18]
49B. SC 9, Ch 1, Turn [-9]
49C. SC 8, SC/BLO [HDC Dec & HDC, SC 3, <Dec>, SC 4], Ch 1, Turn [-18] [27]

Giant Snail with Round Shell

50. SC 17, SC/HDC Dec & HDC, SC 8, Ch 1, Turn [27]

51. BLO [SC 27], Ch 1, Turn [27]
52. SC 27, Ch 1, Turn [27]
53A. BLO [SC 20], Ch 1, Turn [-20]
53B. SC 13, Ch 1, Turn [-13]
53C. SC 12, SC/BLO [HDC Dec & HDC, SC 6], Ch 1, Turn [-20] [27]
54. SC 19, SC/HDC Dec & HDC, SC 6, Ch 1, Turn [27]
55. BLO [(SC 4, Inc, SC 4) x 3], Ch 1, Turn [30]
56. SC 30, Ch 1, Turn [30]

57A. BLO [SC 25], Ch 1, Turn [-25]
57B. SC 20, Ch 1, Turn [-20]
57C. SC 19, SC/BLO [HDC Dec & HDC, SC 4], Ch 1, Turn [-25] [30]
58. SC 24, SC/HDC Dec & HDC, SC 4, Ch 1, Turn [30]
59. BLO [SC 30], Ch 1, Turn [30]
60. SC 30, Ch 1, Turn [30]

61A. BLO [(SC 5, <Dec>, SC 5) x 2], Ch 1, Turn [-22]
61B. SC 11, Ch 1, Turn [-11]
61C. SC 10, SC/BLO [HDC Dec & HDC, SC 4, <Dec>, SC 5], Ch 1, Turn [-22] [33]

62. SC 21, SC/HDC Dec & HDC, SC 10, Ch 1, Turn [33]

63. BLO [SC 33], Ch 1, Turn [33]

64. SC 33, Ch 1, Turn [33]

65A. BLO [SC 30], Ch 1, Turn [-30]

65B. SC 27, Ch 1, Turn [-27]

65C. SC 26, SC/BLO [HDC Dec & HDC, SC 2], Ch 1, Turn [-30] [33]

66. SC 29, SC/HDC Dec & HDC, SC 2, Ch 1, Turn [33]

67. BLO [(SC 5, Inc, SC 5) x 3], Ch 1, Turn [36]

68. SC 36, Ch 1, Turn [36]

69A. BLO [SC 24], Ch 1, Turn [-24]

69B. SC 12, Ch 1, Turn [-12]

69C. SC 11, SC/BLO [HDC Dec & HDC, SC 11], Ch 1, Turn [-24] [36]

70. SC 23, SC/HDC Dec & HDC, SC 11, Ch 1, Turn [36]

71. BLO [SC 36], Ch 1, Turn [36]

72. SC 36, Ch 1, Turn [36]

73A. BLO [(SC 4, Inc, SC 4) x 3], Ch 1, Turn [-30]

73B. SC 20, Ch 1, Turn [-20]

73C. SC 19, SC/BLO [HDC Dec & HDC, SC 3, Inc, SC 4], Ch 1, Turn [-30] [40]

74. SC 29, SC/HDC Dec & HDC, SC 9, Ch 1, Turn [40]

75. BLO [SC 40], Ch 1, Turn [40]

76. SC 40, Ch 1, Turn [40]

77A. BLO [SC 35], Ch 1, Turn [-35]

77B. SC 30, Ch 1, Turn [-30]

77C. SC 29, SC/BLO [HDC Dec & HDC, SC 4], Ch 1, Turn [-35] [40]

78. SC 34, SC/HDC Dec & HDC, SC 4, Ch 1, Turn [40]

79. BLO [(SC 5, <Dec>, SC 5) x 4], Ch 1, Turn [44]

80. SC 44, Ch 1, Turn [44]

81A. BLO [SC 34], Ch 1, Turn [-34]

81B. SC 24, Ch 1, Turn [-24]

81C. SC 23, SC/BLO [HDC Dec & HDC, SC 9], Ch 1, Turn [-34] [44]

82. SC 33, SC/HDC Dec & HDC, SC 9, Ch 1, Turn [44]

83. BLO [SC 44], Ch 1, Turn [44]

84. SC 44, Ch 1, Turn [44]

85. BLO [SC 44], Ch 1, Turn [44]

86. SC 44, Ch 1, Turn [44]

87. In this row, you will Dec along the entire unfinished edge, working through both sides at once to make a long, thin cone shape. Fold the entire long triangle in half the long way, with the visible ridges of BLO stitches on the outside. You will be working through both halves of the long triangle at the same time, working one Dec for every 2 rows. You can tell you're working only one Dec per 2 rows by placing each Dec between the BLO ridge lines, as shown. Once you get past the midpoint of the shell, begin stuffing the bottom of the shell with fiberfill starting around 2 in/5 cm from the end (leave the very end of the widest part of the shell unstuffed for now). Continue stuffing toward the narrow end as you go. Stuff the wider section of the shell medium-firm, stuffing more lightly as the shell tapers to a point.

256 • GIANT SNAILS

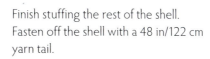
Finish stuffing the rest of the shell. Fasten off the shell with a 48 in/122 cm yarn tail.

Gently curl the shell into a spiral, starting at the thinnest end. Pin in place as you work. The very center of the spiral (where the shell is thinnest) will be stacked on top of the wider part, making a slight cone shape.

The bottommost edge of the shell should fold in on itself a little bit, and you can use it to help shape the shell to fit against the back of the snail.

Once you are pleased with the shaping of the shell, use the yarn tail to sew along the spiral, securing the spiral shape in place.

GIANT SNAILS • 257

Pin the shell to the back of the snail. The front edge of the shell opening should rest at the point where the Snail Body angles upward. The back of the shell should not extend beyond the back edge of the snail "frill" (foot). Sew around the shell opening to secure the shell to the Snail Body. (For more information, see the Giant Snail Assembly section starting on page 261.)

Giant Snail with Round Shell

258 • GIANT SNAILS

Giant Snail with Round Shell

GIANT ROUND SNAIL SHELL OPTIONAL CLOSURE (MAKE 1)

Any Color Yarn for the Shell: Approximately 14 yd/12.75 m worsted/medium weight yarn

Use this piece to close the Giant Round Snail Shell option without attaching it to the Giant Snail Body. This is just used to make a single shell without the snail.

Insert the disk into the wide shell opening. The disk should be slightly inset into the shell. Pin in place. Use the yarn tail to sew in place. If your shell is made with variegated yarn, take care to catch only the parts of the stitches that are inside the shell as you sew. Weave in ends.

1. SC 6 in Magic Circle, Sl St to beginning stitch, Ch 1 [6]
2. Inc x 6, Sl St to beginning stitch, Ch 1 [12]
3. (SC, Inc) x 6, Sl St to beginning stitch, Ch 1 [18]
4. (SC, Inc, SC) x 6, Sl St to beginning stitch, Ch 1 [24]
5. (SC 3, Inc) x 6, Sl St to beginning stitch, Ch 1 [30]
6. (SC 2, Inc, SC 2) x 6, Sl St to beginning stitch, Ch 1 [36]
7. (SC 5, Inc) x 6, Sl St to beginning stitch, Ch 1 [42]
8. (SC 3, Inc, SC 3) x 6, Sl St to beginning stitch, Ch 1 [48]
9. (SC 7, Inc) x 6, Sl St to beginning stitch, Ch 1 [54]
10. FLO [SC 54], Sl St to beginning stitch [54]

Fasten off with a 24 in/61 cm yarn tail.

Giant Snail with Round Shell

260 • GIANT SNAILS

Giant Snail Assembly

1. Finish stuffing the center of the body shape before closing up the head. You will have already sewn around the inner edge of the center of the body to prevent fiberfill and flat glass marble gems from migrating to the edges.

Shape and close the top of the head. Close the underside by tucking the bottom part of the body piece under the edge of the top piece, as shown.

Next, pin the center of the mouth, between the two arched pieces, down about 5 rows from the top edge of the bottom piece, as shown.

Fold the right side in toward the center so that the point where the flap meets the arched piece rests at the center of the body, as shown. These pins can be adjusted. It is okay if these sides are not pinned in to touch in the center of the Giant Snail's body. It is also okay if there is some small amount of space between the edges in the center.

Repeat this shaping on the left side.

Next, put a puff of fiberfill inside each rounded part of the head—do not overstuff.

Then pin the front center stitch of each rounded part of the head down, as shown.

GIANT SNAILS • **261**

Here are a couple examples of finished faces with different shaping options:

2. Using leftover yarn tails, sew the head in place as you have pinned it so that it stays in this exact shape without the pins and without leaving any openings for the fiberfill to escape. Weave in ends.

3. Pin the short antennae in place, as shown on the head of the Giant Snail, centered on each of the two rounded parts at the front of the head. Sew to attach. Weave in ends.

4. Pin the long antennae in place, as shown on the head of the Giant Snail, just before the start of the two rounded parts at the front of the head. Sew to attach. Weave in ends.

5. Pin the shell in place on the back; see photos on pages 263 and 264 to orient it. Whipstitch in place around the entire edge of the shell that touches the snail's body, using the yarn tail from the shell. Weave in ends. The pins on the bodies depicted in the photos show the edge of where the shell should be positioned, without the shell pinned in place.

Giant Snail with Round Shell

262 • GIANT SNAILS

Giant Snail Body with Pointed Snail Shell Assembly

> The pins in these photos show exactly where the edges of the pointed shell are attached to this snail body. You can use these photos as a guide.

GIANT SNAILS • 263

Giant Snail Body with Round Snail Shell Assembly

> The pins in these photos show exactly where the edges of the round shell are attached to this snail body. You can use these photos as a guide.

264 • GIANT SNAILS

Giant Snail with Pointed Shell

Giant Snail with Pointed Shell

SADDLES AND OTHER ACCESSORIES

❶ Mushroom Sprite with Arms Style 10, Body Style 1, Cap Style 1, holding steady another ❷ Mushroom Sprite with Arms Style 7, Feet/Legs Style 10, Body Style 4, Cap Style 6, riding a ❸ Giant Snail with Pointed Shell on a saddle

OPTIONS

Removable Leash... 268

Sew-to-Attach Leash... 269

Giant Snail with Pointed Shell and Full Saddle

Close-up of Giant Snail's Full Saddle

Saddle Blanket:
  Round... 274
  Pointed... 275
Saddle Seat... 275
Saddle Flap... 277
Seat Back (not pictured)... 277
Seat Handle (not pictured)... 280

Saddle Horn... 281
Saddle Support
  (not pictured)... 282
Saddle Bags... 284
Saddle Straps... 284
Reins... 289

SADDLES AND OTHER ACCESSORIES • 267

Leashes

REMOVABLE LEASH (MAKE 1)

Leash Color Yarn: Approximately 2–6 yd/1.75–5.5 m worsted/medium weight yarn

1. Starting with a long enough yarn tail to weave in later, Ch 8, Sl St to the beginning stitch.

> This is the handle of your leash. This loop can be held by, looped over, or pinned/sewn to attach to the hand of the Mushroom Sprite leading a snail. If you want the loop to be bigger, make a longer set of Ch stitches for Row 1 before slip stitching to the beginning stitch.

2. In Row 2, you will chain a length that will include what will be looped around the snail's "neck" and the length of the leash.

For a Small Snail, it is recommended to Ch 48 and then Sl St into the 8th Ch from hook.

For a Medium Snail, it is recommended to Ch 60 and then Sl St into the 8th Ch from hook.

For a Giant Snail, it is recommended to Ch 84 and then Sl St into the 8th Ch from hook.

> The number of chains in Row 2 can be altered for a longer or shorter leash, depending on the yarn, tension, and personal preference.

3. It is optional to then Sl St all the way back along the available chains to the first Sl St in Row 1.

Fasten off with a long enough yarn tail to weave in.

Assembly

1. Weave both yarn tails into the leash.

❶ Mushroom Sprite with Arms Style 3, Feet/Legs Style 2, Body Style 5, Cap Style 14; ❷ Medium Snail with Pointed Shell and removable leash; ❸ Giant Snail with Pointed Shell

2. Wrap the leash around the "neck" of the snail you want to put a leash on, push the loop created in Row 1 through the loop created in Row 2, and pull the leash through that 2nd loop.

3. Help your Mushroom Sprite learn how to gently and slowly walk their new snail.

Giant Snail with Pointed Shell and sew-to-attach leash with optional spikes (for more information on adding spikes, see the "Tips and Tricks" section beginning on page 2)

SEW-TO-ATTACH LEASH (MAKE 1)

***Leash Color Yarn:** Approximately 2–9 yd/1.75–8.25 m worsted/medium weight yarn*

> Row 1 creates the piece that will be sewn to attach to the back of the "neck" of your snail and will serve as the base of your leash.

For the Small Snail

1. Starting with a long enough yarn tail to weave in later, Ch 6, starting in the 2nd Ch from hook, Inc, SC 3, work 4 SC in the last available Ch stitch, continue to crochet around to the unused side of the Ch stitches, SC 3, Inc in the same Ch stitch as the first Inc in this row, do not Sl St, do not Ch 1 [14]
2. Working into the stitches from Row 1, Sl St 4 [4]

> Row 2 takes you to the front-center edge of the base of the leash.

3. Ch 48 (or more), Sl St into the 8th Ch from hook, Sl St all the way back along the chains to where Row 2 ended.

> Row 3 creates the leash length and the loop that the Mushroom Sprite will hold. If you want the leash longer, work more chains. If you want the leash loop handle to be larger than the loop created in Row 3, you can instead Sl St into the 12th stitch from hook. See page 272 for Assembly instructions.

Fasten off with a 12 in/30.5 cm yarn tail.

❶ Mushroom Sprite with Arms Style 8, Feet/Legs Style 9, Body Style 7; ❷ Upright Small Snail with Pointed Shell and Antennae Style 2 with sew-to-attach leash with spikes

SADDLES AND OTHER ACCESSORIES • 269

For the Medium Snail

1. Starting with a long enough yarn tail to weave in later, Ch 10, starting in the 2nd Ch from hook, Inc, SC 7, work 4 SC in the last available Ch stitch, continue to crochet around to the unused side of the Ch stitches, SC 7, Inc in the same Ch stitch as the first Inc in this row, do not Sl St, do not Ch 1, continue to Row 2 [22]

2. Working into the stitches from Row 1, Sl St 6 [6]

> Row 2 takes you to the front-center edge of the base of the leash.

3. Ch 60 (or more), Sl St into the 8th Ch from hook, Sl St all the way back along the chains to where Row 2 ended.

> Row 3 creates the leash length and the loop that the Mushroom Sprite will hold. If you want the leash longer, work more chains. If you want the leash loop handle to be larger than the loop created in Row 3, you can instead Sl St into the 12th stitch from hook. See page 272 for Assembly instructions.

Fasten off with a 12 in/30.5 cm yarn tail.

❶ Mushroom Sprite with Arms Style 7, Body Style 2, Cap Style 13, optional dots; ❷ Upright Small Snail with Round Shell and Antennae Style 1; ❸ Medium Snail with Pointed Shell with two sew-to-attach leashes

❶ **Mushroom Sprite with Arms Style 7, Feet/Legs Style 10, Body Style 4, Cap Style 6;** ❷ **Giant Snail with Pointed Shell and sew-to-attach leash with optional spikes**

For the Giant Snail

1. Starting with a long enough yarn tail to weave in later, Ch 16, starting in the 2nd Ch from hook, Inc, SC 13, work 4 SC in the last available Ch stitch, continue to crochet around to the unused side of the Ch stitches, SC 13, Inc in the same Ch stitch as the first Inc in this row, do not Sl St, do not Ch 1, continue to Row 2 [34]

2. Working into the stitches from Row 1, Sl St 9 [9]

> Row 2 takes you to the front-center edge of the base of the leash.

3. Ch 84 (or more), Sl St into the 8th Ch from hook, Sl St all the way back along the chains to where Row 2 ended.

> Row 3 creates the leash length and the loop that the Mushroom Sprite will hold. If you want the leash longer, work more chains. If you want the leash loop handle to be larger than the loop created in Row 3, you can instead Sl St into the 12th stitch from hook. See page 272 for Assembly instructions.

Fasten off with a 12 in/30.5 cm yarn tail.

SADDLES AND OTHER ACCESSORIES • 271

Assembly

1. Pin Row 1 to attach to the neck of the snail you want to put a leash on. You can attach to the back of the neck or to the front of the neck, between the body's flaps.

Small Snails

Medium Snails

Giant Snails

2. Once you have verified placement of the leash, sew to attach to the snail using the yarn tails, and weave in ends.

3. Help your Mushroom Sprite learn how to gently and slowly walk their new snail.

Giant Snail with Round Shell with a sew-to-attach leash with optional spikes (for more information on adding spikes, see the "Tips and Tricks" section beginning on page 2)

272 • SADDLES AND OTHER ACCESSORIES

Saddle and Accessories for Giant Snail

Read through this section and choose which pieces you'd like to make for your snail mount. It is recommended to make at least a saddle blanket, saddle seat, and saddle flaps. Once you've made all the saddle pieces you want, proceed to the Saddle Assembly instructions beginning on page 285.

SADDLE BLANKET FOR GIANT ROUND SNAIL SHELL (MAKE 1)

Saddle Blanket Color Yarn: Approximately 28 yd/25.5 m worsted/medium weight yarn

1. Using Saddle Blanket Color yarn, starting with a long enough yarn tail to weave in later, Ch 21, starting in the 2nd Ch from hook, SC 20, Ch 1, Turn [20]

2–17. (16 rows of) SC 20, Ch 1, Turn [20]

18. SC 19, Inc, continue to crochet down the unfinished edge of the work toward the OC, SC, HDC 2, DC 10, HDC 2, SC, working along the chain side of the OC, Inc, SC 18, Inc, continue to crochet up the unfinished edge of the work, SC, HDC 2, DC 10, HDC 2, SC, SC in the same stitch as the first SC of this row, Sl St to beginning stitch [76]

Fasten off with an 18 in/45.75 cm yarn tail.

The HDC and DC stitches in the final row will be at the sides of the blanket. Consider embellishing your Saddle Blanket by slip stitching around the edge of the blanket with an accent color or adding a short fringe to the sides of the blanket in the DC stitches from the final row.

Giant Snail with Pointed Shell with saddle. The saddle blanket is red and sits under all parts of the saddle and saddle accessories.

SADDLE BLANKET FOR GIANT POINTED SNAIL SHELL (MAKE 1)

Saddle Blanket Color Yarn: Approximately 22 yd/20 m worsted/medium weight yarn

> This Saddle Blanket is shorter to accommodate the narrower spiraling shell.

1. Using Saddle Blanket Color yarn, starting with a long enough yarn tail to weave in later, Ch 21, starting in the 2nd Ch from hook, SC 20, Ch 1, Turn [20]
2-13. (12 rows of) SC 20, Ch 1, Turn [20]
14. SC 19, Inc, continue to crochet down the unfinished edge of the work, SC, HDC 2, DC 6, HDC 2, SC, working along the chain side of the OC, Inc, SC 18, Inc, continue to crochet up the unfinished edge of the work toward the OC, SC, HDC 2, DC 6, HDC 2, SC, SC in the same stitch as the first SC of this row, Sl St to beginning stitch [68]

Fasten off with an 18 in/45.75 cm yarn tail.

> The HDC and DC stitches in the final row will be at the sides of the blanket. Consider embellishing your Saddle Blanket by surface slip stitching around the edge of the blanket with an accent color or adding short fringe to the sides of the blanket in the DC stitches from the final row.

SADDLE SEAT (MAKE 1)

Saddle Color Yarn: Approximately 22 yd/20 m worsted/medium weight yarn

    For Part 1: 8 yd/7.25 m worsted/medium weight yarn

    For Part 2: 14 yd/12.75 m worsted/medium weight yarn

Part 1

1. Starting with a short yarn tail, Ch 7, starting in the 2nd Ch from hook, Inc, SC 4, work 4 SC in the final Ch stitch, continue to crochet around to the unused side of the starting chain, SC 4, work an Inc in the same Ch stitch as the first Inc in this row, continue in spiral [16]
2. (Inc x 2, SC 4, Inc x 2) x 2 [24]
3. (SC, Inc, SC, Inc, SC 4, Inc, SC, Inc, SC) x 2 [32]
4. (SC, Inc, SC 2, Inc, SC 6, Inc, SC 2, Inc, SC) x 2 [40]

Sl St into the next available stitch, fasten off with a short yarn tail.

Part 2

1. Starting with a short yarn tail, Ch 7, starting in the 2nd Ch from hook, Inc, SC 4, work 4 SC in the final Ch stitch, continue to crochet around to the unused side of the starting chain, SC 4, work an Inc in the same Ch stitch as the first Inc in this row, continue in spiral [16]

2. (Inc x 2, SC 4, Inc x 2) x 2 [24]
3. (SC, Inc, SC, Inc, SC 4, Inc, SC, Inc, SC) x 2 [32]
4. (SC, Inc, SC 2, Inc, SC 6, Inc, SC 2, Inc, SC) x 2, Sl St into the next available stitch, Ch 1 [40]
5. Starting into the same stitch you slip stitched into (as normal), BLO [SC 12, HDC 16, SC 12], Sl St to beginning stitch, Ch 1 [40]

6. Hold the Part 1 piece against the Part 2 piece, wrong side to wrong side. Working through the first stitch on Part 2 and the last SC on Part 1, and, continuing through both pieces at the same time around the entire row, SC 10, HDC 4, DC 12, HDC 4, SC 10, Sl St to beginning stitch [40]

Fasten off with an 18 in/45.75 cm yarn tail.

> The edge of the saddle with the HDC and DC stitches is the back of the saddle and should be oriented toward the back of the snail.

Giant Snail with Pointed Shell and saddle. The saddle is the gray seat on top of the snail's back.

SADDLE FLAP (MAKE 1)

Saddle/Flap Color Yarn: *Approximately 12 yd/11 m worsted/medium weight yarn*

1. Starting with a long enough yarn tail to weave in later, Ch 16, starting in the 2nd Ch from hook, HDC Inc, HDC 2, SC 9, HDC 2, work 4 HDC stitches into the final Ch stitch, continue to crochet around to the unused side of the starting chain, HDC 2, SC 9, HDC 2, HDC Inc into the same Ch as the first stitch in this row, Sl St to beginning stitch, Ch 2 [34]
2. DC Inc x 3, DC & HDC, SC 9, HDC & DC, DC Inc x 6, DC & HDC, SC 9, HDC & DC, DC Inc x 3, do not Sl St, do not Ch 1 [50]
3. Sl St 4, Inc, SC & HDC, HDC, DC 11, HDC, HDC & SC, Inc, Sl St 4 [29]

Fasten off with a 24 in/61 cm yarn tail.

> Consider embellishing your flap by slip stitching around the edge of the flap with an accent color.

❶ Mushroom Sprite with Arms Style 4, Feet/Legs Style 9, Body Style 5, Cap Style 11, riding a ❷ Giant Snail with a Round Shell and a saddle. The flap is on top of the saddle blanket, underneath the saddle, at the front edge of the saddle setup.

SEAT BACK AKA CANTLE (OPTIONAL) (MAKE 1)

Saddle Color Yarn: *Approximately 9 yd/8.25 m worsted/medium weight yarn*

> This piece elevates the height of the back of the saddle, turning it from a more horizontal saddle into a seat or chair back. This piece is entirely optional and cosmetic.

1. Starting with a short yarn tail, work 12 HDC into a Magic Circle, Sl St to beginning stitch, Ch 1 [12]
2. HDC Inc x 12, Sl St to beginning stitch, Ch 1 [24]
3. (HDC, HDC Inc) x 12, Sl St to beginning stitch, Ch 1 [36]

SADDLES AND OTHER ACCESSORIES • 277

4. Fold the piece in half and, working through both sides of the piece at the same time into the BLO of the closest side and the FLO of the farthest side, SC 18 to close the piece to make a half-circle shape [18]

Fasten off with an 18 in/45.75 cm yarn tail.

Assembly

Pin to attach to the inside edge of the back of the saddle (where the DC stitches are along the back edge of the saddle). This step will elevate the back of the saddle, creating a chair back. Sew the piece in place with the yarn tail securing it to the saddle. Weave in the end.

Giant Snail with Round Shell with saddle. The seat back is at the rear edge of the saddle.

❶ **Mushroom Sprite** with Arms Style 3, Feet/Legs Style 10, Body Style 4, Cap Style 7, riding on a ❷ **Giant Snail** with a Round Shell and a saddle

SEAT HANDLE (OPTIONAL) (MAKE 1)

Saddle Color Yarn: Approximately 4 yd/3.75 m worsted/medium weight yarn

> Do not make both a handle and a saddle horn. Pick one or the other, or neither.

Assembly

Pin to attach to the outside edge of the front of the saddle. This step should create an arched handle at the front/center of the saddle. While the handle can be pinned either way, it is recommended to pin the side of the handle that faces you as you crochet Row 3 inward to face the rider/back of the saddle, and the back of Row 3 should face forward toward the snail's head. Sew the piece in place with the yarn tail securing it to the saddle. Weave in ends.

1. Starting with a 12 in/30.5 cm yarn tail, Ch 13, starting in the 2nd Ch from hook, Sl St 12, Ch 1, Turn [12]

2. Working around the Sl Sts and into the Chs from Row 1, SC 2, Inc, SC 6, Inc, SC 2, Ch 1, Turn [14]

> When you work the SC around the Sl Sts and into the Ch stitches from Row 1, you will encase the Sl Sts inside the SC stitches in Row 2. For more information, there's a video on this technique here: https://www.youtube.com/watch?v=khed-Ni_AjM&t=4s

3. Sl St 14 [14]

Fasten off with a 12 in/30.5 cm yarn tail.

280 • SADDLES AND OTHER ACCESSORIES

SADDLE HORN (OPTIONAL) (MAKE 1)

Saddle Color Yarn:
Approximately 7 yd/6.5 m worsted/medium weight yarn

> Do not make both a handle and a saddle horn. Pick one or the other, or neither.

1. Starting with a short yarn tail, HDC 8 in a Magic Circle, Sl St to beginning stitch, Ch 1 [8]

2. BLO [SC 8], Sl St to beginning stitch, Ch 1 [8]

3. (SC, Dec, SC) x 2, Sl St to beginning stitch, Ch 1 [6]

4-5. (2 rows of) SC 6, Sl St to beginning stitch, Ch 1 [6]

6. SC 2, Ch 4, starting in the 2nd Ch from hook, SC 3, SC into the same stitch you last single crocheted into just before the Ch 4 instruction, SC 3, Ch 4, starting in the 2nd Ch from hook, SC 3, SC into the same stitch you last single crocheted into just before the Ch 4 instruction, SC, Sl St to beginning stitch, Ch 1 [14]

7. SC 2, SC 3 up the chain side of the Ch 4 instruction from Row 6, working back down the SC stitches from Row 6 that were worked into the Ch stitches and continuing into the next available stitches from Row 6, SC 7, SC 3 up the chain side of the Ch 4 instruction from Row 6, working back down the SC stitches from Row 6 that were worked into the Ch stitches and continuing into the next available stitches from Row 6, SC 5, Sl St to beginning stitch [20]

Fasten off with a 12 in/30.5 cm yarn tail.

Assembly

Pin in place at the front/center of the saddle. The base of the saddle horn should be compressed/folded in half and should follow the contour curve of the front edge of the saddle. Verify placement. Sew in place using the yarn tail. Weave in the end.

❶ Mushroom Sprite with Arms Style 7, Feet/Legs Style 10, Body Style 4, Cap Style 6, riding a ❷ Giant Snail with Pointed Shell on a saddle

SADDLES AND OTHER ACCESSORIES • 281

SADDLE SUPPORT (OPTIONAL) (MAKE 1)

Saddle or Shell Color Yarn: Approximately 18 yd/16.5 m worsted/medium weight yarn

> This piece will allow you to seat the saddle closer to the head of the Giant Round Snail Shell. It is not intended for use with the Giant Pointed Snail Shell or for saddle placement on the center of the Giant Round Snail Shell.

Part 1

1. Starting with a short yarn tail, Ch 7, starting in the 2nd Ch from hook, Inc, SC 4, work 4 SC into the last available Ch stitch, continue to crochet around to the unused side of the chain stitches, SC 4, work an Inc in the same Ch stitch as the first Inc in this row, Sl St to beginning stitch, Ch 1 [16]

2. Inc x 2, SC 4, Inc x 4, SC 4, Inc x 2, Sl St to beginning stitch [24]

Fasten off with a short yarn tail.

Mark the 14th stitch on Row 2 for reference in Row 8 of Part 2.

Part 2

1. Starting with a short yarn tail, Ch 7, starting in the 2nd Ch from hook, SC 5, Inc in the last available Ch stitch, continue to crochet around to the unused side of the Ch stitches, SC 4, SC in the same Ch stitch as the first SC in this row, Sl St to beginning stitch, Ch 1 [12]

2. SC 12, Sl St to beginning stitch, Ch 1 [12]

3. (Inc, SC 4, Inc) x 2, Sl St to beginning stitch, Ch 1 [16]

4. SC 16, Sl St to beginning stitch, Ch 1 [16]

5. (SC, Inc, SC 4, Inc, SC) x 2, Sl St to beginning stitch, Ch 1 [20]

6. SC 20, Sl St to beginning stitch, Ch 1 [20]

7. (SC, Inc, SC 6, Inc, SC) x 2, Sl St to beginning stitch, Ch 1 [24]

❶ Mushroom Sprite with Arms Style 3, Feet/Legs Style 9, Body Style 4, Cap Style 8, riding on a ❷ Giant Snail with a Round Shell on a saddle supported by a saddle support piece, herding an ❸ Upright Small Snail with a Round Shell with Antennae Style 1, an ❹ Upright Small Snail with a Pointed Shell with Antennae Style 1, and a ❺ Medium Snail with a Pointed Shell

> Stuff the saddle support lightly with fiberfill as you crochet Row 8 to close the piece.

8. Holding Part 1 and Part 2 together, wrong side to wrong side, work through Row 7 of Part 2 (current piece) and the marked stitch on the last row of Part 1 at the same time and, continuing through both pieces around, SC 24, Sl St to beginning stitch [24]

> To make the first SC in Row 8, you will insert your hook first through the next stitch of the current piece (Part 2) and then through the marked stitch of Part 1, and SC both pieces together.

Fasten off with an 18 in/45.75 cm yarn tail.

> For placement and how to attach, go to the Saddle Assembly section beginning on page 285.

❶ Mushroom Sprite with Arms Style 4, Feet/Legs Style 12, Body Style 4, Cap Style 6, riding on a ❷ Giant Snail with a Pointed Shell with a full saddle and reins

SADDLES AND OTHER ACCESSORIES • 283

SADDLE BAGS (OPTIONAL)

Saddle Bag Color Yarn: Approximately 20 yd/18.25 m worsted/medium weight yarn (for two)

Saddle Bag Strap Color Yarn: Approximately 6 yd/5.5 m worsted/medium weight yarn

Part 1: Saddle Bag (Make 2)

1. Starting with the Saddle Bag Color yarn and a long enough yarn tail to weave in later, Ch 9, starting in the second Ch from hook, SC 7, Inc, continue to crochet around to the other side of the starting chain, SC 6, SC in the same Ch stitch as your first SC in this row, Sl St to beginning stitch, Ch 1 [16]
2. BLO [SC 16], Sl St to beginning stitch, Ch 1 [16]
3–6. (4 rows of) SC 16, Sl St to beginning stitch, Ch 1 [16]
7–9. (3 rows of) SC 9, Ch 1, Turn [9]
10. Skip the 1st stitch, SC, HDC, DC 3, HDC, SC, Sl St [8]

Fasten off with an 18 in/45.75 cm yarn tail to weave in later.

If you want to tie the bags closed, after sewing the saddle bag to attach to the saddle bag strap in the Assembly section (page 285), you can weave the yarn tails through to the edge of the last row of the saddle bags at two points, as shown. Then weave another yarn tail through the bag so that it sticks out on either end where you want to tie the bag shut, and use the yarn tails to tie small bows, which will keep the bag closed. If you do not want to tie the bag closed, you can weave in the ends after sewing the saddle bag to attach to the saddle bag strap in the Assembly section.

Part 2: Saddle Bag Strap (Make 1)

1. Starting with a long enough yarn tail to weave in later, Ch 17, starting in the 2nd Ch from hook, HDC Inc, HDC 14, working into the last available Ch stitch make 4 HDC, continuing to crochet along the unused chains, HDC 14, work a HDC Inc into the same Ch stitch that you worked the first HDC Inc into in this row, Sl St to beginning stitch [36]

Fasten off with a 12 in/30.5 cm yarn tail.

SADDLE STRAPS (OPTIONAL)

Saddle Strap Color Yarn: Approximately 10 yd/9 m worsted/medium weight yarn

    For a Giant Round Shell: Make 1 of each Piece.
    For a Giant Pointed Shell: Make 2 of Piece 2.

> These pieces are meant to give the look of the saddle strapped in place against the snail's shell. The first piece will need to be long enough to reach from under the saddle to the inside of the spiral of the shell or down to the first ridge of the shell spiral. If the piece needs to be longer, chain more and work more HDC stitches along the length of it. If the piece needs to be shorter, chain less and work fewer HDC stitches along the length of it.

Piece 1

1. Starting with a 12 in/30.5 cm yarn tail to weave in later, Ch approximately 33, starting in the 2nd Ch from hook, HDC 32 [32]

Fasten off with a 12 in/30.5 cm yarn tail.

Piece 2

1. Starting with a 12 in/30.5 cm yarn tail to weave in later, Ch approximately 25, starting in the 2nd Ch from hook, HDC 24 [24]

Fasten off with a 12 in/30.5 cm yarn tail.

Proceed to Saddle Assembly.

284 • SADDLES AND OTHER ACCESSORIES

Left to right: ❶ Mushroom Sprite with Arms Style 3, Feet/Legs Style 2, Body Style 5, Cap Style 14, holding onto ❷ Mushroom Sprite with Feet/Legs Style 2, Body Style 8; ❸ Giant Snail with Round Shell and saddle, ridden by ❹ Mushroom Sprite with Arms Style 3, Feet/Legs Style 10, Body Style 4, Cap Style 7

SADDLE ASSEMBLY

Saddle Blanket and Saddle Flap Placement for Giant Snail with Round Shell

1. Choose where you want the saddle to sit—either on the top center of the spiral shell or closer to the head of the snail on the shell. If you are positioning the saddle closer to the head of the snail, first pin the saddle support in place.

2. Pin the saddle blanket in place either on the top center of the shell or on top of the saddle support. The curved sides of the blanket should be on either side of the shell. The straight sides of the blanket should be at the front and back of the shell.

SADDLES AND OTHER ACCESSORIES • 285

3. Pin the flap in place, centered at the front of the saddle blanket, closest to the head of the snail. The curving edge of the flap should be oriented to the front edge of the saddle blanket, not overlapping the front edge. The straight edge of the flap should be oriented toward the back of the snail.

Saddle Blanket and Saddle Flap Placement for Giant Snail with Pointed Shell

1. Pin the saddle blanket in place on the top center of the shell, on the widest section of the spiraling shell, closest to the head of the snail. The curved sides of the blanket should be on either side of the shell. The straight sides of the blanket should be at the front and back of the shell.

2. Pin the flap in place centered at the front of the saddle blanket, closest to the head of the snail. The front curving edge of the flap should overlap/go slightly past the front edge of the saddle blanket. The flat edge of the flap should be oriented toward the back of the snail.

Horn, Handle, and Seat Back Placement for Either Type of Shell

1. If you are using a saddle horn, handle, or seat back, and you have not already done so, pin them in place on the saddle. It is okay to pin the saddle in place on top of the flap for now, but do not sew in place yet.

Optional Saddle Strap Placement for Giant Snail with Round Shell

1. For a Giant Round Shell, position Saddle Strap Piece 1 starting under the saddle and reaching deep inside the concave spiral side of the shell. Position Saddle Strap Piece 2 starting under the other side of the saddle and reaching the first ridge of the spiral of the shell.

286 • SADDLES AND OTHER ACCESSORIES

Optional Saddle Strap Placement for Giant Snail with Pointed Shell

1. For a Giant Pointed Shell, position one Saddle Strap Piece 2 starting under the saddle and reaching around the side of the shell to the base of the shell where it touches the body of the snail. Position the other Saddle Strap Piece 2 starting under the other side of the saddle and reaching around the side of the shell to the base of the shell where it touches the body of the snail.

Saddle Bag Placement for Any Shell

1. Pin the saddle bag strap to the saddle blanket under the saddle, toward the back/center of the saddle blanket. From the front to the back of the saddle blanket, you should have the flap first, then the saddle straps, and then the saddle bag strap.

Saddle Placement for Any Shell

1. Pin the saddle on top of the pieces pinned to the saddle blanket. The saddle strap ends should be tucked/hidden under the saddle.

Just because you put a saddle on your snail doesn't mean they'll go where you want.

❶ Mushroom Sprite with Arms Style 6, Body Style 1, Cap Style 3, pulling the reins of a ❷ Giant Snail with a Round Shell and saddle

SADDLES AND OTHER ACCESSORIES • 287

2. Pin both saddle bags in place on either end of the saddle bag strap. It is recommended to keep the saddle bag largely positioned over the saddle blanket so the saddle bag will not be centered on the saddle bag strap. Adjust the positioning per your preference.

3. Verify final saddle placement.

4. Using yarn tails, sew everything to attach, one piece at a time. Sew the saddle blanket first, unpinning whatever you need to unpin to be able to sew it to the Snail Body. Then sew the flap, saddle straps, and saddle bag strap. Then sew the saddle accessories to the saddle. Then sew the saddle in place on the straps and blanket. Then sew the saddle bags in place. Weave in all remaining ends.

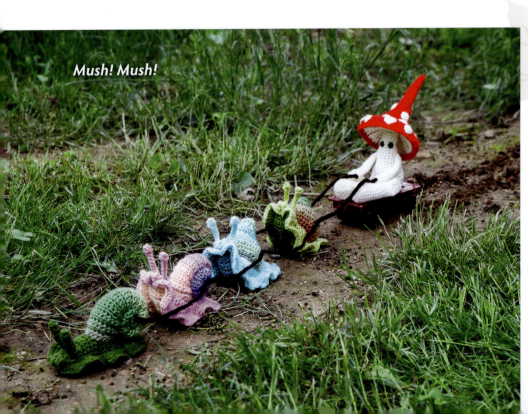

Mush! Mush!

❶ Mushroom Sprite with Arms Style 6, Feet/Legs Style 12, Body Style 4, Cap Style 8, optional dots, driving a sled pulled by four Small Snails. From left to right: ❷ Horizontal Small Snail with Round Shell and Antennae Style 1, ❸ Upright Small Snail with Round Shell and Antennae Style 2, ❹ Upright Small Snail with Pointed Shell and Antennae Style 2, ❺ Upright Small Snail with Pointed Shell and Antennae Style 2. The snails are linked together by two sets of reins!

Reins (Make 1 Set)

Reins Color Yarn: Approximately 6 yd/5.5 m worsted/medium weight yarn

1. Starting with a 12 in/30.5 cm yarn tail, Ch 115 [115]

> You can make this chain shorter if you want a shorter set of reins.

Fasten off with a 12 in/30.5 cm yarn tail.

Assembly

Pin to attach to the face of your snail, either in the center of the face, sort of hidden between the two bobbles, or under each bobble. Once placement is verified and the length of the reins is confirmed, sew to attach the ends in those two places where the reins are pinned on the face of the snail. Weave in ends.

The reins can also be knotted to give the mushroom something shorter to hold on to.

❶ Mushroom Sprite with Arms Style 7, Feet/Legs Style 10, Body Style 4, Cap Style 6, riding a ❷ Giant Snail with a Pointed Shell and saddle; ❸ Mushroom Sprite with Arms Style 3, Feet/Legs Style 10, Body Style 4, Cap Style 7, riding a ❹ Giant Snail with a Round Shell and saddle; ❺ Mushroom Sprite with Arms Style 4, Feet/Legs Style 12, Body Style 4, Cap Style 6, riding a ❻ Giant Snail with a Pointed Shell and saddle

ACKNOWLEDGMENTS

Special thanks to my husband, best friend, and partner, Greg. There are not enough ways to thank you for supporting me unconditionally, and there's no one else I would rather stumble through life with. Thank you for taking care of me, even as I fall apart.

And to my children, Riley and Harper: I love you. I know so much of my time over the past few years has been dedicated to my work. You are so much more important than any of it. However many times I've told you I love you and I'm proud of you, it's not enough.

Special thanks to my brother, Brendan Conway, who supported me through the process of creating this book, and to my wonderful sister-in-law, Grace Jacobson, and my beautiful niece, Naomi. I love you guys so much.

Thank you to my parents, Velma Conway and Richard Conway, and to my in-laws, Joy Lapp and Jim Lapp, for all of your love and support.

Special thanks to Jen Starbird, Sarah Constein, Tammy Simmons, Morgan Carpuski, and Amie Fournier-Flather for being moderators for my Facebook group, being dear friends, and also helping check over this book in advance, test patterns, and make this book the best it can be. You're amazing, and I am deeply grateful.

Special thanks to Lauren Lewis for traveling across an ocean more than once to help photograph the creatures for this book. You're wonderful and talented, and I'm extremely lucky to get to work with you.

Special thanks to my Facebook group moderators and friends:

Kat Bifield	Alix Frere	Stephanie Norby
Morgan Carpuski	Jeremy Leon Guerrero	Amy Panikowski
Sarah Constein	Daniel Jagoda	Tammy Simmons
Chantal DeFrancesco	Elizabeth Keane	Mandy Smith
Heather Flint	Lauren Lewis	Jennifer Starbird
Amie Fournier-Flather	Ashley Lodge	Jennifer Steyn
Austin Foursha-Wentworth	Laura Marshall	Sandi Willoughby

Special thanks to my agent, Christi Cardenas.

ABOUT THE AUTHOR

Megan Lapp has been creating creatures since she was small—first using paper and pencil, then clay and plaster, and later felt and fabric, before finding that yarn and hook are the Goldilocks medium for her art. She began publishing her own digital crochet patterns in 2017 with one small octopus, and she now has over 200 patterns available digitally and has published four books, including *Crochet Snails and Mushroom Sprites*. She lives with her family in Lancaster, Pennsylvania, and her website can be found at https://www.craftyintentions.com

More information available here:
https://linktr.ee/CraftyIntentions

Also available

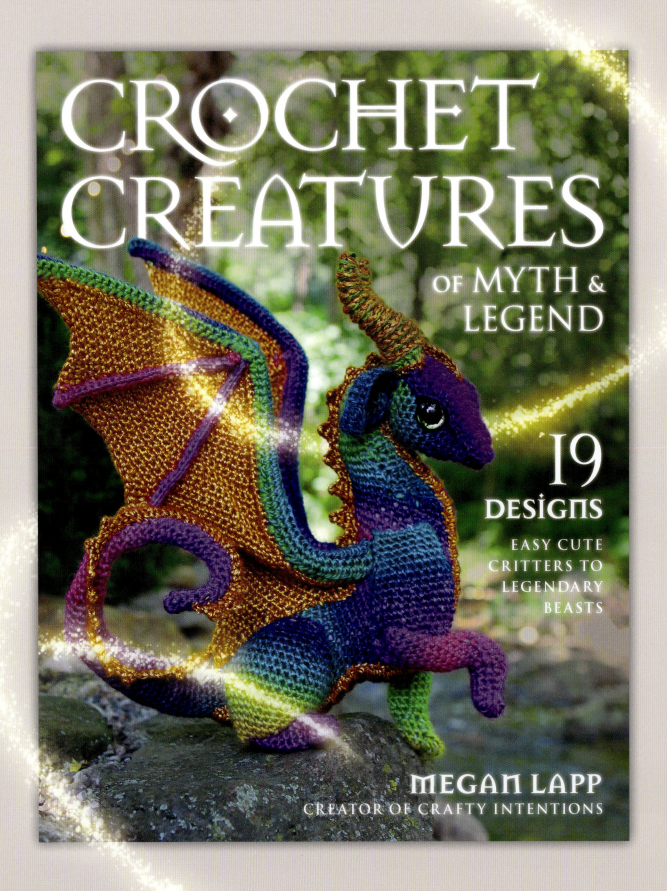

OVER A MILLION POSSIBLE COMBINATIONS! YES, REALLY!

CROCHET IMPKINS

MEGAN LAPP

CREATOR OF CRAFTY INTENTIONS